*People in business organisations –
a student-based course*

People in business organisations –

a student-based course

Christopher E. Stafford

Senior Lecturer, Dept of Business Studies,
Plymouth College of Further Education,
Devon.

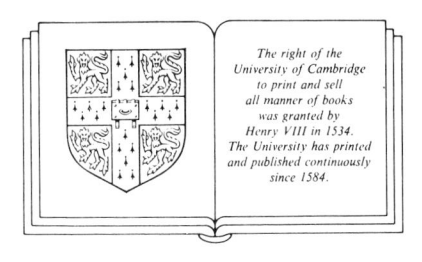

CAMBRIDGE UNIVERSITY PRESS
Cambridge
New York   Port Chester
Melbourne   Sydney

Published by the Press Syndicate of the University of Cambridge
The Pitt Building, Trumpington Street, Cambridge CB2 1RP
40 West 20th Street, New York, NY 10011, USA
10 Stamford Road, Oakleigh, Melbourne 3166, Australia

© Cambridge University Press 1990

First published 1990

Printed in Great Britain by Scotprint, Musselburgh, Scotland.

British Library cataloguing in publication data
Stafford, C. E.
　People in Business Organisations.
　1. Organisations personnel management aspects
　I. Title
　658.3

ISBN 0 521 377552

GO

Contents

Preface vi

Section 1 The organisation, systems theory and communication 1

1. The individual and the organisation 3
2. Systems 6
3. Types of organisation 12
4. Organisational structure and communication 17
5. The functional areas of a business organisation 30

Section 2 Office services, systems and methods of communication 39

6. Office functions and support 41
7. Operational systems, procedures and the O & M function 50
8. Practical communication skills (1) 60
9. Recording information, standard documents and form design 72
10. Information handling and transmission 86

Section 3 The working environment 107

11. People, organisations and change. Case study: Renaissance Kitchens 109
12. Practical communication skills (2) 124
13. The workplace and the law 133
14. Management, human relations and conflict 143
15. Motivation, working in groups, and practical appraisal 153

Section 4 The job 171

16. The job and the individual 173
17. Filling a vacancy 179
18. The job application 194
19. Selection and induction 213
20. Practical communication skills (3) 222

Preface

People in business organisations is about life in the real world of work. It requires an appreciation of the many concepts, ideas and practical applications which provide the basis for a realistic awareness of how business operates.

This book puts emphasis upon student-centred learning, which not only meets BTEC requirements for developing effective work-patterns but also gives scope for each student to develop his/her own ideas in a tutor-guided, investigative environment. Opportunities are provided for individual work, group co-operation, discussion sessions, out-of-college research, work-place studies, and tutorial-based teaching strategies.

The aim of the text is to provide a comprehensive two-year package of student-centred activity, supported by effective guidelines and 'lead-in' information for assignment work. The factual material is not designed to cover every detail of a topic, but is intended to give enough background knowledge to facilitate further investigation – the student must be prepared to **research**, **think** and **apply knowledge** in order to complete assignments satisfactorily.

The tutor will be free to concentrate on his/her vital role as a source of additional 'input', and as an essential guide/counsellor to each individual student; using this book will provide the time for this to be done effectively.

In order to encourage a full range of communication skills, specialist chapters have been included in addition to the guidelines given elsewhere as requirements for particular assignment work. This reference material is not necessarily intended to be 'worked through' by students, but can be 'dipped into' as and when required.

The approach taken in *People in business organisations* has been tested in the classroom by a number of tutors over the last two years and its recognised success is in providing practical and demanding work-programmes for students, and in creating enough classroom time for tutors to implement an effective tutorial-based, student-centred teaching strategy.

SECTION 1

The organisation, systems theory and communication

CHAPTER 1
The individual and the organisation

You are an 'organisation person'! You might not have thought of yourself in this light, and you might not like to be classified in this manner, but if you weren't an 'organisation person' you wouldn't be a student, you wouldn't have a job, and your recreational or social activities would be severely limited.

If you think about it carefully, a considerable part of each individual's life is involved with organisations of various kinds. Children go to Play School, Primary School, and Secondary School. They may belong to the Girl Guides, Scouts, or other youth organisations, play for the local football team or belong to the local swimming club. Workers spend a large proportion of their working hours in work organisations, and after work they commonly become involved in more social organisations such as sports clubs, social clubs, hobby clubs and evening classes. Indeed it would be very difficult to think of people in our society who do not belong to any kind of organisation, and to imagine what their life-style would be like.

As a member of any organisation you take on certain responsibilities, and invariably agree to abide by certain rules and regulations. In return 'the organisation' has certain responsibilities towards you, and in the initial stages of any relationship between an individual and an organisation it is good policy for both sides to find out what the other can offer. In the work situation, the organisation assesses what you can offer before it appoints you (i.e. through standard interviewing and selection procedures); but it often falls on the organisation again to ensure that you, as a prospective employee, can find out what you want to know – not only about the job, but also about the organisation in general and the environment in which you will be expected to work. If you were taking a job in an area away from your home town, you would want additional information about the area in which you were going to live, its amenities and facilities.

The college at which you are studying is an organisation. In choosing your course you have probably looked at brochures, had discussions with tutors, talked through your needs with your employers, and eventually enrolled on the course. In getting to this point you have had to demonstrate a range of communication skills, and experience (suffer?) the essential two-way nature of communication. The time has now come for you to prove your ability! Your tutors can make certain assumptions based on entry qualifications, work experience, personal presentation, etc., but they don't really know how you can perform. As in most real-life situations, an assessment of your abilities is essential to establish how you think, how you communicate, how aware you are, how effectively you can seek out information, how realistically and intelligently you can identify the needs of a situation. The initial assignment for this unit is just such an assessment, and is designed to involve you in nine to twelve hours' work.

ASSIGNMENT: Public relations

Situation

You are employed as an administrative assistant to the Public Relations Officer at the Head Office of an international Insurance Group. It has recently been decided that the company should produce informative brochures dealing with each area in which a Branch Office is situated. The aim is to give prospective employees, or employees being transferred, an insight into the area in which they will be living and working, and the general work of the branch.

Task

Select a suitable city/town in which a Branch Office of the Beacon International Assurance Corporation is situated. Ideally, base the branch in your 'home' town.
Produce a short, informative brochure giving essential/useful information and persuasively pointing out the advantages of living and working in the chosen area.

Notes for guidance

(a) General

Do not attempt to cover too wide an area. Select an identifiable district of the town/city if necessary.

(b) Content

An introductory section could give a descriptive introduction to the area. You should use your discretion as to the rest of the content, and to help you in this the following questions are designed to guide you towards the information you could include. Remember, you are writing for people of all age-groups. These questions are in *no particular order*, and you are free to include any other information you think desirable.
The actual structure/sections of your brochure should be discussed in detail with your tutor before you finally decide.

Questions

What is the population of the area?
How far are you from the nearest city centre?
How far are you from London?
Does the area have any special historical significance?
What are communications like?
How far are you from open country?
Are any new housing developments in progress?
What is the average price for a house in the area?
Are properties easily available?

Where would be a convenient area to live?
Is commuting difficult?
Are you far from the sea?
What kinds of education are available?
What cultural/entertainment facilities are available?
Are there a reasonable number of churches? What denominations?
Is there a railway station?
Is there a major river nearby?
Are continental links available nearby?
What is the health service like?

Note It would be helpful to provide, on the final page, a list of useful telephone numbers which should include the following:

local Electricity Board
local Gas Board
local Water Authority or provider
local telephone information centre
Local Authority/Civic Centre
Education Offices
plumber
electrician
taxi firm
railway information
coach/bus terminus – information
AA
RAC
three local garages
College of Further Education – the nearest

(c) Presentation and format

It could be useful for the cover of your brochure to show a map of your chosen area. The name of the company should also appear somewhere on the cover. The information can be presented/displayed in any way, but you should aim to make it as visually effective as possible. The appropriate use of headings, different types of print and other display techniques will be given credit.

Your brochure will finally appear as a booklet, presented on plain A4 paper, written on one side only.

Sources

You can use *any* sources you feel appropriate, but it is suggested that useful places to visit could be the local reference library, the college library, and the tourist information centre. Any booklets and guides to the area could provide useful background material. Entertainment guides can give an indication of the area's amenities. However, please remember that the aim of this assignment is not to provide a descriptive holiday-type brochure, but to provide essential/useful information to meet the needs of prospective employees from all age-groups – some young and single; some older, married with children. They will need somewhere to live, schools for their children, health and care facilities, etc.

CHAPTER 2

Systems

The 'public relations' assignment should have given you an awareness of the close inter-relationship between organisations and individuals, and how this relationship needs to be constantly nurtured if it is to be effective and mutually beneficial. Every organisation, however, has other considerations which affect its existence and operation. Just as organisations and individuals are almost impossible to conceive of without one another, so an important conceptual link exists between the organisation and its wider environment. The **systems approach** to business organisations stresses the interdependence between:

a   the organisation and its component parts (its **sub-systems**), and
b   the organisation and the factors operating on it from outside (its **environment**).

There is, of course, more than one type of system, and an organisation can embody the characteristics of one or more basic systems. The general classification of systems is as follows:

Deterministic systems

These are the simplest systems of all and tend to be mechanical in nature – clocks, mechanical typewriters and bicycles are typical examples of these. If the present state of the machine is known, the next state can be determined. (If you look at your watch and note the position of the minute hand, assuming your watch is working properly, you can safely predict where the next position of the minute hand will be.)

Probabilistic systems

These are the systems where only certain predictions are possible. For example, if we throw a dice we can be certain that a number will come up between one and six, but not precisely which one.

Adaptive systems

These are systems which are probabilistic in the sense described above and also adapt themselves to changes in the environment. In the animal world a chameleon is the classic example of this, but human beings also share this adaptive ability. We adapt to the cold by putting on another layer of clothing, to fear by flight, to falling in a lake by swimming (or screaming for help!).

Closed systems

These are systems where there is no communication whatsoever with the wider environment; where nothing enters or leaves.

Open systems

Conversely, open systems are those which do interact with other systems outside of them.

A business organisation is one kind of open and adaptive system. This is illustrated in the case of a furniture manufacturer, Build It, Ltd, in fig. 2.1.

Fig. 2.1
Wood, laminates, glue and other raw materials are INPUT into the system, where they are CONVERTED by the manufacturing process to produce the OUTPUT of the system – fitted bedroom furniture.

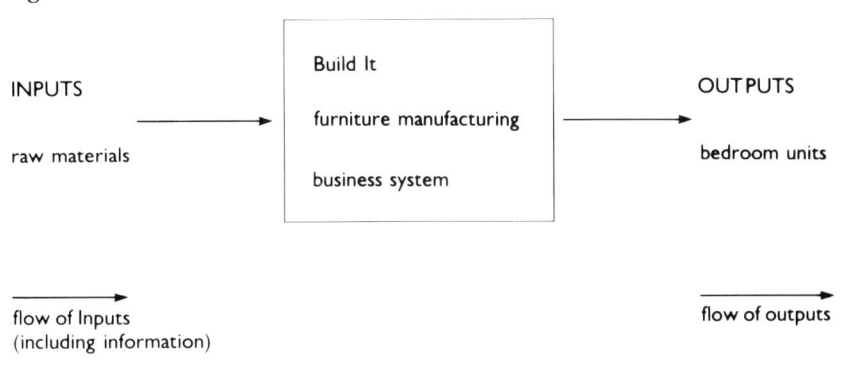

INPUTS → Build It furniture manufacturing business system → OUTPUTS

raw materials → → bedroom units

flow of Inputs (including information) → flow of outputs →

The organisation and external influences

'No man is an island' it is said, and this is also particularly true of a business organisation. Some external influences may be within its sphere of control – for example, a firm's choice of supplier. Others, such as the weather or population structure, are not. The systems approach to the business organisation as an **open** and **adaptive** system highlights the importance of taking external influences into account. Fig. 2.2 illustrates some of the many external factors operating on a firm.

Fig. 2.2

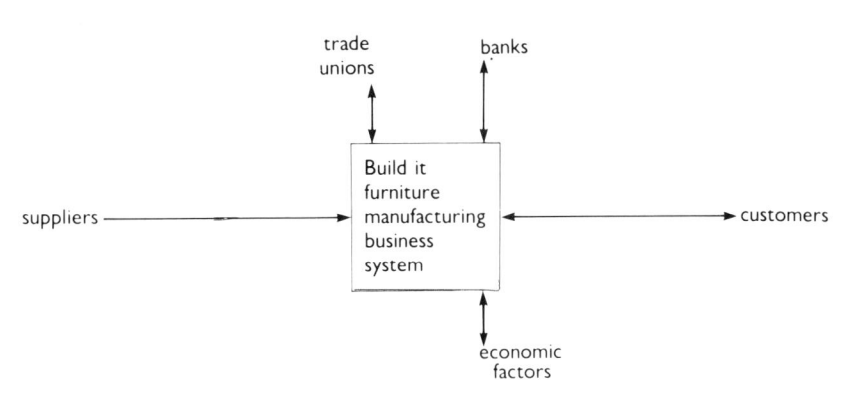

suppliers → Build it furniture manufacturing business system → customers

trade unions ↕   banks ↕

economic factors ↕

Let's consider a very simple example of how an organisation is open and adaptive in its relationship with, and reactions to, its customer system. Referring to the company shown in fig. 2.2, last year consumer research revealed that customers were dissatisfied with the finish of the bedroom furniture. 'Too clinical' and 'too shiny' were typical comments. Build It, Ltd reacted by incorporating two new types of finish in their range: one natural wood, the other satin-finish laminate. By doing this the company hoped to meet consumer requirements more precisely.

ACTIVITY

(suitable for groups of four or five students)

1. In addition to those given in fig. 2.2, can you think of any other external factors which might infuence the operation of a business like Build It, Ltd?
2. For two of these additional factors, and each of those specified in fig. 2.2, describe at least two situations in which they could affect the business. Suggest in what ways the organisation may adapt.

Each member of the group can submit a written answer to question 2, or the group can make an oral presentation to the rest of the class.

The organisation and its sub-systems

A sub-system is a system in its own right, but also a component in a larger system. Fig 2.3 shows the major sub-systems of a small manufacturing company, and how they relate to one another and to two important systems in the firm's immediate environment: the customers' system and the suppliers' system.

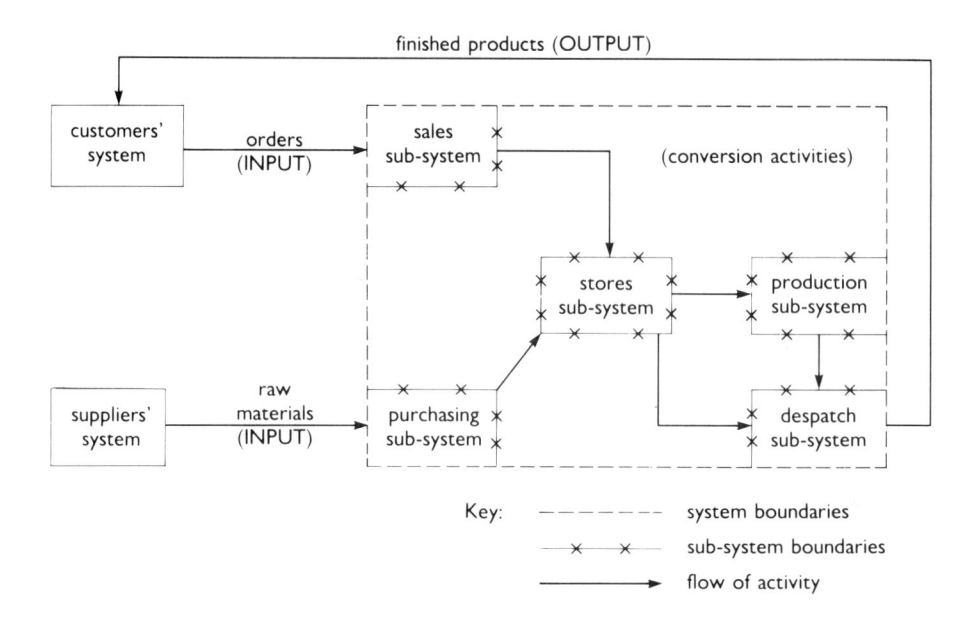

Fig. 2.3

Each of these sub-systems could in turn be drawn as a system in its own right in terms of its interaction with its own particular environment. For example, sub-systems of the sales system in fig 2.3 may include customer reception and advice, customer order processing, and the invoicing of goods and acceptance of payment.

Equilibrium

The business organisation is thus seen as a collection of systems and sub-systems interacting with one another as well as a complete system reacting to, and acting on, its environment. When there is a steady flow of inputs to, and outputs from the business, the system is said to be in equilibrium – i.e. in a state of balance. This is not a static concept; rather it describes a situation where the organisation is in a 'steady state', making continual adjustments to forces inside and outside itself. You will be able to consider these concepts in more practical terms when the work of the various departments (sub-systems) of an organisation is dealt with later in the section.

System control

The control of a system involves **measuring** the output, **comparing** this with the planned output, and **adjusting** the input in the event of under-achievement. This is carried out by means of a **control-loop**. Fig. 2.4 illustrates such a method of feedback control with respect to quality control.

Build It, Ltd's bedroom units are inspected to see if they meet specified quality standards. If they do not, they are returned to the factory for further work to be carried out.

Fig. 2.4

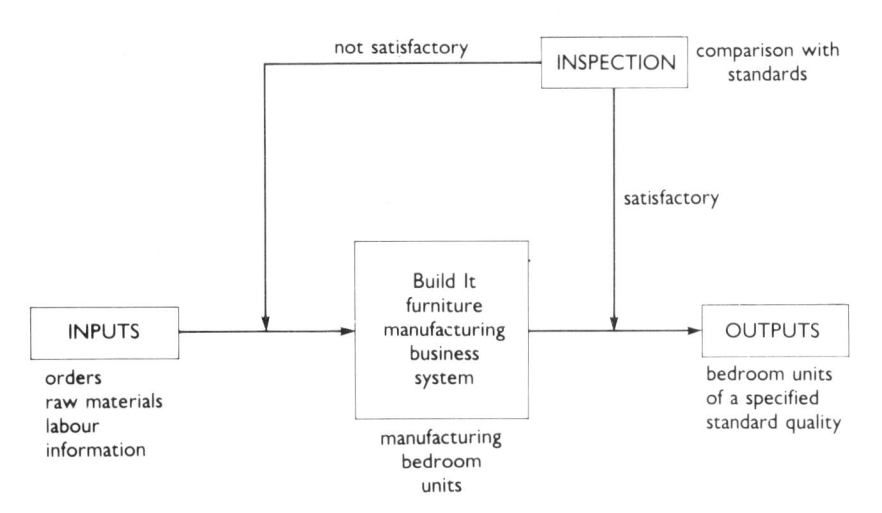

People in business organisations

Bearing in mind the basic systems concepts you have been thinking about, you should be able to apply them to a business situation in the following simple assignment. It is appreciated that you will probably have no specialist knowledge of the type of business, but this shouldn't inhibit discussion and ideas.

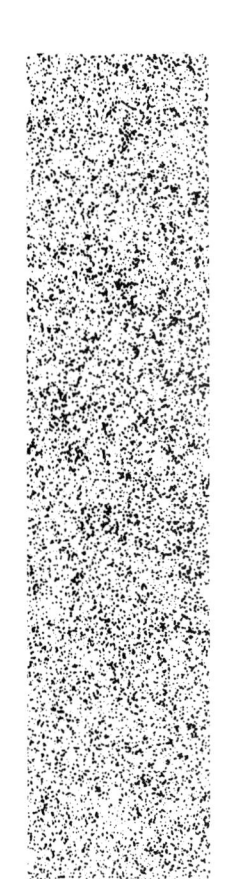

ASSIGNMENT: Gentle giant?

Situation

'Gentle' is a leading soap powder for automatic washing machines, with a long-standing reputation for getting clothes 'deep down clean' while being 'gentle enough for even baby's delicate clothes'. Until comparatively recently this brand image, coupled with a competitive pricing policy, helped it sustain a 40% share of the automatic washing powder market. Last year was, however, a disappointing one for 'Gentle', in which sales fell by almost 50% as the result of market penetration by several 'biological' powders.

The management team decided to re-launch the product, giving it a more up-to-date image, and claiming new and improved performance. To substantiate this claim a 'biological' ingredient was added, but the consumer was not informed of this.

The Board of 'Gentle' was delighted. Within two months of the re-launch sales had reached a new high. Unfortunately however, it soon became apparent that the new improved 'Gentle' was causing problems for people with sensitive skin who had previously relied on the product for its mildness and non-allergenic properties. The media found this story most newsworthy! Indeed, much to the horror of the 'Gentle' directors, it was reported nation-wide on the six o'clock news.

Preliminary considerations

In groups of four or five discuss the 'Gentle' sketch, making sure that you explore the following areas from the point of view of:

1 Considering a way in which the business system may **adapt** to meet this new situation.
2 Assessing the likely effects of your solution on the following **sub-systems**:
    (a)   production,
    (b)   marketing.
3 In hind-sight, determining what **control** procedure(s) could have been implemented to prevent this situation arising in the first place.

Task

As an administrative assistant to the Marketing Director, you often need to liaise between her and the Production Manager, and you have been involved in some of the meetings that have been held in preparation for a full Board Meeting in three days' time. The Marketing Director wants to have some information at her fingertips to be able to put forward at the meeting, and asks you to prepare a **short informal report** for her, covering the three areas discussed above. Present the information in an appropriate format (see below), including your ideas on control procedures as part of the main body, *not* as recommendations. Your concluding paragraph should be very general, simply indicating that if appropriate changes were made, any similar situation could be avoided in the future.

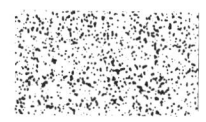

Notes for guidance

A summary of the general presentation, layout and content of a **short informal report** is given below.

For the attention of ....

SUBJECT/TITLE

The introductory paragraph has no section heading and will include information on the reasons for submitting the report, the scope, any source material, and how information was collected (if appropriate).

<u>Section heading</u>

  (a) <u>Sub-heading</u>
      (i)
     (ii)
    (iii)

  (b) <u>Sub-heading</u>
      (i)
     (ii)
    (iii)

<u>Section heading</u>

  (a) <u>Sub-heading</u>
      (i)
     (ii)
    (iii)

  (b) <u>Sub-heading</u>
      (i)
     (ii)
    (iii)

> *Notes*
>
> This main body of the report will be presented schematically under appropriate headings and sub-headings, with numbered points/ statements/comments. This does *not* mean that you can write in an abbreviated note-form. Grammatical accuracy is important to ensure reader comprehension.
>
> The number of sections, sub-sections and numbered points will depend on the requirements of the question and the complexity of the information you are dealing with. The decision is *yours*.
>
> A decimal numbering system is used by many organisations, and you can adopt this if you wish. Section headings will be numbered 1, 2, 3, etc. Sub-headings will be numbered 1.1, 1.2, 2.1, 3.1, etc. Individual points will be numbered 1.1.1, 1.1.2, 2.1.1, 2.1.2, 2.1.3, etc.

The concluding paragraph has no section heading and should aim to 'round off' the report in an appropriate manner. It can be a general conclusion, specific conclusions, or an indication of 'action required'. There is no need to summarise your findings, but any concise conclusions or recommendations should be included (if appropriate).

                                              Signature (of the sender/writer)

Designation (sender's job/position)

                                                                   Date

CHAPTER 3
Types of organisation

What type of organisation do you work in, or would you like to work in? Would you find it easy to classify it as Commercial, Industrial, or Service? Can you see how it fits into general economic activity around you? Did you know it is one contributory element of our **mixed economy**? What is a mixed economy?

Consider fig. 3.1 and see which area your chosen organisation fits into. Our 'mixed economy' is demonstrated by the varied, inter-related, and often interdependent, sectors of economic activity.

Fig. 3.1

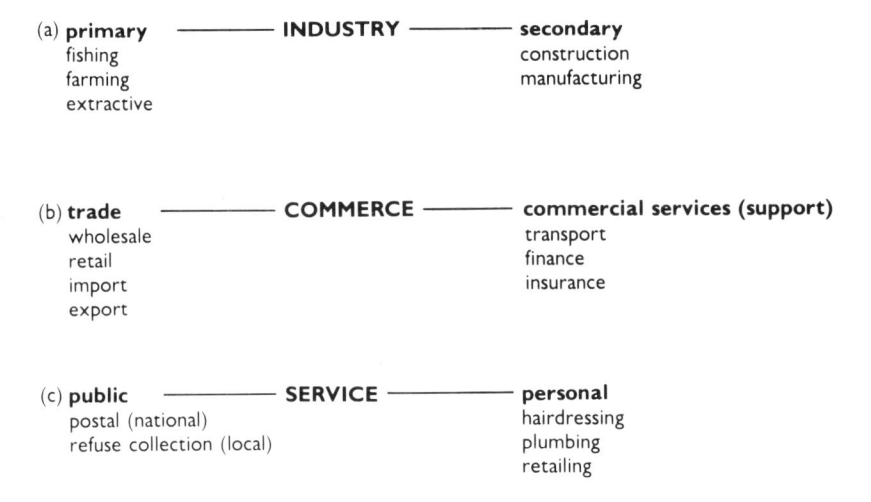

```
(a) primary  ————— INDUSTRY ————— secondary
    fishing                        construction
    farming                        manufacturing
    extractive


(b) trade    ————— COMMERCE ————— commercial services (support)
    wholesale                      transport
    retail                         finance
    import                         insurance
    export


(c) public   ————— SERVICE  ————— personal
    postal (national)              hairdressing
    refuse collection (local)      plumbing
                                   retailing
```

Within these main sectors there are, as you can see, many different types of organisation, each of which has its own particular characteristics, functions, and benefits. Some are easily recognised as **private enterprise**; some are definitely **public enterprises**.

Types of organisation

Private Enterprise

Fig. 3.2

Type of organisation	Functional area	Characteristics
Sole proprietor	Usually personal services such as hairdresser, corner shop, painter and decorator.	1 The owner provides the necessary capital, operates the business, takes the profits, and is liable for debts. 2 Problems can be limited capital and unlimited liability. 3 Advantages can be independence, direct customer contact, and the ability to change quickly, according to market demands.
(Unlimited) partnership	Can be personal services, small industrial concerns, and small commercial organisations.	1 The provision of capital is easier with 2 – 20 partners, and liability for debts is spread. 2 Management of the business is shared and there is wider expertise available. 3 Liability for debts is unlimited. 4 Problems can arise on death or withdrawal of partner.
(Limited) Partnership	Same basic principles as unlimited partnership, but some partners, who must not be involved in managing the business, have limited liability for debts.	

(Limited) private company	Medium-sized or small organisations:
	e.g. building
	     wholesalers
	     manufacturing
	     transport
		1 The company must be registered.
		2 Capital comes from the shareholders, and more is usually available.
		3 The company is a legal entity in itself – separate from the shareholders.
		4 One or more directors are appointed to run the business, but control still lies with the shareholders.
		5 There is limited liability for debts.
		6 Profits are shared through a dividend paid on shares.
		7 Disadvantages are that the company must adhere to quite complicated legal formalities and it is forbidden to advertise for share capital.

Public limited liability company (plc)	Large-scale organisations: e.g. construction manufacturing commercial services	1. Anybody can become a shareholder, and there is no limit on the number. 2. Information on the company must be available to the public, and shares are bought and sold on the Stock Exchange. 3. Much more capital becomes available. 4. Ownership of shares can be transferred without affecting management. 5. Management is through Board of Directors specially appointed to run the business.
Multi-national company	Large-scale organisations: Variety of activities within the general 'interest areas' of the company(ies).	1. Produces goods in more than one country. 2. Owns and controls the producing agencies. 3. Can contribute enormously to the economy of a country by 'importing' capital and technology. 4. If a multi-national decides to move resources (e.g. capital, or a production process) from one country to another, it can damage the economy of the original country.

Public Enterprise

Fig. 3.3

Type of organisation	Functional area	Characteristics
Public corporation e.g. National Coal Board	Usually **key** areas of economic activity. Can provide goods or services which would not be profitable for a private concern.	1. Run by a Board appointed by the government. 2. Ownership rests with the public. 3. Unlimited liability. 4. Any losses are borne by the public. 5. The government (Parliament) determine the aims and objectives of the organisation.

Types of organisation

Mixed enterprise (organisations in which the government has a substantial stake) e.g. BP ICI	Any area, but often production.	1 The State is a shareholder in the company (i.e. **public** and **private** enterprise together). 2 The state usually provides capital but can influence aims and objectives. 3 Usually the company still has to compete in the marketplace. 4 Sometimes a 'privatised' public organisation ends up as a mixed enterprise.
Central government departments e.g. Employment Health Social Services	1 Basically an administrative role in a specialist area on a nationwide basis. 2 Can exert influence over the activities of all organisations, both public and private, and therefore affects all economic and social life.	1 Usually bureaucratic and slow to change. 2 It can be difficult for members of the public to get access to information they require.
Local government departments e.g. Rates Housing Education	Usually have a statutory duty to provide services to local community.	1 There are likely to be differences in the level of service offered by different Local Authorities. 2 Subject to political influences. 3 Local people can have direct access to essential services.

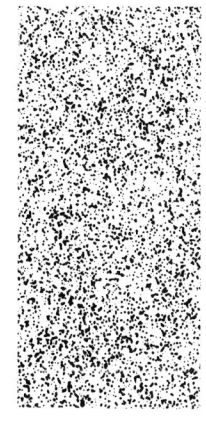

ASSIGNMENT: Local employment

You work for the Town Clerk's Department as an administrative assistant and have become involved in a project to draw up an analysis of the types of business that can be found in your particular area. One of the objectives of the exercise is to establish the range of employment opportunities available to people living in, or moving to, the area, and you and two colleagues have been asked to do some of the 'spadework'.

Task 1

Working as a team, you should draw up a street plan of your area and indicate what organisations are operating, 'plotting' them on the plan. Use a detailed key to indicate what type of business each is. There is no need to give the names of the businesses, unless these indicate the function.

People in business organisations

It might be useful to choose the same area you worked on in the public relations brochure, but do not try to deal with too large an area. In discussion with your tutor, establish the limits within which you are going to work.

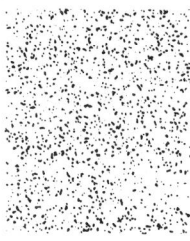

Task 2

In order to give clear guidance to the researchers on the range of organisations operating in your area, draw up a table similar to the one in fig. 3.4 giving all the information indicated for each organisation. An example is given to show the type of information required.

Fig. 3.4

Organisation	Sample activities	Public or private enterprise	Industrial commercial or service sector	Type of organisation
Bank	personal accounts business accounts investments mortgages loans	private	commercial	public company

Note: This assignment should be completed in six hours (including field research).

CHAPTER 4
Organisational structure and communication

Two main characteristics of any organisation are (a) the division of labour, and (b) the distribution of authority. The 'division of labour' refers to the variety of operations that the organisation must carry out in order to achieve its main objectives. The 'distribution of authority' refers to the decision-making apparatus required to plan and control these operations. Both of these characteristics may be shown in an **organisation chart**.

The purpose of organisation charts

An organisation chart can be thought of as a two-dimensional model of an organisation. No such model can effectively convey the reality of executive responsibilities or the complexity of the inter-relationships that exist between the different sub-systems. Organisation charts are, therefore, an *attempt* to illustrate the formal relationships in an organisation, the main lines of communication, and the flow of authority and responsibility through all levels of the management hierarchy. Above all, organisation charts provide a complete picture of the organisation in a way that is simple to understand.

Charts are used to show the whole organisation (system), the departments (sub-systems) within an organisation, or details of one department or section only. Some organisation charts concentrate on the functions of the organisation as opposed to the structure of personnel (see fig 4.3). Certain conventions are normally followed, examples of which are given in fig. 4.1.

Fig. 4.1

(a) formal (line) relationships are shown by a continuous line

(b) Personnel Officer K. Janes — a position, function or unit is often enclosed by a box; where appropriate, boxes should contain names as well as job titles

(c) broken lines are used to denote informal (functional) relationships

(d) where practicable the number of subordinates each manager/supervisor has should be clearly shown.

or

← 6 joiners → If the number is large then figures can be used

(e) Key red lines — production
green lines — purchasing

a key should be given where appropriate

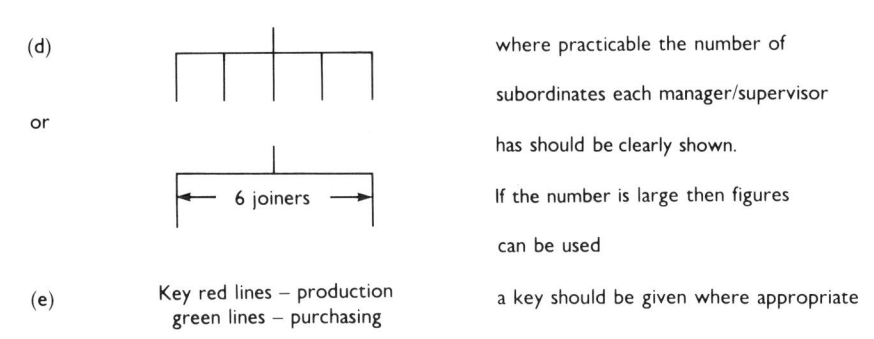

Types of organisation chart

Figs. 4.2(a) (b) and (c) show three different types of organisation chart depicting the structure of a drug manufacturing company, Rayco Ltd, whose main products are toothpaste and anti-dandruff shampoo.

a **Vertical charts** ('T' charts) are the traditional method.
b **Horizontal charts** are read from left to right and minimise the idea of hierarchical levels.
c **Concentric charts** are read from the centre outwards, the closeness to the centre reflecting the relative 'importance' of the posts.

ACTIVITY

Copy and complete the concentric chart (fig. 4.2(c)) using information given in the vertical chart (fig. 4.2(a)).

The interpretation of organisation charts

For simplicity, the following points relate to a vertical chart:

1 **Authority** is the right or power to make decisions or give orders. It flows from the top downwards.
2 **Accountability** is the obligation to follow such decisions or orders. It flows from the bottom upwards.
3 To assume that one post is inferior to another because it occupies a lower level in the chart is incorrect (this can lead to problems with those who are 'status conscious', and is a recognised disadvantage of vertical charts).
4 It is important to keep in mind that a chart is only a simplistic model of an organisation, and too narrow an interpretation can contribute to a rigidity of outlook by staff.

Note   The net result of points **3** and **4** above is that many companies deliberately avoid issuing organisation charts to their staff, retaining them for management use only.

Fig. 4.2(a)

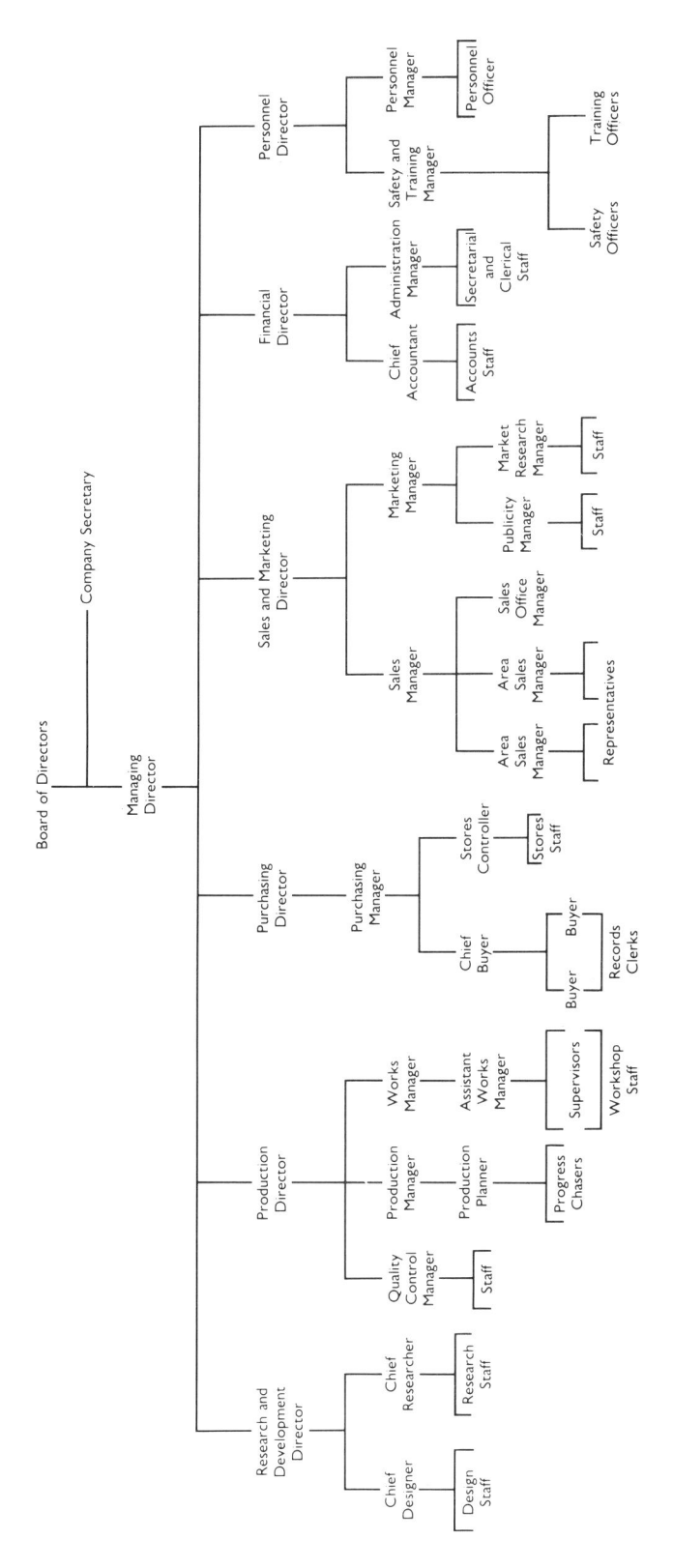

Organisational chart:

- Board of Directors
  - Managing Director — Company Secretary
    - Research and Development Director
      - Chief Designer
        - Design Staff
      - Chief Researcher
        - Research Staff
    - Production Director
      - Quality Control Manager
        - Staff
      - Production Manager
        - Production Planner
          - Progress Chasers
      - Works Manager
        - Assistant Works Manager
          - Supervisors
          - Workshop Staff
    - Purchasing Director
      - Purchasing Manager
        - Chief Buyer
          - Buyer
          - Buyer
          - Records Clerks
        - Stores Controller
          - Stores Staff
    - Sales and Marketing Director
      - Sales Manager
        - Area Sales Manager
          - Representatives
        - Area Sales Manager
          - Representatives
        - Sales Office Manager
      - Marketing Manager
        - Publicity Manager
          - Staff
        - Market Research Manager
          - Staff
    - Financial Director
      - Chief Accountant
        - Accounts Staff
      - Administration Manager
        - Secretarial and Clerical Staff
    - Personnel Director
      - Personnel Manager
        - Personnel Officer
      - Safety and Training Manager
        - Safety Officers
        - Training Officers

20   *People in business organisations*

Fig. 4.2(b)

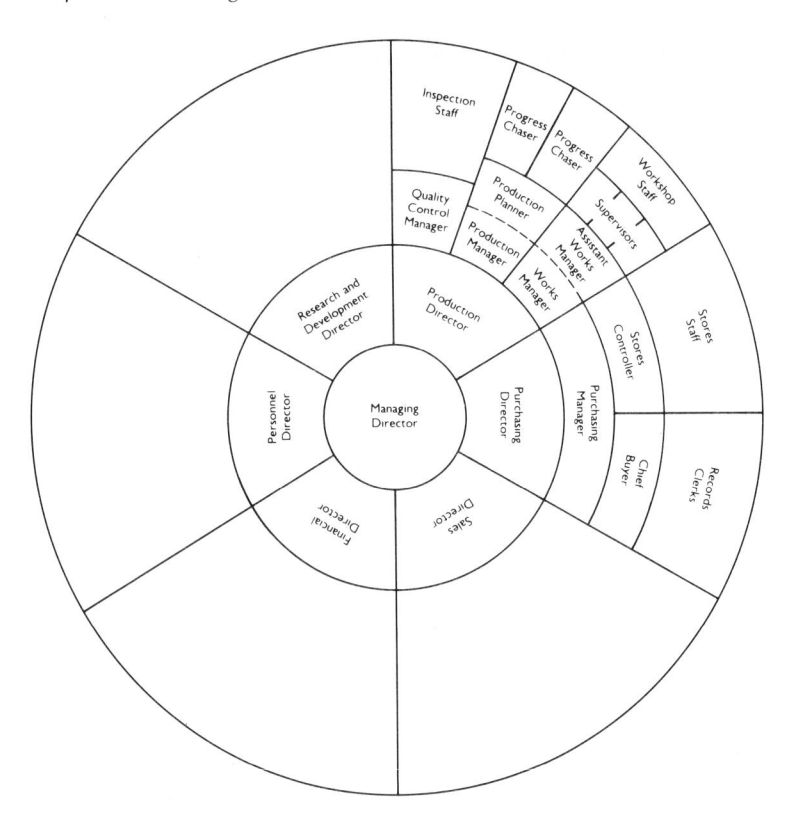

Fig. 4.2(c)

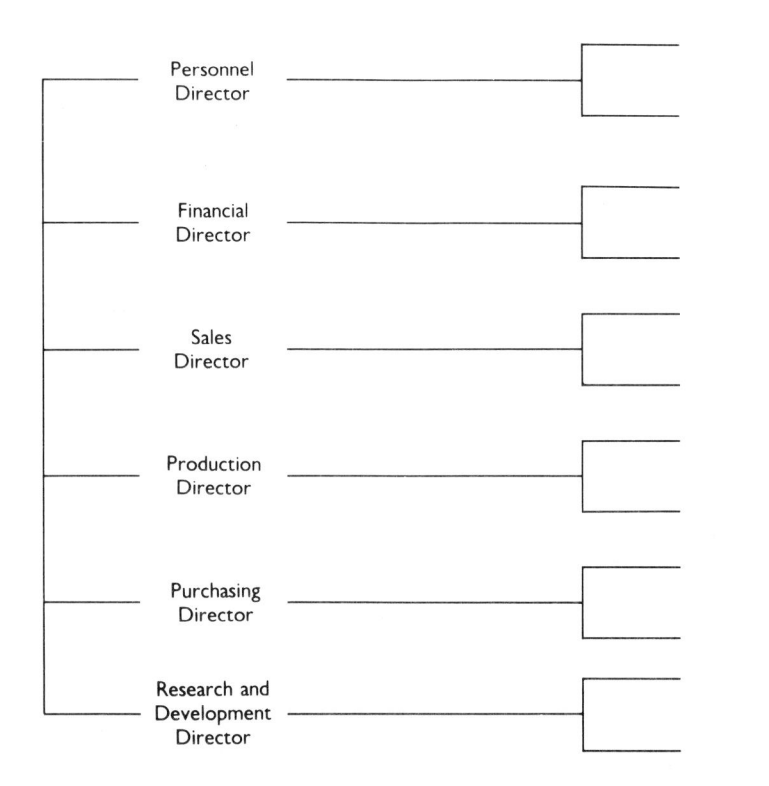

Molecules versus pyramids

Workers have a much greater say in decisions about their factory or workplace than they used to have. Work has become so specialised that senior members of staff have to trust junior staff who have specialist skills which they do not understand, or have not got time to learn. Therefore all the staff often have to be involved in the decision-making process. To reflect this, as well as to avoid the problems of interpretation previously described, some firms favour a molecular representation of their structure. Fig. 4.3 shows the Marketing Department of a large manufacturing company. The people in the striped circles all work in Marketing. Those in plain circles are in other departments, and only part of their work is to do with Marketing. As in other types of chart, where people are joined by a solid line, one is directly responsible to the other. Where people are joined by a broken line there is no direct responsibility, but their work brings them into regular contact with each other.

Fig. 4.3 Part of a molecular chart.

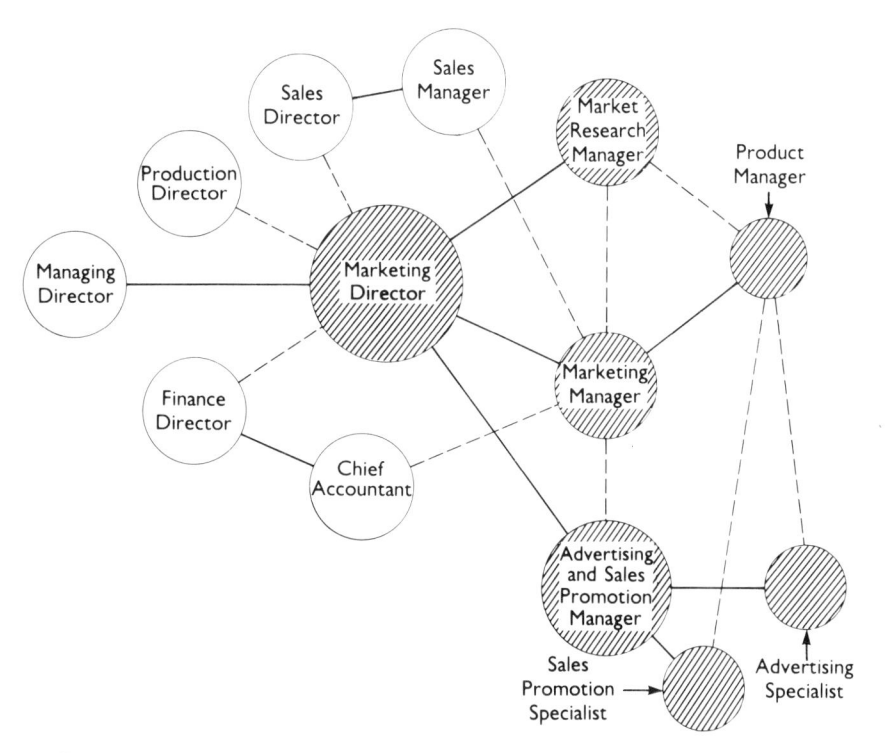

ACTIVITY

1. Draw up a horizontal organisation chart of the organisation for which you work, setting out the main functional areas only.
2. Draw up a detailed organisation chart for the section or department in which you work, depicting job titles and present occupants.

(If you are a full-time student, use the college as a basis for the charts, unless you have access to a suitable commercial organisation.)

Charting the growth of a business organisation
ASSIGNMENT: Toms Enterprises

Mrs and Mrs Toms buy a shop in Plymouth with a view to selling furniture. After a hectic six months they engage two sales assistants.

Task 1

Chart the organisation (use horizontal type charts throughout).

The business goes from strength to strength. Mr and Mrs Toms buy shop premises in Truro and Exeter and take on managers for each of their three shops, plus four sales assistants (two for each of the new shops).

Task 2

Chart the organisation.

Six months later it's going even better. The Toms employ someone to do the purchasing for the three shops, plus a book-keeping clerk.

Task 3

Chart the organisation.

One year later, and what a year it has been! Mr and Mrs Toms decide that in addition to the furniture from the manufacturers they will market their own. They open a small factory in Bodmin for the manufacture of simple standard ranges of furniture. They employ an experienced joiner as the Works Manager, and twelve additional joiners who are subordinate to him. One of their Shop Managers is promoted to overall Sales Manager, and a further Shop Manager is appointed to fill her previous position.

Task 4

Chart the organisation.

The furniture being produced by the Toms' factory is selling like 'hot cakes' (because the quality is very good relative to price). Encouraged by their success, Mr and Mrs Toms decide to employ a very well-qualified designer to head a team of three draughtsmen and women, so that they can offer a wider range of their own products. They also promote the best joiner to the position of Assistant Works Manager, and engage a further six joiners. Finally, at this stage they decide to put the Purchasing Manager (who will be spending less time buying ready-made furniture and more time buying materials) in a subordinate position to the Works Manager, but of equal status to the new Assistant Works Manager.

Task 5

Chart the organisation.

Task 6

As a company expands, the need for greater specialisation emerges – for example, a separate purchasing department may be set up. Assuming Toms' turnover doubles over the next two years, what new specialist departments are likely to be created? Draw up a full organisation chart, showing the structure of the company in two years' time.

Relationships in a business organisation

a Line relationship

This is a relationship which exists between a senior and his/her subordinate at any level of the organisation. For example, in Rayco Ltd (fig. 4.2) such a relationship exists between the Production Director and Production Manager, and between the Works Manager and the Assistant Works Manager.

b Functional relationship

This is the relationship which exists between those holding functional (or specialist) posts and those with direct executive responsibilities. For example, in Rayco Ltd the post of Personnel Director is a line management post only in the sense that the holder has authority over the staff in his own department. His main function is to advise and assist all the other departments on personnel matters. Because he is an expert in his field he is also empowered to make rulings which must be complied with by staff over whom he has no direct line authority. If, for example, the Personnel Director has grounds for refusing to recruit a particular job applicant (because, possibly, of poor references), his authority for recruitment will over-ride the line director's responsibility for selection.

c Lateral relationship

This is the relationship between personnel working at the same level — that is, none is superior or subordinate to others. In Rayco Ltd such a relationship exists between the Production Manager and the Works Manager.

d Staff relationship

The word 'staff' here is used in the sense of a support (as in 'wooden staff'). Such a relationship occurs, for example, between a managing director and her personal assistant. The holder of such a post has no formal relationship with other persons within the organisation, nor does she possess authority in her own right. This kind of relationship exists between the Managing Director and the Company Secretary in Rayco Ltd.

e Span of control

The number of people who are *directly* accountable to the same person constitutes the 'span of control' of that person.

f Informal relationships

Although, in theory, communication should pass up and down the line, if this were carried out in practice every supervisor would become a potential bottleneck. To avoid this, a sensible working arrangement may allow, for example, for a Progress Chaser in Rayco Ltd to establish an **ad hoc relationship** with one or more of the Supervisors. Similarly, the line can be

by-passed on occasions: the Sales Director may, for example, find himself in a situation which would benefit from direct contact with one of the representatives.

The modern approach to relationships within an organisation stresses flexibility as far as sub-system boundaries are concerned. It is one of the tasks of management to link the various sub-systems together, to ensure integration and co-operation, and to act as boundary agent beween the organisation and the environment. The area of contact between one system and another is called an **interface**.

ACTIVITY

As the afternoon shift at Spanner Manufacturing, Ltd got into full swing, there was a sudden flash and crack from the main junction box on the wall, and the lathes whined to a halt.

Bob Wallingford, the foreman, identified the problem as being a leak from a central heating pipe which ran above an electrical junction box. The water had 'shorted out' the system and blown a fuse. He turned his attention to the fuse box and decided that he could make an immediate repair which would enable the busy afternoon shift to continue work.

Having replaced the fuse, he was about to put the main power back on when Jane Prendergast, the Safety Officer, came in. She had been told of the problem, and immediately instructed Bob to leave the power off. She then told two people to leave their lathes and fetch a mobile scaffolding tower from the maintenance section so that some temporary repair could be made to the leaking central heating pipe. As the two operators left the workshop, they met the Production Supervisor, Arthur Malford, who was just returning from a meeting with the Production Manager. When he discovered what was happening, he accused Jane Prendergast of interfering in the running of his workshop, and pointed out that Jane had no authority to 'order my staff about' or take them off their specified tasks. Jane Prendergast replied that where the safety of employees was concerned her authority overruled other considerations, and she was expected to take such action in such circumstances.

Consider this difficult situation in small groups of four or five, paying particular attention to the following comments and questions:

- 'Jane Prendergast had no right to stick her nose in when she did. It was none of her business.'
- Can you suggest what kind of authority Jane Prendergast was exercising when she 'stepped into' the situation?
- What rights did Arthur Malford have? Was he justified in arguing against Jane Prendergast's action? How do you see the role of the Safety Officer in this sort of situation?
- 'This problem could have been avoided if it had been tackled in the right way.'
  Suggest what course of action could have been taken.

The organisation and communication

The channels of communication outlined in the previous section and the case sketch indicate the desirability of co-operation and free information flow throughout an organisation. However, in reality, communication is often seen as a downward process whereby 'management' tell 'workers' what to do and what is happening. This attitude can sometimes be reinforced by the misuse, or misinterpretation, of an organisational structure as delineated in an organisation chart. Unfortunately, misconceptions like this can lead to dissatisfaction, an unwillingness to co-operate fully, and unnecessary disputes.

Such an authoritarian approach to management means that any interference or suggestions from below are resented, there is an unwillingness to confide in 'subordinates', and employees are told only what is essential for them to do their jobs.

Fortunately, as management thought has become more enlightened, the benefits of consultation, participation, and person to person communication have been recognised and taken advantage of. However, many instances still occur where downward communication is regarded as the norm, with little appreciation of the fact that communication must be a **two-way process** – the person giving the message must be willing to pass on the information (and therefore make a determined effort to overcome misunderstanding, apprehension, antagonism and other barriers), and the recipient must be prepared to listen, think about the information, and reach a point of understanding or agreement with the initiator.

In this context there are many things which can 'block' effective communication. Some examples are:

Barrier	*Possible effect*
language	misunderstanding/ambiguity
intelligence	inability to understand or make oneself understood
suspicion	refusal to 'get involved'
distrust	immediate antagonism
refusal to listen/accept	total breakdown in communication
prejudice	failure to accept logical argument
unsympathetic attitudes	unwillingness to listen to alternative points of view
inattention	inappropriate/incorrect action taken
use of inappropriate medium (e.g. memo, when personal interview would be better)	no opportunity for questioning/ discussion/further explanation

If barriers are not overcome, communication failure leads to conflict and dispute. Therefore (although there are always likely to be disagreements in any working environment), there will be less chance of a disruptive 'flare-up' if all employees know what is happening and why it is happening, and are given the opportunity to discuss problems and express their opinions in the knowledge that their ideas will be listened to. If communication failure between individuals escalates to the point where it influences the working relationship between sub-systems (Departments), the effective running of the whole organisation can be affected, with a consequent drop in efficiency, work-flow, profitability and – in the longer term – viability.

You will have the opportunity of considering the problems of communication breakdown further in case studies later in the text.

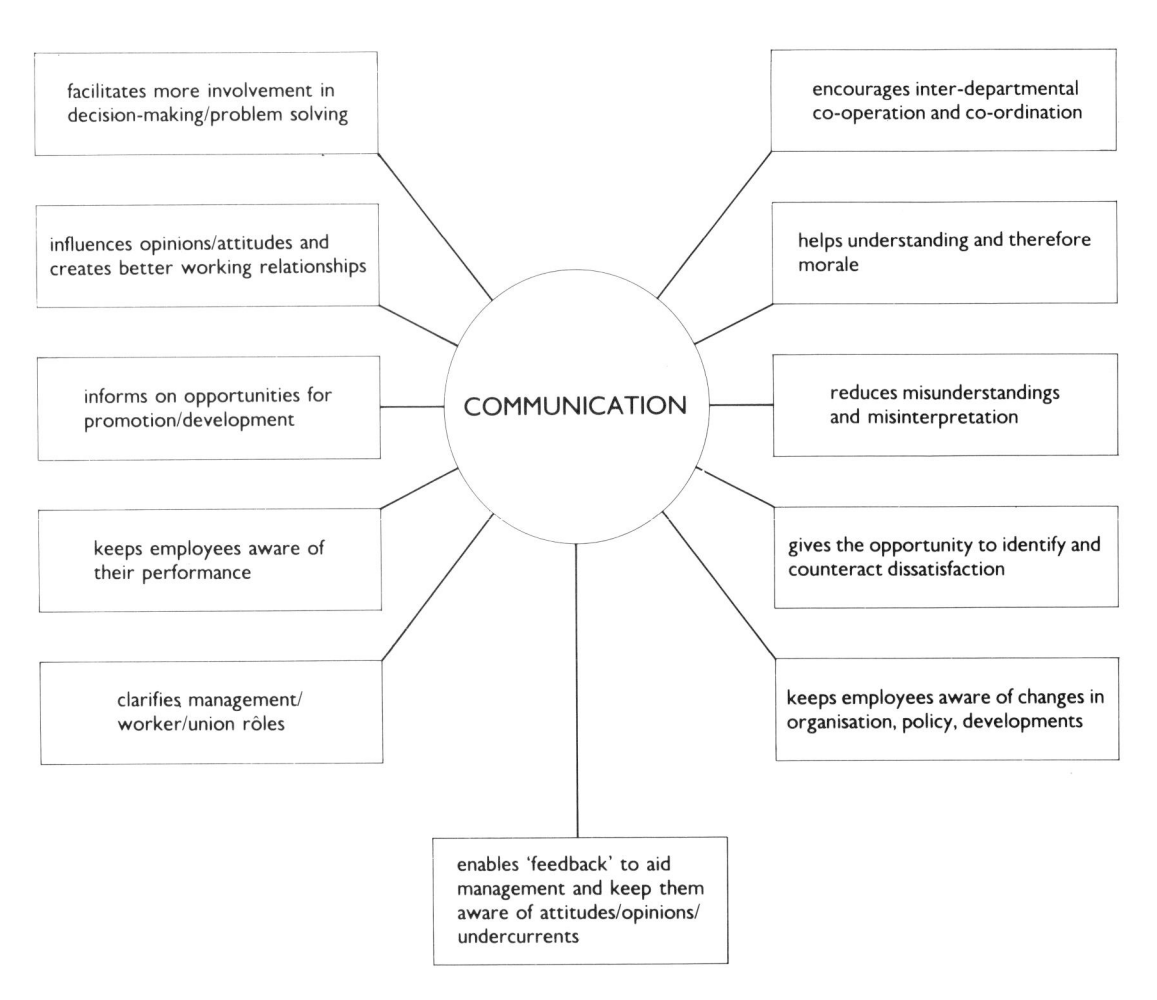

Fig. 4.4 Some benefits of good communications.

COMMUNICATION

- facilitates more involvement in decision-making/problem solving
- influences opinions/attitudes and creates better working relationships
- informs on opportunities for promotion/development
- keeps employees aware of their performance
- clarifies management/worker/union rôles
- encourages inter-departmental co-operation and co-ordination
- helps understanding and therefore morale
- reduces misunderstandings and misinterpretation
- gives the opportunity to identify and counteract dissatisfaction
- keeps employees aware of changes in organisation, policy, developments
- enables 'feedback' to aid management and keep them aware of attitudes/opinions/undercurrents

The rumour factory?

No matter what is happening through the more formal communications procedures in an organisation, anyone concerned with administration must be aware of the **grapevine** – the most informal (and hazardous!) route that the information can take.

The grapevine reaches all levels of an organisation, and information is often passed on by people who don't have all the facts, or who might give them a slightly different emphasis to that intended. This doesn't mean

Fig. 4.5   THE GRAPE VINE

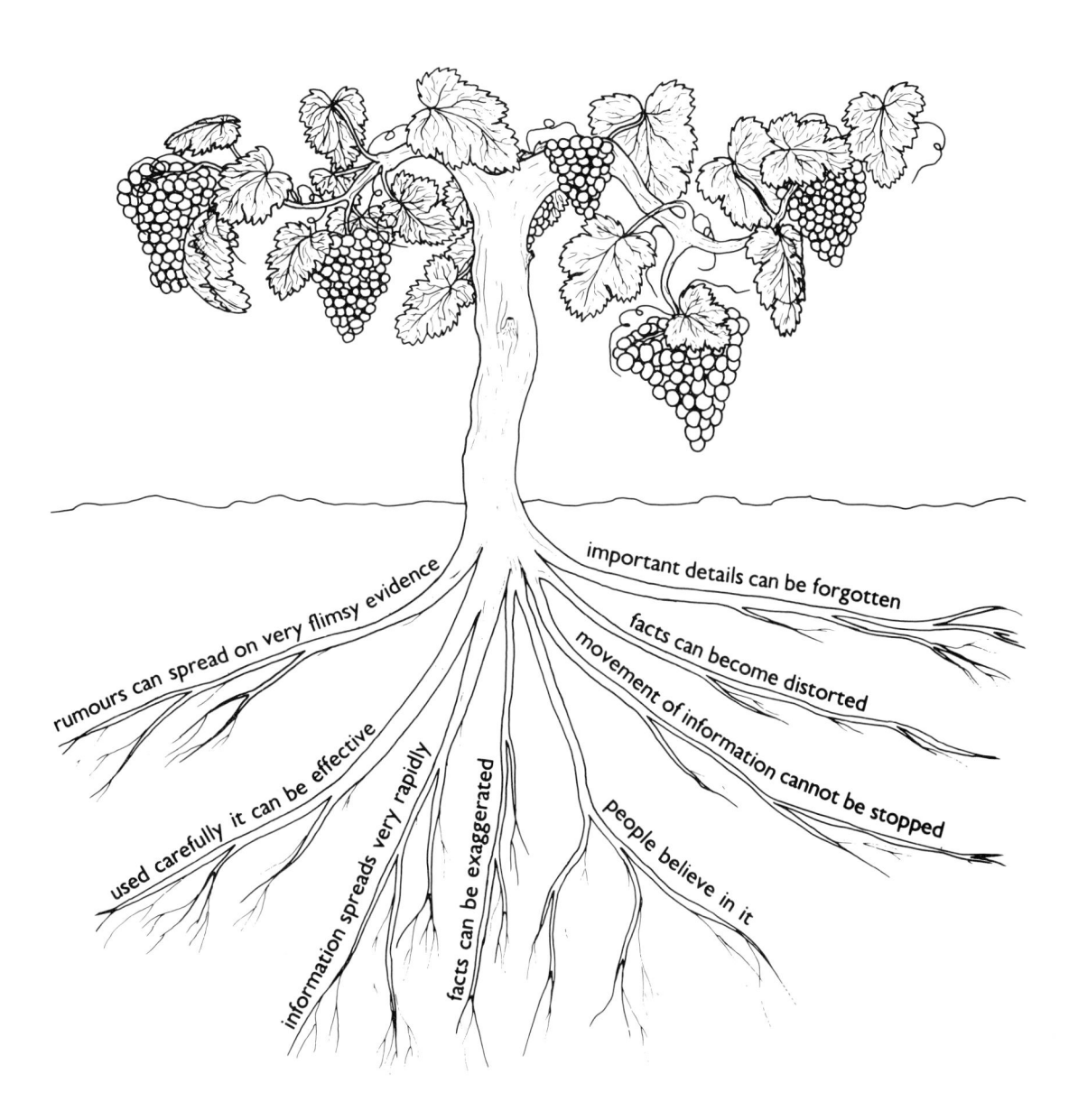

- rumours can spread on very flimsy evidence
- important details can be forgotten
- facts can become distorted
- movement of information cannot be stopped
- used carefully it can be effective
- information spreads very rapidly
- facts can be exaggerated
- people believe in it

that frequent and direct person-to-person communication is always bad – in fact it is accepted as a normal process of keeping people informed of what is happening, and as long as it is used carefully, such informal channels can have advantages. If, for example, an idea or course of action is only tentative, an appropriate rumour fed into the grapevine could provide the opportunity to identify attitudes and observe reactions before making a final decision.

ASSIGNMENT: Rayco

Some ways in which in-company communications can be developed are listed below. Using fig. 4.2 (Rayco) for reference, consider the overall structure of this organisation, and think carefully about how good relationships and useful communication processes could be encouraged within the workforce. Gather as much information as you can on each of the 'methods' listed below (using the college library or *any* other sources) and consider how appropriate they are, and their implications for the company.

As a Personnel Officer, and on your own initiative, inform the Personnel Manager of your thoughts and ideas, and recommend what you consider to be the *minimum* requirements for establishing an effective communications policy. Specify what procedures you consider appropriate, and suggest how any consultative 'groups' should be constituted.

Methods of communication

notice boards	manager's newsletter
in-house magazine	consultative committee
company newspapers	employee handbooks
briefing groups	regular person-to-person interviews
suggestion scheme	informal 'meetings' (e.g. over lunch, etc.)
worker-directors	union newsletter
appraisal interviews	induction programme
'open door' policy	information sheets
regular social events	progress meetings
section/departmental meetings	policy meetings

Notes

a You should consider the needs of new employees, established employees, management, and workers.
b Do not attempt to incorporate *all* the methods mentioned above. Assume that there are few, if any, formal procedures at present, and suggest *minimum* requirements for setting up a workable system.

Format

As this is an internal, person-to-person, self-initiated document, a memo-report format should be adopted. A suggested structure for this is illustrated in fig. 4.6.

Fig. 4.6

CONFIDENTIAL

To: (name and designation)   Ref:

From: (name and designation)   Date:

Title/subject

This first section should be presented as a normal paragraph and will contain the terms of reference i.e. essential introductory and background information; why you are submitting it; what procedures have been followed in acquiring the information; what the purpose or function of the document is. If more than one paragraph is appropriate, this is acceptable.

Section heading

    (a) sub-heading

        (i)
        (ii)
        (iii)

    (b) sub-heading

        (i)
        (ii)
        (iii)

The main body of the report can be presented schematically under relevant section headings in order to aid comprehension and speed of assimilation. Each of the sections, sub-sections and numbered points can be as long as you require to put across your information. This must *not* be in note-form.

Section heading

    (a) sub-heading

        (i)
        (ii)
        (iii)

The final sections should be normal narrative paragraphs incorporating your conclusions and recommendations. If you feel it would be useful to present any of these as a list of numbered points, they should be indented and presented for maximum visual effect.

                                  Signature (for validation)

CHAPTER 5
The functional areas of a business organisation

This chapter describes the major functions of each of the sub-systems of Rayco Ltd. For the sake of simplicity we shall take Rayco to represent a 'typical firm' while remembering that, rather like the family with 2.4 children, no such entity truly exists! The departments shown reporting to the Managing Director in fig. 4.2 are those commonly found in a medium-sized manufacturing firm. However, you may find that your own organisation is different, either because of the nature of the enterprise (e.g. banks, and local government departments) or because the arrangement of the sub-system is different.

Production

This department is responsible for manufacturing the finished goods. Its main activities are described below.

Purchasing

This is carried out on the principle of finding the best quality goods for the purpose for which they are intended, at the cheapest possible price. In one year Rayco uses over a tonne of typing paper, skips-full of soap and toilet paper, and millions of cardboard cartons. Chemicals are delivered in 32 tonne truckloads, and up to 30 company cars are bought every year for senior managerial staff and the sales force. When purchasing on such a scale, most organisations would appoint specialist buyers to maximise the efficiency of this section.

Stock control

It is essential to have effective control over stocks of raw materials and supplies. In Rayco the Purchasing Manager is also ultimately responsible for stock control. This part of the organisation is concerned with receiving and storing finished goods before despatch, as well as dealing with supplies from outside agencies. (All of Rayco's packaging materials, for example, are bought-in.) The issue of stock for internal use or delivery to customers is another aspect of this work. In large companies like Rayco, a computerised system would be the most effective method of stock control. The computer file would have data on re-order levels for each item, and all receipts or issues would be keyed into a computer terminal so that the file would be constantly updated, and stock levels known.

Production planning

An important activity in this section involves planning the lay-out and use of manufacturing plant so that the orders gained by the Sales Department are produced in the most efficient way. Main activities include:

a **Scheduling** – establishing priorities for work that has to be done and timetabling the work according to these priorities;
b **Loading** – balancing the work between work stations and individuals so that they each perform a reasonable amount of work, and bottlenecks are avoided.

Production control

This aspect of the process ensures that the planned production is achieved. Activities include:

a **Progress control** – ensuring that tasks are completed on schedule;
b **Quality control** – ensuring that the quality of the output meets specific standards. This is a vital activity for Rayco as its type of production is subject to strict health and safety regulations. An experienced, highly-qualified biochemist would be in charge of this section.

Work study

In large organisations this can be an on-going activity, involving the scrutinising and monitoring of the work content of each job to ensure that it is done in the most efficient manner.

Maintenance

This department is responsible for the maintenance of the plant and machinery.

Marketing and sales

The Marketing Department is often considerd to be the king-pin of the manufacturing organisation. It is concerned with finding out precisely what goods the consumer wants so that the research and development, and production sub-systems of the organisation can be geared to producing them. After this, the next most important step is to sell the product at a profit. The tasks of the Marketing Department include the following main areas.

Market research

Activities involved in this area are:

a **Consumer research** – learning of consumers' preferences;

b **Market research** – obtaining facts relating to marketing possibilities and prospects. (This is particularly important for export trade, as facts relating to a foreign market must be studied before the preferences of consumers can be taken into account.)

Advertising

Whatever form advertising may take, its primary function is **communication**. The most appropriate type of advertising in any particular market will be indicated by the results of the market research conducted by the company.

Public relations

The task of this section is to establish and maintain an appropriate public image of the company. Methods used may include:

a **Press releases** – relating to aspects of the company's activities which it wants to publicise;
b **Exhibitions** – at trade fairs, conferences, industry exhibitions, etc.;
c **Direct consumer contacts** – personal goodwill missions may sometimes be appropriate. Regular telephone contact and sampling can be useful;
d **Sponsorship** – e.g. sports events, individuals, charity appeals, etc.;
e **Literature** – e.g. brochures, pamphlets, leaflets, direct advertising, handouts, etc. (NB – closely tied in with marketing.)

Sales

Obtaining orders for the company's products is one of the most basic and essential activities. In Rayco this is achieved mainly by a network of representatives, organised in geographical areas.

Research and development

'Development' is usually taken to mean all the work needed to turn a new idea into something that can be produced/manufactured profitably. It is often called 'Research and Development', but for most firms, except the very biggest, the research aspect is minimal. Very often 'development' means taking a product which the company already makes, and improving it. For example, the Research and Development Department of Rayco might concentrate on developing their existing brand of dandruff control shampoo to produce an everyday preventative shampoo, as opposed to an occasional 'treatment' shampoo.

Finance

Money is a key resource, and the Finance Department is responsible for its efficient management. Cash must flow from the customers into the business, and flow out of the business to staff and suppliers (together with tax payments to the Government, and rates to the local authority, etc.). In its simplest form, managing the finance consists of controlling these flows and ensuring that, after they have occurred, a surplus is left. In Rayco some of the activities performed by the Finance staff include:

a **Financial accounting** – keeping the books.
b **Cost accounting** – keeping a check on the costs involved in the running of the business, particularly the production process.
c **Management accounting** – providing financial information on past, present and possible future performance of the firm.
d **Financial management** – including monitoring cash flow and credit control.
e **Wages** – most sections of the accounting function in large organisations like Rayco use computerised procedures.

Personnel

Whilst everyone in charge of people has some responsibility for and to them, Personnel staff are specialists in the field. They work to create the best climate for people to work in and to give of their best. Main activities include:

a **Staff planning** (often referred to as manpower planning) – planning the supply of suitably trained personnel to fill posts.
b **Recruitment and selection** – obtaining the right person for the job.
c **Training** – of new and established staff. A progressive company goes on training staff of all ages and at all levels. Even senior managers may require re-training when new technology is introduced.
d **Health and safety** – interpreting and applying the law with regard to people's rights, security, safety and health.
e **Records** – maintaining up-to-date records on all personnel.

The Company Secretary

By law, every limited company must have a Company Secretary. His/her functions, as laid down in various Acts of Parliament, are restricted to the legal and financial side of the business, though nowadays he/she may perform other tasks. The Company Secretary is responsible for convening and minuting meetings of the Board of Directors as well as the Annual General Meeting of shareholders. He/she is also responsible for the correspondence of the Board, completing statutory books and returns, and carrying out the firm's legal work.

Data processing/management services

The functions and operation of this important department are dealt with in detail in Section 2, Chapter 10.

ASSIGNMENT: Local industry

(Read the complete assignment before you start.)

In a previous assignment you will probably have identified a range of organisations operating in your area, and it is likely that one or more fall into the industrial/manufacturing/production category. The aim of this assignment is to enable you to gain a knowledge and understanding of the structure, activities and operation of such an organisation, other than your own. If you have *not* identified this type of organisation, then you should look further afield and select an appropriate one.

Task 1

Contact the organisation *by telephone* and establish who you should write to in order to request information about the company and its activities. You should *not* be persuaded to speak directly to the person concerned at this stage – merely establish who is responsible for general public relations, his/her name and position.

If more than one person intends to contact any particular organisation, those concerned should co-operate and share information so that no company receives more than one call.

You should bear in mind that a 'cold' approach like this is very difficult, and needs to be thoroughly prepared (see 'Notes for guidance' below).

Task 2

Write a letter to the appropriate person, explaining briefly who you are, why you are contacting him/her, and asking for any information which will enable you to draw up a profile of the company. The letter can be handwritten or typed, but should be well-presented and conform to accepted business conventions (see 'Notes for guidance' below).

Task 3

See what information you can find about the company using other sources, e.g. local knowledge, library, advertising features in the press, recent company reports, advertisements, leaflets, brochures, etc.

Task 4

Produce a folder profiling the company, and giving information on its aims, structure, activities, etc.

Any information about the company will be relevant, and you should aim to collate, classify and present the material as a coherent and easy-to-follow package, with identifiable sections. Obviously, the main content of your profile will be written by you, but any support materials and illustrative information you can acquire can be incorporated. The profile can be structured in any way you think appropriate, but the following guidelines indicate main areas you ought to consider:

- the company's aims and functions
- geographical location
- company structure (include an organisation chart)
- the management team
- the rest of the workforce
- the departments
- the product(s)
- the customers
- company performance (see recent Company Report if available)
- research and development
- the future

The functional areas of a business organisation 35

Notes for guidance

1. Your task will be made much easier if you choose a fairly large organisation.
2. If possible, arrange a visit to the company as part of your research.
3. For Task 1, make sure you are prepared. We all think we can use the telephone competently, but you need to be quite certain of what you want to say, and what responses you are looking for, before you make the initial contact. The first telephone call could determine whether or not the company will co-operate with you. You would be well advised to produce some brief **notes for a telephone call**, which will give you a checklist of points you want to raise. Even if it seems a little long-winded, try a format similar to the one in fig. 5.1 below – it will pay dividends.

Fig. 5.1

> **Notes for telephone Call**
>
> **Tel no:** 01 734 8754
>
> **Company:** South East Motor Supplies,
> 21 Ivatt Place,
> London SW3
>
> **Contact:** Mr Thistlethwaite (Mail Order Dept.)
>
> 1. Ordered headlamp for BMW motorcycle – 75/6 model – 4 weeks ago. Cheque sent with order.
> 2. No confirmation of order received – no goods arrived.
> 3. Have checked with my bank and the cheque has been cashed (cheque no. 827352)
> 4. Have the goods been sent?
> 5. If not, request immediate dispatch
> 6. If lost in post, ask for replacements to be sent.

For Task 2, bear in mind that the visual impact of any written communication determines the recipient's impression of the writer. The conventions and components of basic business letters are given after the general layout diagram (fig. 5.2).

You will notice that although the writer's address is on the right-hand side of the page, it is still 'blocked', i.e. the beginning of each line is directly below the beginning of the previous line. This matches the receiver's address and gives the visual impact of the letter a degree of consistency.

Fig. 5.2

```
                                    Writer's
                                    address


           Reference                 Date

           Recipient's
           address


           Salutation
_____
_____
                        Main
_____
                            body
_____
                                of
_____
                                    letter
_____
_____

                       Subscription

                       Signature
                       Designation
```

The writer's address

- **a** It is not normal practice for the name of the individual sending the letter to appear at the beginning of this address.
- **b** If a house number is used, it is not necessary to put a comma between this and the street name. Avoid abbreviations such as St. (Street), Ave. (Avenue), and Rd. (Road).
- **c** There should be a comma at the end of each line, except for the last line *before* the postcode. A full stop is used here.
- **d** No punctuation is required in the postcode.
- **e** In handwritten letters the address should not be printed completely in capital letters. However, it is acceptable to use printed capitals for the name of the town.

f If a house *name* is used instead of, or in addition to, a number, this name is written on a separate line.

g If there is a recognised abbreviation for the county, this can be used, e.g.

17 Youldon Way,
Plymford,
WATERHAVEN,
Herts.
HE7 8PJ

The reference

a In a typed letter from a firm, this should contain the initials of the person authorising (dictating) the letter and those of the typist. Sometimes other symbols are used to help with identification, e.g. document code.

b In a handwritten letter a reference is not normally required unless this is quoted from some previous communication related to the subject of your letter. In this case it should be written as 'Your Ref.' and positioned at the left-hand margin.

c Some printed letter heads have spaces for 'Our Ref.' and 'Your Ref'. This is self-explanatory, but the writer's reference should always be placed at the left-hand margin, e.g.

Ref: PMC/CES
Your Ref: ACT/BRJ
Our Ref: SMS/KCS/154

The date

a Present the date in the correct order – day, month and year.

b The only standard punctuation necessary in the date is a comma after the month.

c There is no full stop after endings used with day numbers such as 1st, 2nd, 3rd, 4th, etc.

The recipient's address

a The same punctuation rules apply here as for the writer's address.

b The name of the person (or his/her official title) should be included. A clergyman should be addressed at The Rev John Smith, or The Rev Mr Smith. A Member of Parliament should be address as Mary Jones MP.

c This name and address is sometimes placed at the foot of the letter – on the left-hand margin – but the most common practice is to position it as indicated in fig. 5.2. For example:

The Customer Services Manager,
Broadway Marketing Ltd,
Broadway Industrial Estate,
NORFORD,
Hants.
HA2 6SN

The salutation

a The standard beginning to a business letter is **Dear Sir**, but others are used in certain circumstances: **Dear Sirs**, when the letter is addressed to a partnership; **Dear Madam**, whether a woman is single or married; **Mesdames**, when a partnership consists of women only.

b The first letter of each word should begin with a capital letter.

c The salutation should be followed by a comma.

The main body of the letter

This is the most important part of the letter, because it contains the **message**. Bear in mind that effective communication should be as simple as possible. Therefore,

a Don't include any unnecessary information.
b Express yourself as concisely as possible.
c Start a new paragraph for each new point you wish to make.
d Conform to all standard puncutation and grammar rules.

Note   Many business letters fall easily into the framework of a three-paragraph plan, which can be generally summarised as:

Paragraph 1   Introduction: this can be an acknowledgement, a reference to previous communication, or any generally informative statement which introduces your main theme.
Paragraph 2   Specific information/facts/reasons.
Paragraph 3   Reference to further action/conclusion.

More detailed analysis of specific types of letters will be given in future sections on correspondence.

The subscription (complimentary close)

a In most circumstances **Yours faithfully** should be used.
b The first word should begin with a capital letter, but the second should begin with a lower case letter.
c The subscription should be followed by a comma.
d **Yours sincerely** can be used if the recipient is known to the writer on a personal basis, or if it is desirable to dispense with formality.
e The subscription should be started at the middle of the page.

The signature

a This should be the normal signature of the writer, and should not include any courtesy title or otherwise.
b A woman can indicate her title in brackets if she wishes, e.g. (Miss: Mrs: Ms).

The designation

This simply gives the official status of the writer and, if required, is best printed directly underneath the signature.

Open punctuation

One trend in the business world which must be mentioned at this point is the use of **open puncutation**. This means that in a typed letter, the date, the reference, the address, the salutation, and the complimentary close (subscription) are presented without any punctuation. The body of the letter is punctuated normally, with certain exceptions.

The main danger for you in using this system is that you might be tempted to carry it over into other work!

SECTION 2

Office services, systems and methods of communication

CHAPTER 6

Office functions and support

When we consider 'the office', we all have our own ideas about what it actually is, and we probably have a picture in our minds of one particular office in one particular organisation. The 'picture' might be of a small general office (dealing with all administrative aspects of an organisation), a specific departmental office (where specialist tasks and duties are carried out), or a large, open-plan centralised office. There are many variations on these themes, but whether an office is general or specialist, large or small, it is an essential co-ordinating and activity centre for any organisation. It provides communication and support services, and the skilled personnel to ensure effective operation. It gives administrative support to whatever the main functions of the organisation might be, and all organisations need 'the office' to maintain and store records, process information and pass it on to internal and external contacts.

ACTIVITY

Using the list of office services and activities below as a basic guide, draw up a table showing the office functions you can identify in your own working environment, and indicate why you think they are essential to the efficient operation of the organisation. Present your answer in the format illustrated in fig. 6.1.

Fig. 6.1

NAME OF ORGANISATION:

Function	This function is essential because:

Office services and activities

This list is not intended to be exclusive or comprehensive, but gives an indication of the range of activities to be found in a business organisation. There should be enough variety for those of you who work in other areas, or are full-time students, to identify office functions relevant to your current work environment. If you can identify other functions you should include them in your table.

computer operating	mailing
establishing staffing levels	preparation of estimates
telephone and telex	preparation of job descriptions, etc.
payment of wages	
reception	meetings
maintaining personnel records	typing
interviewing (recruitment/selection)	production of financial statements
interviewing (appraisal)	training
reprography (photocopying)	filing
wages calculations	producing statistics
induction	contacting customers
contacting suppliers	stock maintenance
checking deliveries (invoices)	placing orders
answering queries	processing orders
balancing statements	preparing advertising material
preparing customers' 'bills' (statements)	writing to customers
	taking/handling cash
giving advice to the public	contacting other departments
drafting memoranda	producing reports
editing documents	maintaining financial records
interpreting statistics	contracts
writing technical information	printing
processing cheques	passing on telephone messages

It is pretty obvious from the range of activities carried out that the office is a centre of information for the various sections of the organisation. On the whole, this information is directly related to the running of the business, but there are times when other information is required, and tasks need to be performed which fall outside the normal working operations.

What would you do, for example, if your Manager asked you to check up on the patent of a competitor's product? If you were asked to find out the regulations covering the export of live animals? If you were asked to suggest the best route for the Managing Director to drive to a conference in Southampton?

Where would you get hold of information which wouldn't normally be available in the office?

Sources of information

Sources of information are many and varied, and can range from personal contacts to official organisations to standard works of reference. In the very first assignment when you started this course, you had to go out and collect information for your Public Relations Brochure. You employed a number of 'sources of information'. It would be impractical to try to list all sources available to you, but, just to give you some idea of the scope of this aspect of information-gathering, consider some of those you might need in a particular area – e.g. travel.

AA Handbook	Local RAC office
RAC Handbook	Road maps
ABC Coach and Bus Guide	car-hire firms
British Rail guides, timetables	ABC shipping guides
'Special offer' brochures	Shipping company brochures
Local travel agents	ABC World Airways Guide
Local airline office	currency exchange bureau
Local AA office	

As well as being able to find information on such a specific topic, it is useful to be aware of what can be gleaned from standard works of reference – not only those exclusive to your area of work or study, but also those which give general information.

Standard reference books

The following list is by no means comprehensive, but will introduce you to some well-known reference books and their contents.

a *Concise Oxford English Dictionary* – alphabetical list of words and their meanings.
b *Fowler's Modern English Usage* – correct English style, grammar and usage.
c *Roget's Thesaurus* – collection of words connected in meaning, grouped under subject headings.
d *A Dictionary of Abbreviations*.
e *Dictionary of the Bible* (J. Hastings) – a full treatment of facts, concepts and beliefs.
f *Oxford Companion to English Literature* – biographies of authors, plots of plays and novels, and characters in fiction.
g *Everyman's Dictionary of Quotations and Proverbs*.
h *United Nations Statistical Yearbook* – statistics relating to various aspects of life in most countries of the world.
i *Whitaker's Almanac* – reference book for assorted information ranging from population statistics to public schools.
j *British Standards Yearbook* – details of British Standards applied to all goods.
k *Who's Who* – biographical dictionary of famous people, published annually.
l *Britain: An Official Handbook* – comprehensive coverage of numerous aspects of life in Britain.

People in business organisations

- m *Scientific and Learned Societies of Great Britain* – arranged by subject and then alphabetically by society or institution.
- n *Telephone Directories* – alphabetical lists of names, addresses and numbers.
- o *Kelly's Directories of Towns* – street directories.
- p *Keesing's Contemporary Archives* – weekly diary of world events.
- q *Kemp's Engineer's Yearbook* – published annually, covers all branches of engineering.
- r *Statesman's Year Book* – general information on most countries.
- s *Post Office Guide* – information on Post Office services and activities, etc.
- t *Official Rules of Sport and Games* – covers rules of most major sports.
- u *The Guinness Book of Records* – world records in almost anything recordable.
- v *Gibbons Stamp Catalogue* – full details of stamps.
- w *The Highway Code* – rules of the road, information and instruction.
- x *Collins' Guide to English Parish Churches* (Betjeman) – descriptions and illustrations.
- y *Everyman's Own Lawyer* – the layperson's guide to the law.

While thinking about general sources of information you should be aware that some of these may be useful to you on a personal level, as well as being an important aspect of the service you can offer as an employee. You never know when it might be important to seek or verify information from organisations such as the Department of Social Security, the Inland Revenue, the Health and Safety Executive, the Commission for Racial Equality, the Office of Fair Trading, or the Equal Opportunities Commission. There are numerous circumstances in working and private lives when individuals or organisations need information from Local Authority services such as Housing Offices, the Environmental Health Offices, Tourist Information Offices, the Social Services, the Police, Consumer Advice Centres or Careers Officers.

Voluntary organisations are also there to help and give guidance – e.g. the National Council for Civil Liberties, the Child Poverty Action Group, the Claimaints Union, Marriage Guidance Centres, the National Society for the Prevention of Cruelty to Children, and Housing Advice Centres – and there is a wealth of private organisations, ranging from societies and clubs, to local companies, to radio, television and the press.

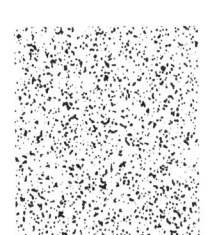

ASSIGNMENT: Electrofit

(Read the complete assignment before you start work.)

As an Administrative Assistant in the Sales Department of Electrofit (an electrical fittings wholesaler) you have recently received a substantial order to supply 30 000 wall sockets, 150 000 three-pin plugs, 100 000 standard light switches, and 50 000 bathroom light switches. Obviously, the customer is expecting quality products, and has specified that all these items must conform to the appropriate British Standard.

Office functions and support

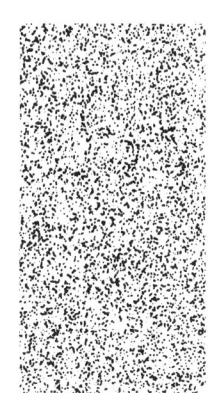

Task 1

It is part of your job to find which British Standards relate to these particular items, and give their numbers. The information needs to be submitted to the Sales Manager and a **memo-format** would be most appropriate.

Another problem is that your company does not normally export components and, therefore, it is necessary to arrange transport. It is decided to rely on an experienced firm to deal with this aspect of the transaction, and you have been advised to consider employing a 'container' operator.

Task 2

As the normal procedure in your company is to obtain three quotations for long-distance deliveries, provide the names, addresses and telephone/telex numbers of three haulage firms which specialise in containerisation and have the necessary experience to arrange the whole process of delivery. This information can be incorporated into the memorandum required for Task 1.

The Sales Manager has been invited to go to Hamburg to meet her German counterpart in order to finalise the deal. It is decided that she can only travel on a Wednesday, because of on-going commitments, and that she should spend two nights there. All arrangements at the Hamburg end will be dealt with by a German company. The Sales Manager, however, has to be back at Head Office for a Board Meeting at two o'clock on Friday afternoon.

Task 3

Draw up a suitable itinerary for her, making sure you cover all stages of the journey from your town/city to Hamburg. The timing and connection of each part of the journey must be realistic, and it is important that you indicate where and when she will be able to take meals. Provide accurate costings for all the travel aspects. Present your itinerary in tabular form, using the layout in fig. 6.2. For each stage, indicate from where you obtained your information.

Fig. 6.2

Method	Leave	Time	Arrive	Time travel	Meal/time/venue	Cost of	Source

Total travel cost: _____

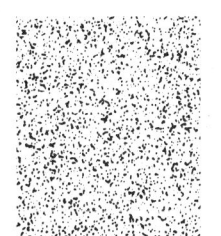

Notes for guidance

Within most organisations the main form of non-specialised written communication is the memorandum. When you send a memo it reflects the general quality and efficiency of your work, and so the drafting of such a document requires a lot of thought and care. Decide first of all on its function. Is it reminding someone of something? Is it drawing someone's attention to particular information or a situation? Is it conveying instructions?

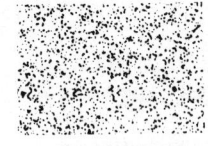

Once you know what you are aiming to achieve you should be able to establish the best approach and an appropriate tone. As far as the layout is concerned, try to acquire a standard memo form from your own organisation, and use it as a pattern for this assignment. In any case, consider the example in fig. 6.3, which gives you further information about writing memos.

Fig. 6.3

THE ORGANISATION

Memorandum

To: All Business Students Date: January 27, 19—
From: The Communications Supervisor Ref: CES/SMS/COMS

Subject: drafting memoranda

The memo is one of the main methods of internal communication, and the aim must be to convey information as clearly and as effectively as possible. As a rule, it should be concise and deal with one basic topic. However, flexibility is an essential quality in business, and you must accept that it will often be more convenient to deal with more than one important point in a single document.

As with any written material, the basic principles of paragraphing should be applied, as long as the memo is long enough to merit this. The first paragraph is the important one, and it will establish what you are talking about, i.e. give background information, and explain why the memo is being submitted. Beyond this, the structure will vary according to the content, but you must get your point across clearly, i.e. the request, the order, the instruction, the reminder, the information.

Memoranda will normally be written in a straightforward narrative style, as demonstrated so far in this example, but if the content is such that you need to give lists, or numbered points or instructions, these can be indented and displayed for visual effect.

All memos should contain certain information as part of the standard layout, separate from the main message.

   (i) the name of the organisation
  (ii) document title (memorandum)
 (iii) name or title (or both) of the recipient(s)
  (iv) name or title (or both) of the sender
   (v) date
  (vi) an appropriate reference

It is generally accepted that a memorandum does not need any salutation, subscription or signature as you would use in a letter, *but* it is useful to develop the habit of initialling or signing at the end for purposes of validation. Remember, an unvalidated document could have been produced by anyone!

Centralised or decentralised services?

In the activity at the beginning of this chapter you were asked to identify the services provided in your own work environment, but you probably hadn't considered whether they were provided from a central resource, or whether each department provided its own.

The decision on how these services were to be provided might have been a planned policy decision, or the situation might simply have developed as the organisation developed. There are a range of arguments for and against centralisation or decentralisation, and it can be useful to be aware of some of the advantages and disadvantages of each system.

Consider the following scenario. You work for an organisation which is entirely based on one site. What is the best way of providing the essential services required by the various departments? It might be quite useful to let each department provide the specific specialist services it needs, with control and responsibility resting with the departmental manager. However, if you analyse the services that need to be provided throughout the organisation, you will immediately recognise that there will be substantial duplication of general services such as secretarial/typing/clerical support, and expensive duplication of equipment such as typewriters, word processors and photocopiers. These thoughts might lead you to another solution. Why not provide all the services likely to be required by the entire organisation from a single resource centre? This would probably mean the creation of another separate department under an Office Manager, but it would enable you to rationalise the provision of staff and equipment, possibly cutting costs in the long term. However, setting up a centralised office services department would need major initial capital investment if it were to run efficiently, and some Departmental Managers would complain that their *own* staff – who have a thorough knowledge of their department's specialised function within the organisation – could do the job far more effectively.

This is the dilemma that Management faces. In some situations it could even be practical to leave certain staff and equipment within the individual departments, while maintaining some in a central servicing unit. In this case it might make sense to make all clerical and typing staff accountable to the manager of the centralised unit.

What is the solution?

To make the decision even more difficult, what would be the best solution if the organisation was based on a number of different sites?

What system, or combination of systems, would provide coherent and co-ordinated office services?

It must be obvious to you now that there is no ideal answer. Each individual organisation must try to arrange its services to the best advantage. Costs, site, physical resources, personnel, the range of organisational functions, established procedures – all these affect what can realistically be done, and the only approach is to assess the advantages and disadvantages of the various methods in the context of the practical work situation.

Figs. 6.4 and 6.5 give some general indication of what centralisation or decentralisation can mean.

Fig. 6.4

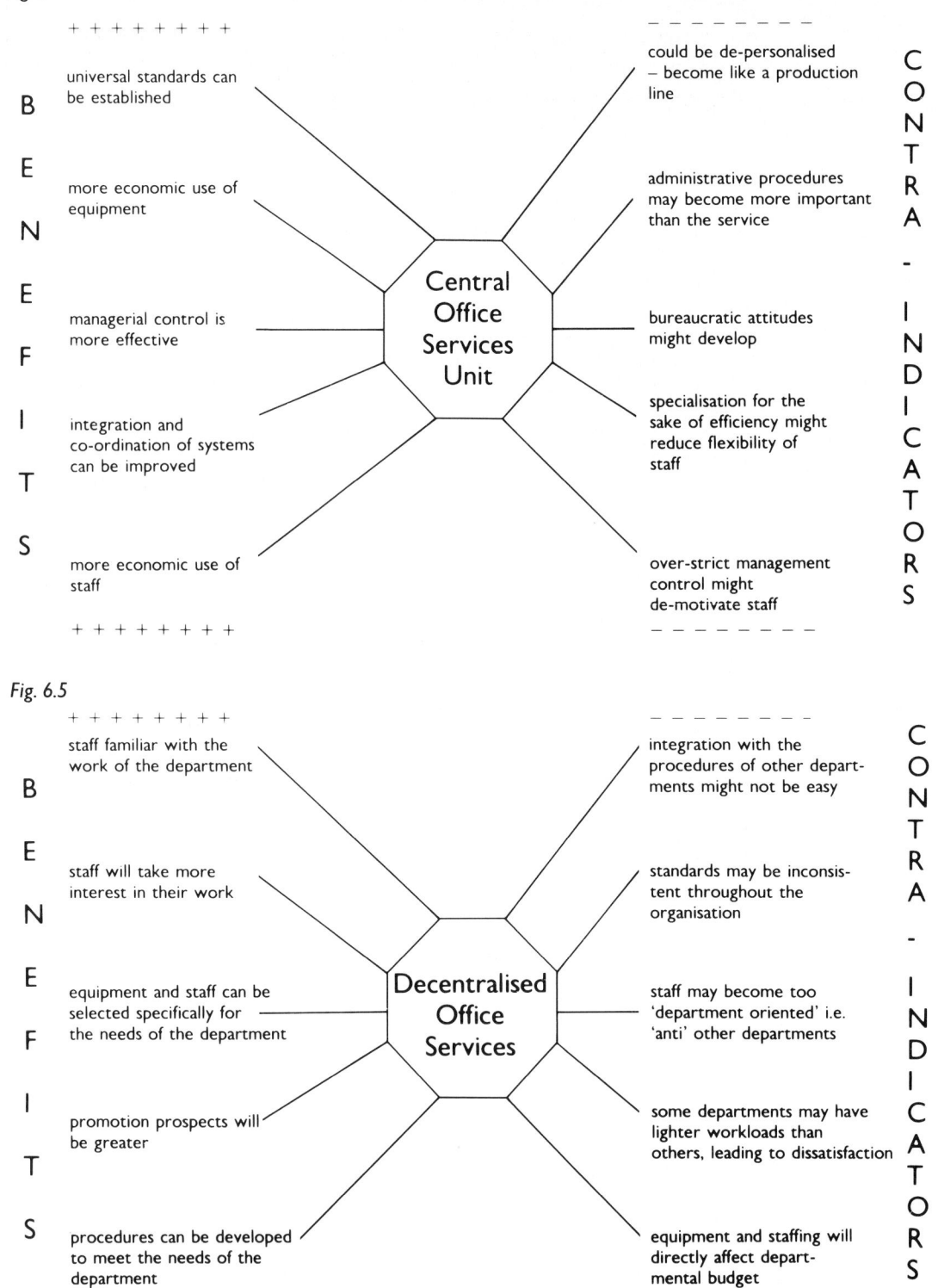

Central Office Services Unit

BENEFITS (+ + + + + + + +)
- universal standards can be established
- more economic use of equipment
- managerial control is more effective
- integration and co-ordination of systems can be improved
- more economic use of staff

CONTRA-INDICATORS (– – – – – – – –)
- could be de-personalised – become like a production line
- administrative procedures may become more important than the service
- bureaucratic attitudes might develop
- specialisation for the sake of efficiency might reduce flexibility of staff
- over-strict management control might de-motivate staff

Fig. 6.5

Decentralised Office Services

BENEFITS (+ + + + + + + +)
- staff familiar with the work of the department
- staff will take more interest in their work
- equipment and staff can be selected specifically for the needs of the department
- promotion prospects will be greater
- procedures can be developed to meet the needs of the department

CONTRA-INDICATORS (– – – – – – – –)
- integration with the procedures of other departments might not be easy
- standards may be inconsistent throughout the organisation
- staff may become too 'department oriented' i.e. 'anti' other departments
- some departments may have lighter workloads than others, leading to dissatisfaction
- equipment and staffing will directly affect departmental budget

Office functions and support

ACTIVITY

Select five of the services you identified in the activity at the beginning of this chapter, and write a commentary (see **Note** below) on the way in which each one is provided – i.e. whether from a central unit or departmentally. Your commentary should include the answers to, or your opinions on, the following questions:

Is your organisation based on a single site?
Is the building in which you are based purpose-built for your work?
Does the nature of your business determine particular procedures?
Why is a particular service provided centrally or departmentally?
Do you think the system could be improved? How?
Are standards consistent throughout the organisation?
Are the services executed swiftly? Accurately?
How many staff are needed to provide the service?
What equipment is needed to provide the service?
What do the senior staff in your department think about the services provided?

Note A commentary is a personal assessment/review of a situation, and has no predetermined format. It gives you the flexibility of layout and structure to present information in a way you think is appropriate. However, it should be written in a fluent, narrative style – not note-form.

CHAPTER 7

Operational systems, procedures and the O & M function

Systems and procedures

In Chapter 2 you considered 'systems' in general, and how a business organisation could be analysed as a series of inter-related systems and sub-systems with identifiable inputs, outputs and control functions. Unfortunately, you can't escape 'systems', and even when you move into the particular area of what *your* job consists of, or what jobs are done in an office environment, it becomes obvious that things run smoothly because appropriate systems and procedures are implemented by all staff. Even the smallest task you perform is related to an established procedure which, in turn, is an integral part of an office system. The office could not function as an information and support system unless its systems and procedures were designed to meet the needs of the work processes (i.e. the 'product' or 'input').

Therefore, when people in any work situation follow an identifiable pattern of activity in order to achieve an aim connected with the business of the organisation, they are working a system. An established system, which has been proved to work well should give the following benefits:

- the office should work more smoothly, with a more **efficient flow of work**;
- because the various stages of any procedure can be identified, **control** over what is done and how it is done, is easier;
- greater efficiency should result in **economies** being made;
- a clearly-defined system makes the **training** of new staff easier.

So we can see that a system must be concerned with *what* is done, *by whom* it is done, *how* it is done, *when* it is done, and *where* it is done, and it is important that all the people involved in the system know exactly what their tasks are, as well as being aware of how the whole procedure fits into the overall system.

Example – the wages system

A relatively simple example of a system can be explained by looking at wages/salaries. In its most basic form, the system might be that payment is made on Thursdays, so that all the necessary information needs to be collated, and calculations made on Wednesday. The calculations can be quite straight-forward – hours worked multiplied by rate of pay – and all the necessary information can be acquired from the time-sheets or clock cards. Once the calculations are made, the appropriate amount is allocated to each employee in cash, by credit transfer, giro, etc. This is a nice easy system, but – as with most systems – complications invariably set in. What about overtime? Sickness benefit? Absences? National Insurance? Pension contributions? Tax rebates? Bonuses? From the basic system a more complex system evolves to cope with most eventualities, and, therefore, the efficient running of the organisation continues.

Basic principles of systems and procedures

Despite the fact that many systems and procedures are quite complex, the principles on which they should be established reflect a common-sense approach, and are outlined below.

- They should be as **simple** as possible, as this makes supervision easier.
- If there is scope for **specialisation** in certain tasks, this should be encouraged for greater efficiency.
- Possible bottlenecks should be identified and avoided so that **maximum 'flow'** is achieved.
- Repetition or **duplication** must be **avoided**.
- **Checking** procedures should be **minimised**.
- The system should be **flexible** in order to adapt easily to changing circumstances.
- There should be continuous **control** over work.
- Tasks should be performed in the most appropriate **sequence**.
- Every task performed should mean that the **work progresses**.
- **Paperwork** should be kept to a **minimum**.

ACTIVITIES

1 Consider the following list of systems common to many organisations, and identify those which apply to the particular work situation you are in at the moment (full-time students can use the college as the basis for this activity, or specify an organisation with which they are familiar). Write out a list of the systems you identify and indicate next to each one how many people are involved in implementing them. You might find it difficult to establish this, but it should help you appreciate the extent and complexity of some of the systems, as well as their inter-related nature.

buying and selling	mail room routines	stationery/requisitions
credit control	work recording	work rotas
stock control	interviewing (selection)	flexitime
data control	merit rating	overtime
filing	job evaluation	petty cash
data processing	recruitment	issuing of payments
reprography	staff appraisal	

> **2** Identify *three* specific procedures that are operated in your work environment and describe them in detail, specifying each task, saying why it is performed, and explaining how the procedure inter-relates/fits in with other procedures or systems.

Organisation and method (O & M)

It is not likely that the operational systems in any organisation will remain static for very long, and there are many influences which can alter their effectiveness. So, close monitoring is necessary to ensure that problems are 'picked up'. Regular reviews are necessary as the organisation expands (or contracts!), as staffing changes, as new legislation requires extra forms and documentation, and as more and more paperwork is moved from place to place. It is here that the Organisation and Method specialist makes his contribution. He may be a member of the Management Services team, or he may be an outside consultant, called in periodically to check on office efficiency. Wherever he comes from, his job is the same – to improve the efficiency and effectiveness of office procedures by simplifying them, cutting out wasteful use of time, labour or materials, and reducing costs. The scope of his investigations can include anything which affects efficiency, but in particular he is concerned with office organisation, systems, procecures, machine/equipment, forms and work measurement.

O & M can be applied to any aspect of the work of an organisation, but we shall concentrate on the office – and this is often where O & M specialists have their hardest task. The problem is that the office embodies such a variety of work, skills and talents that straightforward work-study or time-study techniques are not seen as appropriate by the staff being 'investigated'. Some typical reactions might be:

- 'I'm not on a production line – I'm an administrator and I know how to do my job best!'
- 'We work with our brains not our hands, so how can that be measured?'
- 'How can I be timed in doing my job when I am constantly interrupted by telephone calls and queries from Accounts?'
- 'You can't compare her job with mine.'
- 'The forms I have to deal with are much more complicated.'
- 'The job is never straightforward – something always crops up to complicate matters.'
- 'I can't take on any more work – I'm already doing overtime.'
- 'I can't work any faster because John can't cope with the forms coming to him in greater quantities.'
- 'All they're trying to do is reduce staffing levels.'

ACTIVITY

> Discuss the merits of the statements on the previous page. Can you identify any false arguments? Do you agree with them? Can you suggest any solution that would invalidate any of the comments?

Applying O & M techniques to office work

Although it is generally accepted that applying O & M techniques to office work is not always successful, this doesn't mean that it is impossible, or that improvements cannot be made. Procedures can be standardised, resulting in savings in staff training and provision of equipment, and facilitating movement of staff from one section to another. Specialisation can improve efficiency and productivity, reduce the error factor, and make savings in time (however we must remember that it can also lead to boredom and lack of flexibility – problems which can lower morale!). There can be a reduction in work or effort necessary, so that resources can be redeployed and used more effectively.

All these things can contribute to a clearer definition of jobs, a rationalisation of procedures, and – if implemented carefully – an improvement in staff efficiency and job satisfaction.

With benefits such as these to be gained, it is obvious that an O & M investigation must be very carefully set up if it is to be accepted by the complete working team – from the newly-appointed clerk to the Office Manager. To start with, the most important step is to establish what the main purpose of the investigation is. Is it to:

reduce costs?

improve management control?

simplify procedures for staff?

ensure effective utilisation of equipment?

reduce the error factor in certain areas?

improve quality of output?

help the business to adapt to a changing environment?

Any or all of these will, in general, improve the efficiency of the office, and if we accept that the work of an office depends on the interaction of a range of procedures, it seems logical that the study of procedures is likely to be a primary activity in any investigation. Often referred to as **Method Study**, this process is carried out in four recognisable stages: the investigation; the report; the implementation of recommendations; the audit.

The investigation

It is essential not to try to investigate too much at once. The systems to be studied should be split up into identifiable procedures, otherwise faults and weaknesses could be disguised and not detected. Another preliminary consideration should be to decide in what detail any procedure is to be investigated – how deep should the O & M expert dig?

Having resolved these questions, the investigator can start work, and should ensure that she looks at all aspects of the situation. Discussions should be held with the operator, and observations made of the tasks being performed. Discussions should also be held with the supervisor, so that both sides of the situation can be appreciated. Comparisons should be made to identify any areas of misunderstanding or misinterpretation. Most important of all, the question must be asked: **why is this job done?**

If there is no satisfactory answer to this, then the investigation might as well stop at once. However, assuming that the job is recognised as being necessary, fig. 7.1 shows certain key questions which the investigator should consider.

Fig. 7.1

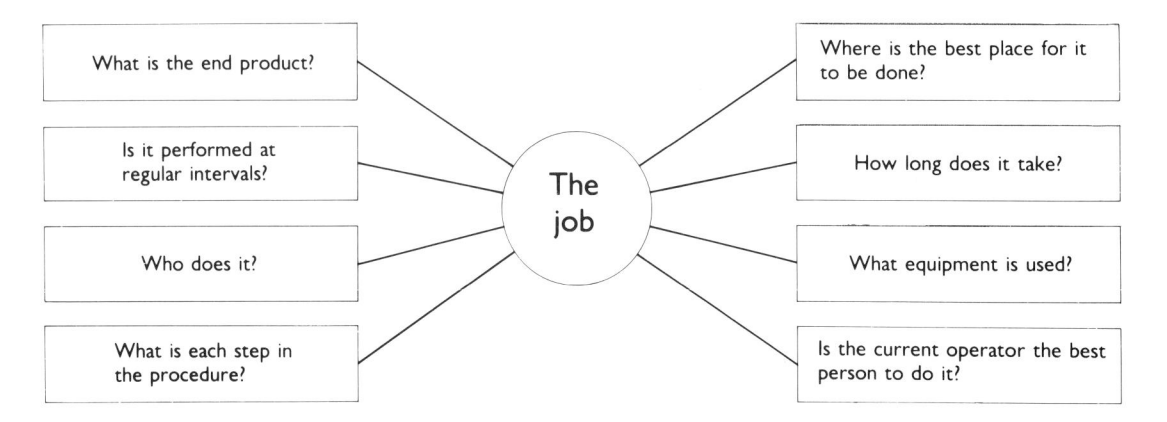

```
What is the end product?              Where is the best place for it
                                      to be done?

Is it performed at                    How long does it take?
regular intervals?
                         The job
Who does it?                          What equipment is used?

What is each step in                  Is the current operator the best
the procedure?                        person to do it?
```

The report

During the investigation the O & M specialist will collect a vast amount of information, including notes on interviews, records of tasks performed and specimens of forms used. The next task is to collate and present the information in an easily assimilated form. The first stage is usually to draw up a **procedure narrative**, which specifies each operator in a procedure, describes and numbers each operation in sequence, and lists each form or document involved in each operation. The easiest way of doing this is to produce a **procedure narrative chart** which could look like that shown in fig. 7.2.

Sometimes a further column is included (fig. 7.3) which indicates the symbol used to represent the type of operation when another element of the report – **a procedure flow-chart** – is drawn up.

The procedure flow-chart maps the sequence of operations by the use of a range of conventional symbols. The systematic graphic representation has the advantage of visual impact rather than a narrative description, and the major symbols used are shown in fig. 7.4.

Flow charts can be as simple or as complex as an operation requires. Fig. 7.5 demonstrates a basic structure.

Fig. 7.2

PROCEDURE NARRATIVE CHART

PROCEDURE: Preparation of goods received note

DEPARTMENT: Purchasing ....

DATE: ....

Operator (function/name)	Operation number	Description	Department name or ref.no.
Clerk (1)	1	picks up folder containing delivery vouchers from in-tray	
	2	takes vouchers from folder	DV 1
	3	sorts vouchers into order number sequence	

Fig. 7.3

PROCEDURE NARRATIVE CHART

PROCEDURE: ....

DEPARTMENT: ....

DATE: ....

Operator (function/name)	Operation number	Description	Symbol	Department name or ref.no.

Fig. 7.4

Symbol	Meaning
	used where a document or a person enters the procedure. The title of the document or the person is written in the box
	an operation in the procedure is performed
	inspection – some form of checking takes place
	movement of a document to another operator

	storage – usually filing – when the document has fully completed its role in the procedure
	temporary storage – where a document will be used again in the procedure
	delay – usually waiting for a document or the completion of a procedure
	decision box – where alternative routes of action can be chosen
	destruction of a document
	end of investigation

*Fig. 7.5
Basic flow-chart to show what happens to a letter after production.*

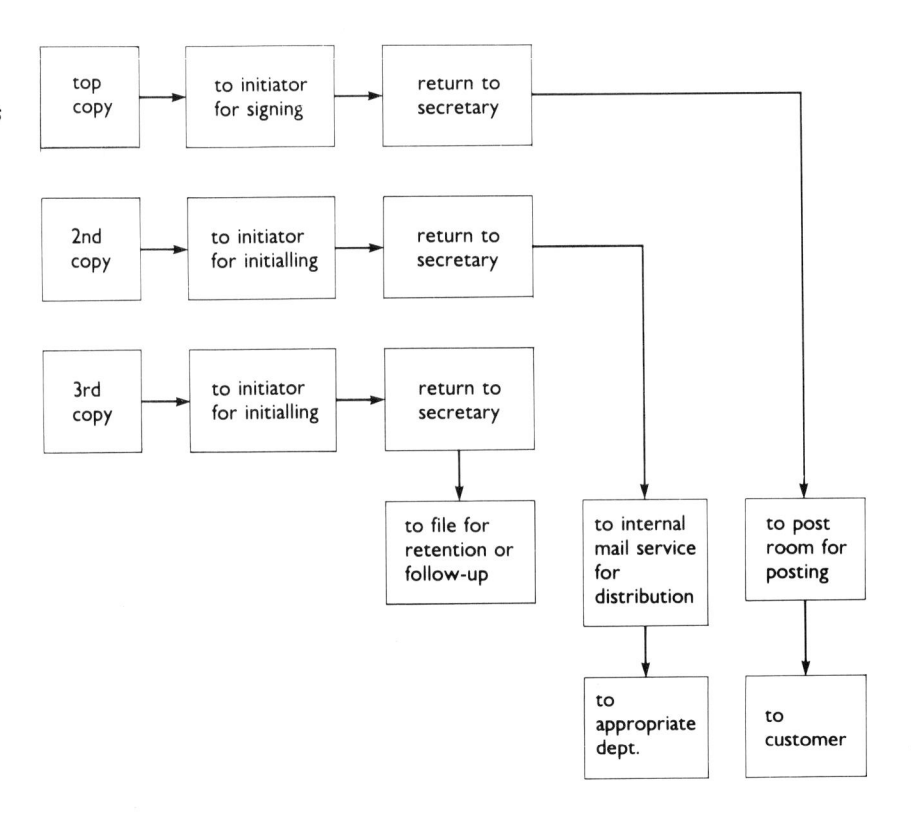

top copy → to initiator for signing → return to secretary →

2nd copy → to initiator for initialling → return to secretary →

3rd copy → to initiator for initialling → return to secretary →

→ to file for retention or follow-up

→ to internal mail service for distribution → to appropriate dept.

→ to post room for posting → to customer

ACTIVITY

Using your college library as the major resource centre, find the section which houses books on Business Administration or Administrative Management and complete the following tasks:

1. List five books by title and author, which give a detailed description of O & M functions/technique, and which give examples of different methods of recording procedure flow in chart form.
2. Reproduce two flow-charts which demonstrate two different types of presentation. You should choose charts which incorporate as wide a variety of symbols as possible, and, therefore, you might find that you need to select fairly complex ones. A *minimum* requirement for this task is that each chart should use the following symbols:

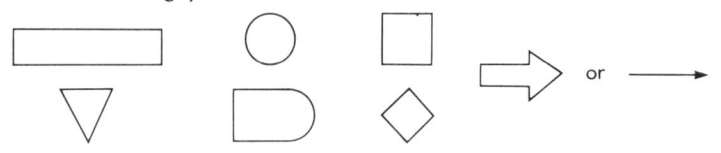

The implementation

Once all the information has been collected, collated and presented as procedure narratives, charts and specimen forms, an analysis is done and report prepared for submission to Management. This report will make suggestions/formal recommendations for change, and should lead to consultative meetings and discussions to decide on the course of action. If changes are to be implemented these should be done with the minimum of disruption, although a certain amount of disturbance is unavoidable if new machinery has to be installed, staff have to be retrained, new stationery has to be printed and old procedures have to be phased out.

As part of this implementation, a useful management aid is **critical path analysis** (CPA) and the drawing up of a CPA flow-chart. It is basically the technique of planning complex procedures or operations very carefully so that they will be carried out in the correct sequence without any, or with the minimum delays. The CPA flow-chart is simple in concept and usually consists of circles (in which each operation is named), and direction arrows showing the flow, overlap, and merging of activities into a coherent procedure. The chart is read from left to right and (in an elementary form) could look like the one shown in fig. 7.6.

As you will see, the chart shows that some of the operations can be performed concurrently by different people, and the whole procedure merges at the point where separate elements *need* to be brought together. Progress is then made to the next stage.

The audit

If an investigation has resulted in the implementation of new procedures, the mere fact of the implementation does not mean that the job is over for the O & M expert. Some problems may arise which it was not possible to foresee; a comparison needs to be made with the old system to check that

Fig. 7.6
CPA chart to show the processing of a circular.

better results are being achieved; the whole work system needs to be monitored closely to ensure that it is operating smoothly. In any case, with the business climate constantly changing there may be a need for further adjustments/investigations.

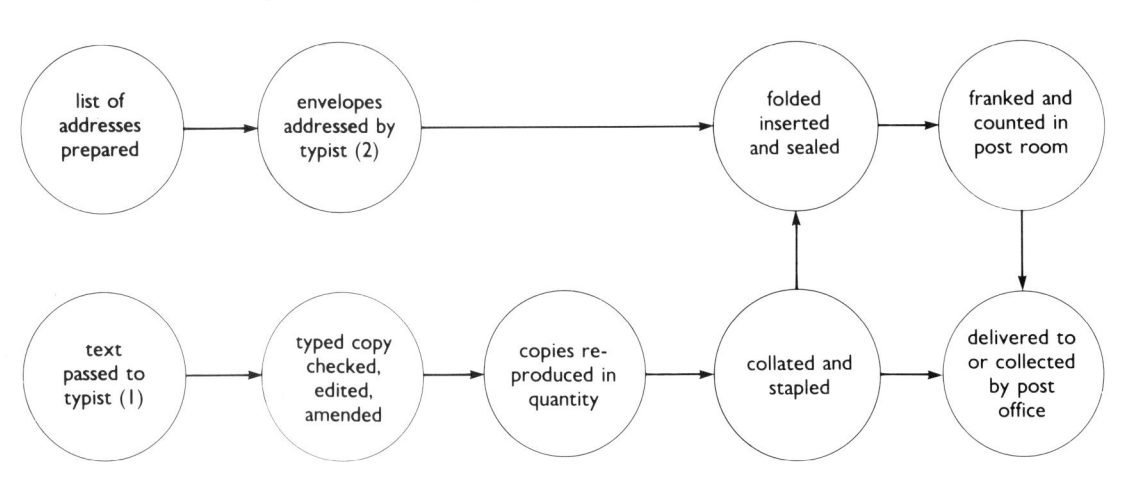

```
list of addresses prepared → envelopes addressed by typist (2) → folded inserted and sealed → franked and counted in post room

text passed to typist (1) → typed copy checked, edited, amended → copies re-produced in quantity → collated and stapled → delivered to or collected by post office
```

ASSIGNMENT: goods received

You are employed as an administrative assistant in the Personnel Department of Sumar Fabrication Limited – a local company which manufactures alloy components to customers' specifications. Within your company, an O & M investigation is currently being carried out in the Purchasing Department, and you have been asked to assist the Chief Investigator in collating and preparing her report. On Thursday of last week she was delayed in getting to work, and sent a message asking you to have a preliminary chat with one of the Purchasing Clerks to establish in general terms what the procedure was for taking goods in. As part of your discussion, you asked the clerk to explain in detail what is involved in preparing a 'goods received note' (GRN). This is what he said:

> Well, in the morning – first thing – I usually find a folder with all the delivery vouchers (DVs) in it, in my in-tray. I pick it up, take out all the vouchers and settle down to sort them into some kind of order – this is done by order number sequence. Once they're all sorted out I go through and stamp each one with the date-received stamp. This isn't a very big job (although it's a bit boring) and once they're done I keep them on my desk until about 10.30. By then the typist is usually ready to deal with them, so I take them to her desk and dump them there.
>
> The folder arrives back in my in-tray – usually after lunch sometime – so I pick it up and extract all the completed GRNs with the vouchers clipped to them. Obviously, I have to check them through for typing errors, and if there are any problems I take the individual forms straight over to the typist for correction. When I'm satisfied that they're all complete, I separate the various copies and deliver the top copy to the Stock Record Clerk's desk, copies 2 and 3 to the General Office out-tray so that they can be taken to Accounts, and I file copy 4 in my Record of Goods Received file. That's it, then. I can move on to my next job.

Having listened to all this, you realised that in order to get a full picture of the complete process, you needed to talk to the typist, so you decided to do this on an informal basis during the coffee break. She said:

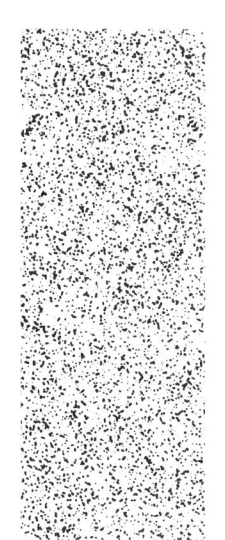

> It's usually about 10.30 before I'm ready to deal with the GRNs, so John usually puts the DVs into my tray at break-time. I remove all the vouchers from the folder and deal with them one at a time, entering the information on to a GRN. The GRN is self-copying with a top copy and three others. Fifteen vouchers can be recorded on each form. As I complete each form I check the details, and then clip the appropriate vouchers to the GRN. When they're all completed I put them together in the folder and put it in John's in-tray. Sometimes he's got to come back to me for corrections, but I always do these at once.

This seems to have given you a reasonable account of the procedure, so you decide to complete the following tasks:

1. Draw up a procedure narrative chart for the procedure currently used to prepare a goods received note. You should use the format shown in fig. 7.2.
2. Produce a procedure flow-chart to give a graphic representation of the operations you have identified in the procedure narrative chart.

You will be assessed on the effectiveness of your presentation, so choose a format which will have the greatest visual impact.

ACTIVITY

Using your work environment as the source of information, identify a fairly straightforward procedure which is carried out regularly as part of an overall system. If you can choose your own job, do so.

Once you have established which procedure you are going to analyse, complete the following tasks:

1. Describe briefly what the procedure is, who carries it out, and how it fits in with the overall system of which it is a part (i.e. why it is carried out).
2. Draw up a procedure narrative chart for the procedure, ensuring that you detail every stage in the operation, and include every task that is performed. Use the form of presentation indicated in fig. 7.3 for this task.
3. Produce a procedure flow-chart for the complete operation, bearing in mind that visual impact is an important element of assessment.

CHAPTER 8

Practical communication skills (1)

This chapter will provide you with a substantial amount of reference material for use in future assignments, and will give you guidance and practice in a range of communications common to most business situations.

Business letters

You have already had an introduction to the structure of basic business letters in Chapter 5, and you will recognise that as one of the most important methods of communication between organisations and the public, the letter has one over-riding function – it is a written record which can be used as documentary evidence if required. Therefore, any letter should be:

clearly expressed – so that it cannot be misinterpreted;

accurate – so that the writer cannot be accused of misrepresentation;

appropriate in style – to suit the particular function of the letter, i.e. what you want it to achieve.

Fig. 8.1

The first letter of complaint you write on any topic must be **tactful** and carefully worded, in case the cause of your complaint is a genuine error which can easily be put right. You should be **calm**, **sensible**, **realistic** and **polite**, and avoid making any threats.

COMPLAINT

Paragraph 1 This should make a general reference to the source of the complaint.

Paragraph 2 You should now move on to comment specifically on the exact reason for your complaint, giving all details and explaining what effect the problem has had on you.

Paragraph 3 At this point you should simply request that the necessary action be taken to put the matter right. You can make specific suggestions if they are reasonable and realistic.

Despite the modern trend towards word-processing, standard or form letters, and computer print-outs, there are still circumstances in which the individual business letter is necessary – particularly in a small business where personal contact with customers is valued, and in our personal lives where there is often a need to communicate effectively with all sorts of business organisations, ranging from the local plumber to Her Majesty's Inspector of Taxes!

Often the most difficult letters to write are **complaints** and **apologies**, and it can be useful to adopt a structure which can be used in most situations.

Fig. 8.2

An apology, particularly on behalf of an organisation, is difficult to construct, because each one is entirely different, and you need to strike a balance between keeping the customer happy and maintaining a **reasonable image** for the firm. To be effective, it should combine an **apology** with an **explanation**, and convince the customer that everything is being done to put the matter right. You should **avoid** getting into a **confrontation** situation, and aim to retain as much **goodwill** as possible.

A P O L O G Y

Paragraph 1 It is usual to refer to the source of the complaint (telephone call, letter, etc.) and it can be useful to thank the customer for bringing it to your attention.

Paragraph 2 This should contain a credible explanation of why the problem has arisen. Remember that you are trying to maintain a good company image.

Paragraph 3 At this point you should state clearly what action you are taking to remedy the situation, and if possible offer the customer some kind of concession to compensate for inconvenience.

Paragraph 4 The formal apology should not be over-apologetic and can contain an assurance that this sort of thing does not normally happen and that greater care will be taken in the future.

ACTIVITY

You and your family have recently moved into a new house which happens to be sited on the edge of an industrial estate. Much to your disgust, within a week of you moving in, the engineering firm which is situated five hundred yards from your property has implemented a night shift, and there has been a lot of noise from a particular machine in the lathe shop. Although it is not noticeable during the day, at night it has been having a dramatic effect on your family and your neighbours.

Write a tactful letter to the Production Manager outlining your complaint, asking for her co-operation in dealing with the problem, and possibly suggesting a reasonable solution. Your letter should be produced on plain paper, ready for posting, using your own address and creating an appropriate address for the factory.

ACTIVITY

As a trainee manager with a local carpet retailer, you have this morning received a complaint by telephone from any angry customer who had been expecting new carpets to be fitted to the whole ground floor of his house yesterday. He had taken a day off work to be there, but no-one had arrived. As your manager is away on a Buyer's conference, you apologised on the 'phone and assured the customer, Mr H. Denby, that you would look into the matter.

On investigation, you discover that the problems did not wholly lie with your company, because Mr Denby's carpets were in stock and ready to be delivered. What had happened was that the firm to whom you sub-contracted the fitting had, because of an oversight in their office, failed to schedule Mr Denby into their work programme for the week. They were fully booked, and would be unable to fit his carpets until Tuesday of next week. Obviously, something had gone wrong with your checking procedure, because it was normal practice for the transport supervisor to check with the sub-contractors each day at 4.30 pm to confirm what work they were doing for your company the next day. In fact, the check had been made, but no-one had thought to inform Mr Denby of the delay.

You feel it is essential to write a letter of apology to the customer as soon as possible, and feel that you should offer him some minor compensation. As a trainee manager, you have a discretionary power to give up to 10% discount on orders over £1,000 and Mr Denby's order falls into that category. However, he has already paid in full.

Write the letter, using your own address as Mr Denby's, and that of an appropriate local retailer for your company's address.

Notices and posters

In any organisation there is often a need to convey general information to staff. This can be done by direct communication with each individual, but more commonly a notice-board system is used. This is simple and effective, with notice-boards being provided centrally, or in each section/department. In some circumstances it can be more effective to use a 'visual' medium to demonstrate a point, and the poster can be an effective way of conveying information – particularly in areas such as health, hygiene, safety or advertising.

An important thing to remember about a **notice** is that it is not an appropriate medium for conveying bad news. Any notice should have the following characteristics:

- the message should be simple in concept and clearly put across.
- the language and sentence structure should not be complex.
- the tone should be appropriate to the intended function.
- the presentation and layout should be attractive and easy to read.
- the whole communication should be kept as short as possible.

ACTIVITY

Think about the following notices and discuss their merits. Are they acceptable or unacceptable? Why? What possible responses could you suggest?

Fig. 8.3

NOTICE

The Management regret that, owing to a back-log of work, all holiday leave during the period December 17th to January 5th will be restricted to statutory holidays only.

B. Wantage,
Managing Director.

NOTICE

We are pleased to inform all staff that the new rest/recreation area next to the canteen will be open at coffee breaks as well as lunchtimes in future.

G. Wilton-Baker,
Personnel Manager.

NO PRODUCTION WORKERS BEYOND THIS POINT

The **poster** relies mainly on visual impact for its effect, and can be purely pictorial, or a combination of pictures and words. Any written message *must* be brief and to the point. No matter what the theme, a number of different approaches can be used – ranging from the humorous to the simply informative, to the visually shocking. One of the most common uses of the poster is as an aid to safe working practices.

Fig. 8.4

see over your load

ACTIVITY

1. Draft a notice informing all staff in your organisation that the Social Committee, of which you are Secretary, is intending to publish a monthly newsletter containing general company news, opinions, comments, personal ads. etc. The newsletter will be available free to all staff and will be distributed with their pay advice.
2. Assume that you have been asked by the president of the Students Union in your college to design a poster advertising the College Magazine, which is produced once a term and contains a wide variety of material ranging from serious commentary on college life, to jokes, poems, anecdotes, and reports of student activities/clubs.

ACTIVITY

Look closely at your own work environment, and identify anything which could be regarded as a hazard or an unsafe work practice. Draft a notice to all staff drawing their attention to the problem and suggesting how the danger can be avoided, and design a safety poster to be displayed in the problem area.

Responses

Responses, both oral and written, form a major part of the communication process between people within organisations and between members of different organisations. However, it is the interaction between an organisation and members of the public which constitutes one of the most important relationships.

Written responses

The written response needs to be a most carefully considered document which reflects a thorough appreciation of the business context, a comprehensive knowledge of the subject (or sound research), and a realistic consideration of the requirements of the organisation and the needs and feelings of the recipient. One of the best ways of appreciating the effect of anything you write is simply to ask yourself how you would react if you were the recipient. Would you feel pleased? Angry? Disappointed? Encouraged? Would you think that the writer was being helpful? Stupid? Insensitive?

Whenever you need to respond personally to an individual's enquiry, think carefully about the guidelines below and adjust your content, tone and approach accordingly. These guidelines can be applied to many situations, but are probably easiest to appreciate if you assume that you have received a general letter of enquiry from a member of the public.

Guidelines: written responses

- Identify the general theme and assess the content. Is it within your range of responsibility? If not, what do you do? Do you have the necessary knowledge or information? If not, where can you get it?
- Decide specifically what the writer wants. Is it simply information? Is it information plus advice? Are any explanations or assurances asked for or required?
- Does the 'background' to the situation affect the way in which you will respond? For example, the writer's circumstances, any previous correspondence or communication, the requirements of other organisations, the requirements of your own organisation, legal restrictions.
- Are there a number of specific points to be answered? Can any be left out? Are any of them automatically answered by implication when you deal with others?
- Select and collate the information necessary for answering each point accurately, and as comprehensively as is practical.
- Decide in what order it is most appropriate to deal with the points raised: e.g. rank order, order of presentation, chronological or logical.
- Be as helpful and encouraging as possible. If you can't be of direct help, recommend another contact or suggest an alternative route of action.
- Always try to end on a positive note. Try to hold out some hope and, as mentioned above, suggest an appropriate course of action if at all possible.
- Above all, remember that any direct contact you have with a member of the public is a **public relations exercise**, conducted by you on behalf of your organisation. If it's done badly, it reflects badly on you and your employer. If it's done well, you personally can take the credit, and the organisation may reap some benefit.

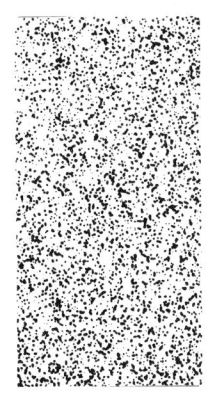

ASSIGNMENT: professional training

(Read the notes for guidance.)

Situation

You are employed at middle-management level in the finance/accounting department of a large organisation, and are involved in the activities of the Association of Certified Accountants during your spare time. This important professional body is not particularly strong in your area, and at a recent meeting you were persuaded to take on the role of Information and Press Officer for the region.

Within a week of your appointment, you received the letter below. Only the main body of the letter is given.

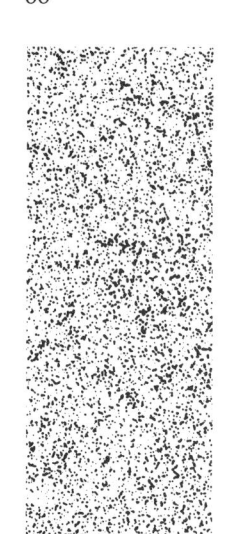

Dear Sir,

I have been advised to contact you for information about achieving qualifications in accountancy.

I am now thirty three, and left school with four O levels to take a job as a Clerical Assistant in the Civil Service. As part of a day-release programme I studied at College for my ONC in Business Studies, and successfully achieved this. I married, and some time afterwards stopped work to devote time to my family. As my children are now older, I have returned to work as an accounts clerk with a major insurance company. I am enjoying this work very much, and feel that I would like to make a career for myself in the accountancy field. My supervisor has recommended that I get in touch with you.

Obviously, I realise that it will take some time to achieve a professional qualification, but I should be pleased to receive any advice/guidance you can give me on routes of study, entry qualifications, and relevant courses. It is essential that I maintain my current job, but I could certainly study part-time and – because of a flexitime system – could possibly get day-release.

I shall be very grateful for any help you can offer.

Yours faithfully,
MARGARET E. WATSON
M. E. Watson (Mrs)

Task

Respond to Mrs Watson's letter, bearing in mind the Public Relations function of what you write. Obviously, you are keen to encourage people to become qualified in the Accountancy field, and – in the longer term – are looking for new members of your professional organisation. Your letter should answer the writer's questions fully, clearly and helpfully, avoiding irrelevant details, giving no unnecessary information, and ensuring that you are encouraging and positive. Aim to give sound advice and clear guidance on an appropriate course of action or route of study Mrs Watson can take.

Notes for guidance

You cannot attempt this assignment until you have completed the following preliminary tasks.

1. Write to the Association of Certified Accountants, Student Services Department, and ask for information on the academic standards necessary for registration with the Association, different methods of study, opportunities for training, and some indication of different routes to achieve membership of the Association. You will be able to get the address from your local reference library or college library.
2. Find as much information as you can on training for accountancy in general, as this will give you good background knowledge and awareness. Investigate the careers advice provision in your college for help on this.

Selection, classification and schematic presentation of information

There are many situations which arise in business and in our personal lives when we have to read through lengthy documents or other textual material, searching for particular items of information. We have all, at some time or another, come across reference material which is badly indexed or ineffectively headed, so that the only way to find specific information is to read right through it. You might already have thought that the heading to this section is unnecessarily complicated – why not simply call it 'Summary' or 'Notemaking'? The reason is that the main aim of this work is to develop your skill of logical and incisive assessment of information, to encourage you to select only essential facts, and to reinforce a method of presentation which is effective (both visually and practically) and which you have already seen in short informal reports and memo-reports.

ACTIVITIES

(**Note:** you should record how much time you spend on these activities.)

1 Using your college library as the resource centre, find a text book which deals with *company shares* and find the sections which describe Ordinary Shares, Preference Shares and Debentures.
2 Time yourself and find out how long it takes you to find out what *Loan Stocks* are.
3 Write down some essential facts about *Cumulative Preference Shares*.
4 What is the difference between *Deferred Ordinary Shares* and *Ordinary Shares*?

Now consider fig 8.5 which gives a schematic presentation in note-form of basic information on shares.

Although there is not as much detail as you will have found in a textbook, these notes on shares provide essential information and present it in such a way that it is quick to read, and easy to select required facts.

The method of presentation is simple in concept, and based on elementary display techniques of progressive indentation, emphasis of important headings, and numbering of points. The 'pattern' on the page gives visual impact, can aid comprehension, and can indicate the rank order of information. This simple layout gives you a sound basis for producing any kind of business communication which would benefit from having information classified under explanatory headings and sub-headings (e.g. reports, briefings, notes for a talk).

Fig. 8.5

SHARES

1 Introduction

A company offers shares for sale in order to raise capital. This allows members of the public to invest in a business with a view to making a profit. The shareholder is entitled to 'share' in the profits of the company. The different shares can be classed in groups.

2 Ordinary shares

(a) Ordinary shares
- (i) also known as equity shares
- (ii) high return on capital
- (iii) high risk
- (iv) capital gains rather than revenue profits

(b) Deferred ordinary shares
- (i) sometimes called founders' shares
- (ii) high risk
- (iii) dividend paid after ordinary shares have had some profit

3 Preference shares

(a) Preference shares
- (i) prior right to payment of dividend
- (ii) less risk
- (ii) security rather than large dividend

(b) Cumulative preference shares
- (i) dividend not lost if company makes no profit one year — it accumulates until profit is made

(c) Participating preference shares
- (i) extra dividend paid if dividend of ordinary shares goes above certain rate
- (ii) holder 'participates' in extra profits

4 Debentures

Not really shares, but loans to companies referred to as 'loan stocks'.

(a) Loan stocks
- (i) minimum risk
- (ii) fixed interest rate
- (iii) 'secured' by firm's assets

(b) Convertible loan stocks
- (i) can be converted to ordinary shares after a certain period of time

5 Conclusion

This is an example of note-presentation in schematic form, *not* a comprehensive guide to shares and their characteristics!

ACTIVITY

(You will need to consult 'law' textbooks for this activity.)

Find out what you can about the *magistracy* and produce a set of notes giving essential information which might be useful to someone who is thinking of putting his/her name forward for selection as a magistrate. Your document should be general in nature, presented in exactly the same format as that shown in fig. 8.5 and should answer as many of the following questions as possible:

- What are magistrates? (Their role and function.)
- Who appoints them? (The role of the Lord Chancellor and the Secretary of Commmissions.)
- How are they selected? (Local Advisory Committees.)
- Can anybody be one? (Qualifications and disqualifications.)
- What type of person is appointed? (The Social Composition of the Magistracy.)
- Do they receive any training? (Current system, any problems, the future.)

ASSIGNMENT: Flexitime

(Read the notes for guidance.)

Your boss, Mr James Hurst, is the Personnel Manager of a group of companies, and is consequently away from the Head Office a fair bit of the time. He is difficult to track down at times, but when he is back in the office, everybody is expected to 'jump' and produce work very quickly as he demands it. Although the pay is quite good, there is quite a high turnover of staff, because of this fluctuating and uneven work load. Many people have objected to working late 'just because Hurst has got a bee in his bonnet again'.

You know that Mr Hurst is currently considering the likely effects of introducing a flexible working hours system into the Head Office, and has been trying to assess its impact on the administrative workings of the organisation. When you come across the following article, you think that some of the points are particularly relevant to your company, and decide to summarise them and present them to Mr Hurst when he is next in the office. Concentrate on the *advantages* of flexitime.

Flexible working hours – an assessment

The principle of flexible working hours has brought about a revolution in people's concept of the working day and in business efficiency across the whole face of industry and commerce. The idea is simple – the working day is divided into two types of time, 'core time' and 'flexible time'. During the core time, all employees should be at their job – say from 10.00 am to 3.00 pm – but the other hours at the beginning and end of the day are flexible so that it is up to the individual when he or she arrives and leaves. The system can remain this simple, or can be made more complex by allowing flexibility over the period of a week, or even longer, and lunch times can be either fixed or used wholly or partially as part of the flexible periods.

For somebody like myself, whose method of working depends on the demands of the day, the flexitime system is invaluable, because my secretary can use her time much more effectively. If I have been away at a conference and am not coming into the office until

10.00 am, there is little point in my secretary starting at 8.30 am. If I decide to come in at 8.30 am and spend an hour dictating to the machine, there is little point in her sitting in the office waiting for me to finish. However, I often need to work until six or six-thirty, and it is not unusual for me to ask Jean to finish a report or come to a meeting with me late in the afternoon. Whatever the pattern of work, it is essential that we co-operate to ensure the best 'attendance' hours to suit both of us. Obviously, debit or credit hours are carried over so nobody loses out.

As can be seen, it is the support staff who are likely to benefit most from a flexible system – particularly administrative and secretarial. One senior secretary I know sums it up like this:

> If my boss has to go to Lyons on, say, a Thursday, I can make sure that I clear up any outstanding work and go home just after lunch. It's much better to do that than sit around getting bored. When she comes back on Monday, however, I might have to work until 8.00 in the evening in order to finish the reports and letters that she wants to catch up on. It all balances out – if I am owed four or five hours by the end of the month, I take an extra half day off, which can be a nice little bonus. Obviously, if you take time off or come in late you need to come to some arrangement with another senior secretary so that he or she can 'cover' your 'phone.

The general feeling is that overall efficiency improves with a system like this, because it is likely that the office will be 'open' for more hours in the day, which means there is a greater time-span during which customers can make contact. Many people feel happier with their travelling arrangements too, because they can avoid the peak periods for traffic and make their journeys much quicker and more comfortable. In one company in Banford, most of the admin. staff arrive at 8.30 am because they travel by bus, and the service is rather irregular after this time. However, in another area, where services are less erratic, many staff in a large insurance company don't get to work until 9.30 am, because it is easier for them to travel in a quieter period.

Many people like the flexitime system because it means they can finish a job once it has been started, without feeling they are giving the company something for nothing. Time is saved because the need to look back over what has been done is avoided, and they know that for the extra time worked, they can take time off or start later another day.

In my experience of chatting to people who work this system, it is often the people with families who get the greater advantage from it – possibly because they have more to arrange. There are the children to cater for, general housework, shopping, and a wealth of other tasks that have to be fitted in with work.

Apart from efficiency, the company can benefit in other ways from having employees on this system. Casual absenteeism, whether it is because of a 'morning after' headache, a dentist's appointment, or an arrangement to have a haircut, is reduced. People can arrange their working day to suit when they perform the best, and as a result they are likely to work with much greater enthusiasm, concentration and even enjoyment. Medical opinion supports this view, at least to the extent that flexible hours must reduce the inevitable stresses and strains of having to work fixed hours at pre-determined times, no matter what the workload or how you feel.

Source: *Administration Monthly* article by Tamsin Rabin, Administration Manager, Simbox Packaging Ltd.

Notes for guidance

1 The most appropriate format for your communication is a memo. Revise the basic principles of memo writing as outlined in Chapter 6.
2 Produce a full heading sequence and subject line, as indicated.

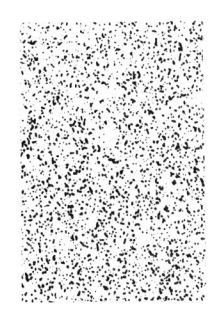

3 Your first paragraph should contain the terms of reference, i.e. a statement of why you are submitting the memo, what the scope of your information is, and an indication of any sources you have used.
4 After the introductory paragraph, you should present the information under a series of headings, sub-headings and numbered points, indicating clearly what the benefits for the organisation are, and what effects it could have on general staff and management. You should consider such aspects as efficiency, absenteeism, travelling, organisation of work, etc.
5 The concluding paragraph can be very general, and should not make any overt attempt to persuade. Your presentation should appear as objective as possible.

CHAPTER 9
Recording information, standard documents and form design

In previous work we have considered the office as a source of information and a centre of information. In practice this means that it receives, records, sorts and disseminates information, which inevitably leads to a vast amount of paperwork. In order to increase efficiency and save time, most organisations use a range of pre-printed documents to deal with recurring situations, and although these might differ in design from company to company, they are 'standard' in concept and always contain certain essential information.

In a commercial organisation, documentation will be necessary at each stage in the process of buying and selling, and fig. 9.1 shows a typical document plan.

Fig. 9.1

THE BUYER   **THE SELLER**

1	A **letter of inquiry** requesting information is sent.	→2	The seller despatches a **catalogue**, a **price list**, or a specifically prepared **quotation**
3	After considering these the buyer will submit an **order**. This might be a further letter or could be a special **order form**.	← →4	On receiving the order the goods will be sent with an **invoice**, or, if necessary, a **credit** or **debit note**.
	When the goods are received, payment will be made to the seller.	← →5	If payment is held up, or a certain amount is still due, a **statement of account** will be issued.
	Payment will then be made usually by cash or cheque.	← →6	The seller will issue a **receipt**.

Recording information, standard documents and form design 73

One further general point is that most forms are produced so that multiple copies can be generated at the same time. Whereas the old carbon paper approach may still be used in some smaller organisations, it is normal now for sets of forms to be produced on NCR (no carbon required) paper, or for panels of carbon to be integrated into the reverse side of forms so that only selected information is transferred to those underneath. In addition, the forms are usually colour-coded to help identification, and distribution to appropriate departments.

The order

Fig. 9.2

```
                    PURCHASE ORDER        No. ____

            INTEGRATED HARDWARE PLC

    ┌─────────────────────────┐   76–84, Southside Road,
    │ To: _____   │   Manchester,
    │     _____   │   ME6 2ST
    │     _____   │   Tel: 0726 854721
    │     _____   │   Date:
    │ Ref:_____   │   Ref:
    └─────────────────────────┘
```

Cat. No.	Quantity	Description	Price per unit

Delivery required by:

Deliver to:

Special Instructions.

....
BUYER

Order forms come in many shapes and sizes, and the number of copies depends on the needs of the organisation. The essential contents are indicated in fig. 9.2. Note that it is not necessary for the total amount of money involved to be mentioned because this is not a bill. It is the start of a transaction from both the legal and accounting point of view. In a typical commercial enterprise a five-copy set might be used as shown in fig. 9.3.

Fig. 9.3

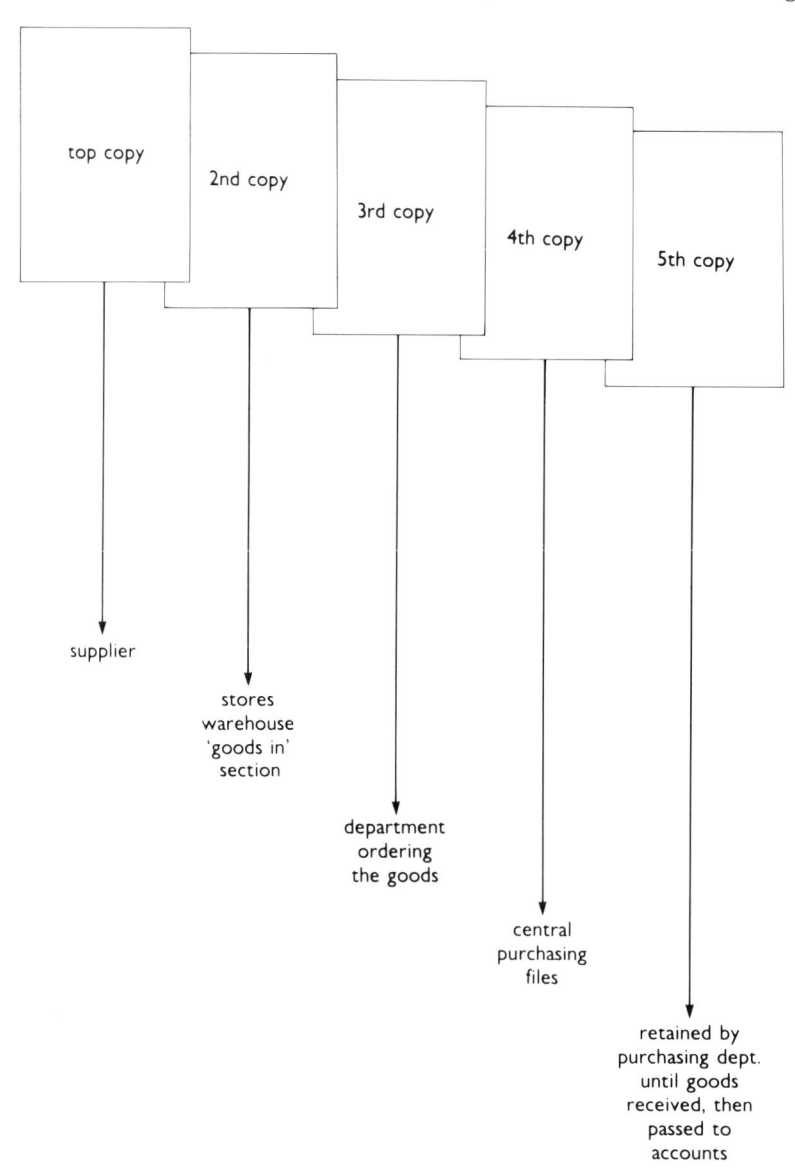

- top copy → supplier
- 2nd copy → stores warehouse 'goods in' section
- 3rd copy → department ordering the goods
- 4th copy → central purchasing files
- 5th copy → retained by purchasing dept. until goods received, then passed to accounts

The requisition

Within an organisation, particular departments may need to requisition goods or consumable items such as stationery from a central store or from another department, and for this purpose there will usually be an internal requisition form. An example of a requisition form is shown in fig. 9.4

Fig. 9.4

INTEGRATED HARDWARE PLC				
REQUISITION				
FROM: DATE: REF:		TO: Central Stores		
Please supply:				
Quantity	Description	Date required	For use by Purchasing Dept. only	
		.... Manager			

Goods received note (GRN)

When goods are delivered to a company, it is important for both the supplier and the recipient to have records of what has passed between them. The supplier will normally ask for a **delivery note** to be signed, which is really a type of receipt. Obviously, goods should be checked before they are signed for, and if this is not possible a statement to this effect should be written on the delivery note – e.g. 'Not inspected'. If inspection indicates any damage, this should also be recorded. The delivery note should be checked against the copy of the order, to see that all is correct, and if this proves satisfactory, a goods received note (example in fig. 9.5) can be made out.

The 'disposal' column is used to indicate what happens to the goods – e.g. 'passed to Production Department'; 'passed into Stock'.

The GRN is also likely to be a multiple copy form, with copies being sent possibly to:

Stores: so that the stock records can be kept up to date.
Purchasing: as notification that the goods have been received.
Accounts: to authorise payment.
The department which placed the order: to act as an internal delivery note – usually signed and returned to the 'Goods In' department.

One copy would be retained for 'Goods In' records.

Fig. 9.5

INTEGRATED HARDWARE PLC

GOODS RECEIVED NOTE

Date: .... No. ....

Cat. No.	Quantity	Description	Disposal

Received from: ...... Order no. ....

....
....
....
....

Carrier: .... Received by: ....

The invoice

This is the 'bill' (fig. 9.6). It should take into account any trade or cash discount and ensure that calculations include appropriate VAT or any other tax which might exist at the time. Value Added Tax has a number of rules and regulations associated with it, such as:

a Every business claiming or paying VAT must register, and the registration number must appear on all invoices.
b An invoice must be issued for every transaction which is subject to VAT.
c VAT is chargeable on the *total value* of the taxable items, and must be shown on the invoice as a *separate* charge.
d VAT is calculated on the actual selling price, i.e. after deduction of any discounts.

One point to remember is that VAT is payable by the seller even if the customer defaults and never pays for the goods received.

Fig. 9.6

INVOICE   No. _____

INTEGRATED HARDWARE PLC

To:

Reference:

76–84, Southside Road,
Manchester,
ME6 2ST
Tel: 0726 854721

Date ....

Delivery ....

....

....

VAT reg. No. 891-736-284

Tax point ....

Cat. No.	Quantity	Description	Unit price	Amount	VAT rate	VAT amount
			Total goods		Total VAT	
			VAT due			
			Amount due			

Goods and services are supplied subject to our normal terms and conditions of sale.

Discounts

It is quite common for discounts to be offered, and these can be 'cash' or 'trade'. A cash discount does not always mean what it says – it can simply be a discount allowed to a company for paying its bill on time! The trade discount can be for quantities of goods, or simply because a trader is acting as an agent and will be retailing the goods to a customer. Another trend nowadays is towards reducing credit periods, i.e. the time allowed between invoice and payment. Normally, an invoice would be followed by a statement which might request payment within 30 days. This could effectively give 60 days of credit in some cases, but many companies now require payment within a certain number of days from the issue of the invoice, and will often offer discount for prompt settlement.

If discount is available, it would normally appear on the invoice as additional columns showing the type of discount and the amount, *before* the VAT information.

Credit note

In some circumstances, such as if a customer is sent damaged goods, is overcharged for a consignment, or returns goods for some other reason, a downward adjustment (reduction) will have to be made to the amount owed by the customer. The issue of a credit note is the most common way of doing this, and, although the note cannot be exchanged for cash, it does guarantee that the amount will be offset against future bills.

Debit note

This document is really a supplementary invoice, and is used if a customer has been under-charged, or an item has been omitted from the original bill. Sometimes a debit note is used to charge the customer for things such as insurance or carriage on a consignment, when the exact amounts involved are not known at the time the original invoice is issued.

Statement of account

The Accounts Department of any organisation will keep records of the amounts owed to the organisation, and a statement is simply a copy of an individual customer's (debtor's) account which shows clearly what is owed, and is sent to the customer when payment is due. Such statements might be sent out at the beginning of each month, or a **cycle billing system** might be implemented, whereby a certain number of accounts are sent out each working day. This latter system has the advantage of spreading the workload more evenly throughout the month.

Fig. 9.7

```
                        STATEMENT

              INTEGRATED HARDWARE PLC

     ┌─────────────────────────┐
     │ To:   ................  │   76–84, Southside Road,
     │       ................  │   Manchester,
     │       ................  │   ME6 2ST
     └─────────────────────────┘
                                   Tel: 0726 854721

                ACCOUNT NO.   ................
```

Date	Details	Debit	Credit	Balance

Abbreviations: Gds Goods   Dr Debit   Bal Balance
                Dis Discount Csh Cash   Cr Credit

Stock control documents

'Stock' is a very general term, and can mean many things, but most organisations hold stock which falls into one or more of the categories shown in fig. 9.8.

Stock is really cash in a different form and, therefore, needs careful control. Security is essential to prevent theft, and on-going records are vital so that stock levels can be maintained to ensure that the organisation does not 'run out' of anything.

The most basic document used is the **stock record card**, and its design varies from company to company. A possible format is shown in fig. 9.9.

Fig. 9.8

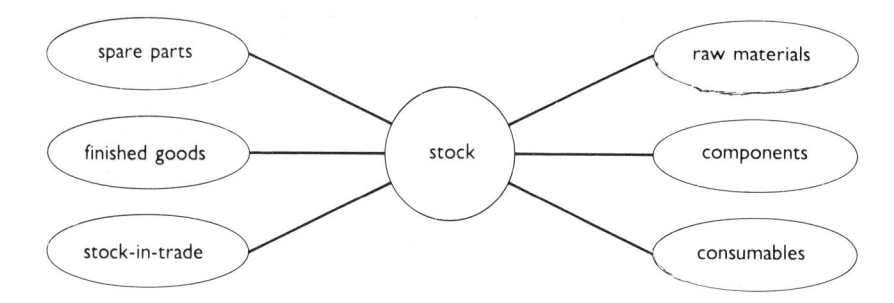

Fig. 9.9

STOCK RECORD CARD

INTEGRATED HARDWARE PLC

Item: ....   Catalogue No. ....
Minimum stock: ....   Maximum stock: ....

Date	Details	Stock in	Stock out	Balance

It is fairly evident that the maintenance of such records is a time-consuming task, and electronic record-keeping can save hours of work, and reduce the amount of paperwork considerably. We are all familiar with the use of bar codes and computerised tills in supermarkets, and there is a whole range of applications of modern technology to all aspects of record-keeping and data handling, which will be considered specifically in a later chapter.

Most organisations need to implement a stock-taking exercise at least once a year for accounting purposes, and an **inventory** is produced, listing the stock held, to help establish whether the actual stock corresponds with what the books indicate should be there. Comparisons can then be made, and any discrepancies investigated.

ACTIVITY

Using any sources and contacts you can find, put together a portfolio of genuine documents used in business. They can come from any types of business, and you should aim to collect a wide variety from as broad a range of businesses as possible. Try to ensure that you obtain examples of all the major documents dealt with in this chapter, but don't hesitate to include any other you might come across.

Your portfolio should be assembled over the next month or so, and if original documents aren't available, photocopies will do. There is no specific written work associated with this activity, but the documents you collect will be useful to you in completing a later assignment.

ACTIVITY

1 The following terms and abbreviations are commonly used on business documents. Referring to a dictionary of business terms, or using a glossary given in some standard Business Studies textbooks, write a brief explanation of each one, and describe the circumstances in which it might be used.

CWO	Carriage Paid
Carriage Forward	COD
CIF	CF
FAS	Ex Works
Terms Net	FOB

2 List any other abbreviations or specific terms you identify on the documents you collect for the preceding activity, and give an explanation for these. Your aim should be to build up as comprehensive a glossary as possible for your own use.

The design of forms

It is not unusual to hear people complaining about having to fill in forms.

- 'What does this section mean?'
- 'I've already told them that!'
- 'That's a bit vague.'
- 'What do they expect me to put in here?'
- 'What do they need that information for?'
- 'Don't they want to know . . .?'

There are always lots of references to 'they', but nobody is really sure who 'they' are. In fact there are three groups of 'them' – the **designers**, **originators**, and **users** of the form – and it is vital that the needs of all three groups are considered carefully when thinking about introducing a form for a particular purpose.

Before this stage is reached, however, certain questions must be asked which might lead to a decision that the whole exercise is unnecessary.

Fig. 9.10

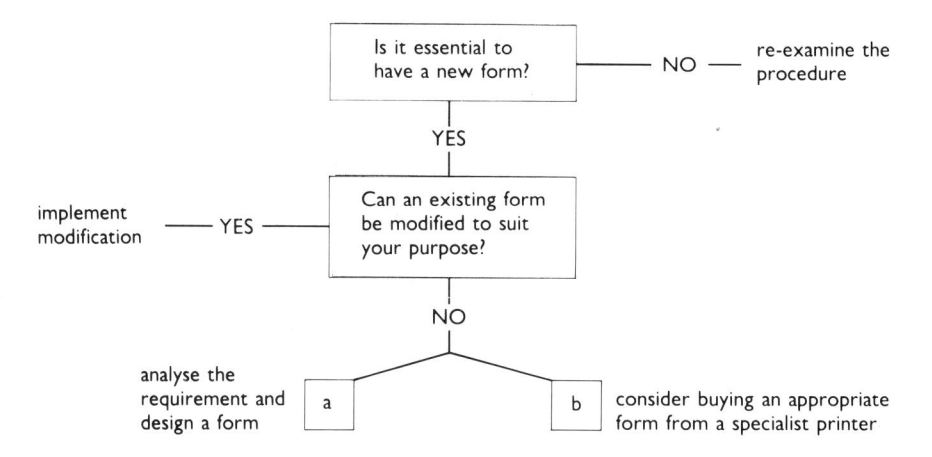

```
                    Is it essential to
                    have a new form? ───── NO ───── re-examine the
                            │                        procedure
                           YES
                            │
implement           Can an existing form
modification ── YES ── be modified to suit
                    your purpose?
                            │
                           NO
                         ╱     ╲
analyse the            ╱         ╲      consider buying an appropriate
requirement and   [a]             [b]   form from a specialist printer
design a form
```

If your initial questioning leads you to alternative (b) in fig. 9.10, you could possibly save a great deal of time and expense. Some types of form which can be bought in this way are given in fig. 9.11.

Fig. 9.11

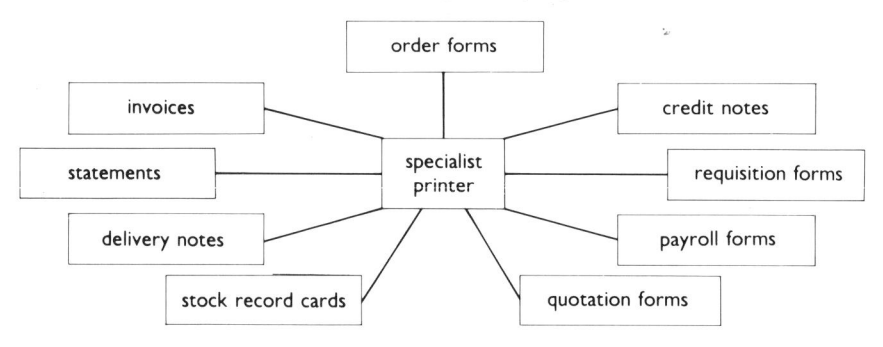

Specialist printer can provide: order forms, invoices, credit notes, statements, requisition forms, delivery notes, payroll forms, stock record cards, quotation forms.

ASSIGNMENT

You have recently joined an expanding company which manufactures and assembles bedroom furniture, and the Administration Manager, John Driscoll, is currently assessing the basic systems and procedures with a view to rationalising and streamlining the administrative side of the business. he calls you into his office and says:

> I've been thinking about the range of forms we use. There doesn't seem to be much consistency in design, and there's a great deal of duplication of information. What we need is a coherent system designed specifically for this business, but that could be an expensive exercise. I seem to remember that there are a number of specialist people who produce standard ranges of forms, and it might be worth finding out what they can offer.
> Will you find out where the nearest ones are who can do this type of work – three will do – and get some idea of the range of forms they can show us. I don't want to waste time and money if I can buy them off the shelf.

Find the necessary information for Mr Driscoll, and incorporate it into a memo to him. The information you submit should be comprehensive enough for him to be able to decide whether or not this course of action seems worth following up, and you should provide him with appropriate addresses, telephone numbers, etc. to facilitate following action.

Recording information, standard documents and form design 83

Designing a form

After careful consideration, you might decide that the only solution is to design a new form to fulfil the requirements of a particular procedure or situation, and to help you there are a number of basic principles that should be borne in mind (fig. 9.12). On top of this, to be a good designer, you will need flair, an eye for visual impact, and a highly developed sense of proportion!

Fig. 9.12

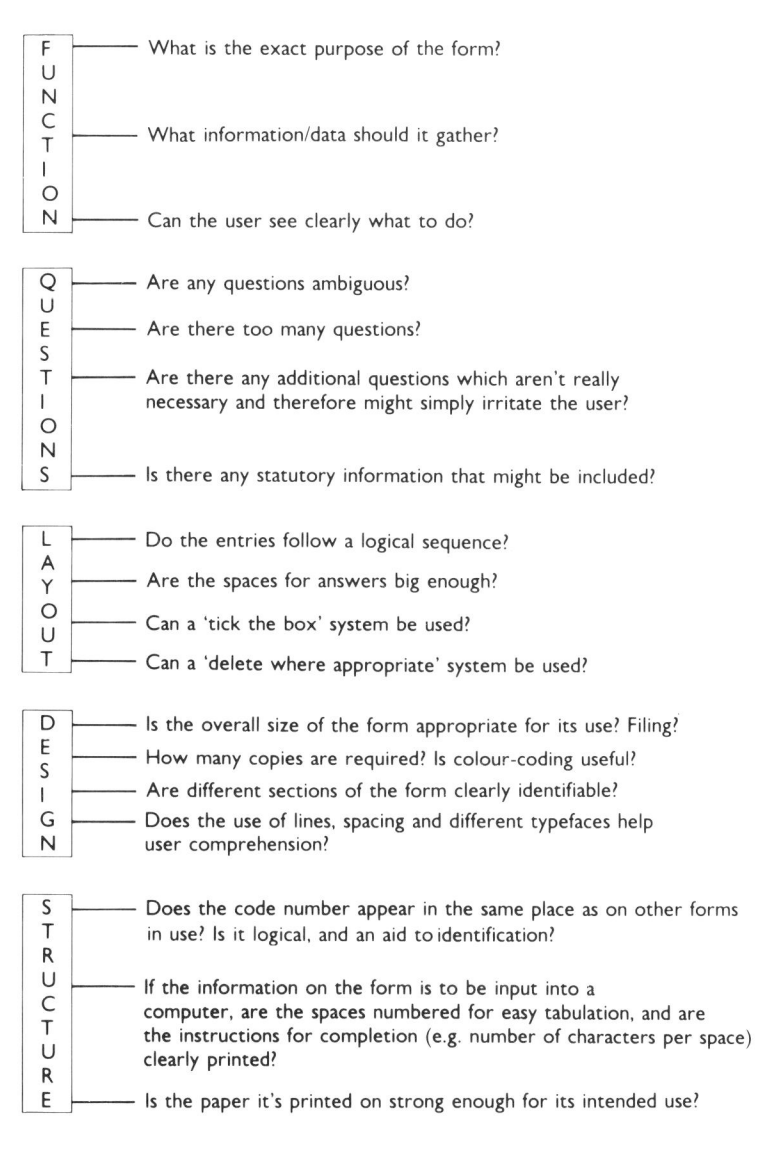

FUNCTION
- What is the exact purpose of the form?
- What information/data should it gather?
- Can the user see clearly what to do?

QUESTIONS
- Are any questions ambiguous?
- Are there too many questions?
- Are there any additional questions which aren't really necessary and therefore might simply irritate the user?
- Is there any statutory information that might be included?

LAYOUT
- Do the entries follow a logical sequence?
- Are the spaces for answers big enough?
- Can a 'tick the box' system be used?
- Can a 'delete where appropriate' system be used?

DESIGN
- Is the overall size of the form appropriate for its use? Filing?
- How many copies are required? Is colour-coding useful?
- Are different sections of the form clearly identifiable?
- Does the use of lines, spacing and different typefaces help user comprehension?

STRUCTURE
- Does the code number appear in the same place as on other forms in use? Is it logical, and an aid to identification?
- If the information on the form is to be input into a computer, are the spaces numbered for easy tabulation, and are the instructions for completion (e.g. number of characters per space) clearly printed?
- Is the paper it's printed on strong enough for its intended use?

These principles are intended for use as a checklist when you embark on the design of any form, and there are certain other techniques which will improve its 'useability':

- in case a typewriter is to be used for making entries, the design

should be compatible with the vertical line spacing of the typewriter (6 lines to the inch).
- horizontal guidelines are not always useful to a typist, but can be helpful for handwritten entries.
- as far as possible, line endings should be aligned vertically with each other.
- forms on which figures are to be entered and totalled should be designed so that amounts can be totalled vertically, with a clear indication given whenever a 'total' is required.
- avoid the user having to do too much writing – much standard material can be printed on the form.

Forms control

In any organisation it would be unwise to allow forms to be produced for special purposes whenever someone thought it was necessary, so a system of control is essential. This can be run by the O & M department, or be the responsibility of a particular section. In any case, all supervisory and management staff should constantly review the forms used in their area to make sure that they still serve a useful purpose; note any changes in procedure which could necessitate a change in form design; and ensure that the most up-to-date version of any form is used so that efficiency is not impaired.

Other control procedures can include issuing forms on requisition only, regular evaluation to establish the time required to understand them, fill them in and use them, and the destruction of all obsolete forms to avoid confusion.

If a form control procedure is to be initiated, all staff must first be informed what is being done. Any 'casual' forms activity should then be stopped, and all requests made to a central control. At the same time, a 'forms file' containing specimens of *all* forms in use (both statutory and in-house) should be assembled, the forms classified and registered. In the **forms register** there can also be a summary of how, where and why the form is used; its code number, title and originating department; how and when it was originally produced/revised; and the size, type and colour of paper it is printed on. There are, of course, many different designs of form control sheets, but the principle of control is an important one which can increase efficiency and decrease costs in almost any organisation.

ACTIVITY

You have been asked by your Section Head to accept responsibility for the purchasing and controlling of all items of stationery used in your company. Describe concisely how you would ensure that stock levels are maintained, and explain what system you would use to control the issuing of stock to various departments. You should produce copies of any forms and/or cards you may use to achieve this.

Recording information, standard documents and form design 85

Accident report forms

Standard forms do not always have to be related to the commercial activities of an organisation, and one of the most common examples which can be found in most organisations is the **accident report form**. As its name indicates, this is a type of formal report which is submitted on a ready-printed form. This makes it much easier to deal with, and if you ever have cause to use one, remember that you should follow the instructions carefully. If you need to give a description of an accident or incident, make sure you say exactly what happened and that your facts are accurate. It is a mistake to exaggerate or try to make things sound worse than they actually are, because if there is an investigation and you are proved wrong, you could prejudice any legal claim to compensation or, at least, destroy your own credibility. Every organisation will have a different design of accident report form to meet its own requirements, so there is no standard format.

ACTIVITY

Bearing in mind the principles of form design you have considered in this chapter, design an accident report form for use either within the college or within your own work environment. You should *incorporate* or *request* the following information as a *minimum*.

form reference number	organisation name
document title	instructions
name of injured person	place of accident
when accident was reported	witnesses' names and addresses
nature of injury	description of accident
names & addresses of others involved	date and time of accident
occupation of injured person	age of injured person
name of injured person	address of injured person
statement of whether hospital treatment was received	signature of person completing the form
	date

If you feel other information is required, you should include it in your design. The report should be produced on plain A4 paper, using a maximum of two sheets (written on one side only).

ACTIVITY

Acquire a copy of an accident report form currently in use within an organisation of your choice. This example should be kept in your file as part of your formal 'written' work. If you can get hold of a number of different examples, all the better!

You should bear in mind that any report should be kept as brief as possible, and that your skill in writing concisely and accurately will really be tested if you ever have to get involved in filling in this type of document.

CHAPTER 10
Information handling and transmission

Traditional record management

Whenever anybody mentions 'filing' as an essential aspect of business administration, a common reaction is for those listening to 'switch off' and start daydreaming, and it is unlikely that phrases like 'alpha numerical' and 'terminal digit' figure very prominently in the scenario.

However, the importance of filing and indexing cannot be over-emphasised in an efficiently run organisation, and for anyone involved in designing and setting up systems it can be quite a complex exercise in logical thought and functional analysis. The thing to remember is that there is no 'best' system, because each organisation, department, section and individual will have different needs and will require a system specifically tailored to those needs.

In general terms, we can identify certain characteristics which will make a filing system work efficiently, but they are really only guidelines which are subject to the vagaries of the real world, e.g. human nature, physical resources, money. Fig. 10.1 summarises these 'essential' qualities.

Fig. 10.1

Characteristic	Reason
accessibility	people must be able to get at them easily
compactness	space is valuable – particularly floor space
simplicity	it's no good having a system or method of classification which nobody can understand
elasticity	it must be possible to expand (and contract) the system as required
speed of retrieval	it must not take a long time for users to find things, as time costs money
economy	the costs of installation, implementation and application can get out of hand
safety	loss, damage and insecurity of documents can be disastrous
recorded removal	documents or complete files cannot be traced unless a system of 'out' guides or 'tracers' is used
daily update	this is the only way to ensure *current* information

Information handling and transmission

As far as the organisation is concerned, a filing system can be centralised (the same system used throughout the organisation) or de-centralised (departmentally based). The centralised system does have a number of advantages, including the elimination of duplication, a specially trained staff, uniformity throughout the organisation, economy of equipment and space, and a close control over all records. Against this, however, a department-based system can offer easy availability, a variety of appropriate storage and classification systems, and immediate up-dating.

No matter how much is written about the importance of filing and efficient information storage, problems always arise, and most organisations can quote examples of files being taken out without a record being kept, individual documents disappearing from a file, or files being returned to the wrong place. Most of these problems can be attributed to human failings, but common causes can be identified in more general terms:

a   The staff are untrained or unsuitable.
b   The wrong system of classification has been used.
c   There is no planned system of retention or disposal of records.
d   The space and equipment are inadequate for the purpose.
e   There are no established procedures for creating new files.
f   There is bad organisation and lack of control over borrowing and return of records.

ACTIVITY

This activity will enable you to collect essential information on basic storage and retrieval systems. In your library you will find relevant information in books on office administration, secretarial practice, office practice, business administration, etc.

Filing equipment and methods of storage

Listed below are a number of standard storage methods. You are required to draw up a table (see fig. 10.2) listing each one, and describing its main characteristics. If possible, produce a diagram to give some idea of what each looks like.

| lateral filing | electrically operated systems | horizontal filing |
| vertical filing | mobile systems | rotary filing (carousel) |

Fig. 10.2

Method	Description	Artists' impression
horizontal filing	Files placed on top of each other in shallow drawers or on shelves. Not a very efficient method. Retrieval not always easy.	

ACTIVITY

Classification systems

No matter what method of storage is used for documentary information, there needs to be an efficient system of classification in order to help people retrieve files as quickly as possible. Obviously, the system chosen depends on the type of information being stored, and it is important to pick the best method for maximum efficiency.

Produce a set of notes on the main classification systems mentioned below. Your notes should be schematically structured (presented under a series of headings, sub-headings, and numbered points, as outlined in Chapter 8). It may well be appropriate to use the name of each classification system as a main section heading, and construct informative sub-headings such as 'Description', 'Characteristics', 'Operation', 'Advantages', 'Disadvantages', 'Example'.

Systems

numerical filing	alphabetical filing
subject filing	alpha-numerical filing
geographical filing	decimal filing
terminal digit filing	

ASSIGNMENT: Data classification

As part of the administrative team working under the Office Manager, you have discovered some drawbacks in the filing classification system used by various departments, which often results in some documents being wrongly filed, and others being difficult to find. Obviously, the whole system of data storage needs to be looked at, but, as a start, you are asked to draw up some basic guidelines for consideration by the Office Services Committee, as a move towards rationalising classification types throughout the company. You have identified the following types of information which need storage:

clients'/customers' records	products
personnel/staff records	supplies/purchases
customers' accounts	contract numbers
technical data	services
sales territories	mail order records
insurance policies	import/export records

Produce your guidelines in tabular form using the structure indicated in fig. 10.3. The 'additional comments' column should be used to express any particular difficulties you envisage in implementing the recommendations, or to describe any circumstances in which the system would need modification (e.g. additional colour coding).

Fig. 10.3

Type of data	Classification system	Reasons for choice	Additional comments
sales area	alphabetical by geographical location	Simple operation. The names of individual firms are not required. No cross-referencing is likely to be needed.	If there are a large number of files, it may be necessary to have a separate file-list for general reference.
customers			

Indexing systems

A necessary complement to any general filing system is an **indexing** system. The basic function of an index is as a guide to the location of information, and there are five main types.

1 Page index

This may be a book or a loose-leaf binder, with one or more pages devoted to each letter of the alphabet.

2 Visible card index (visible edge index)

The basic principle of visible card indexes is that each card overlaps the next, allowing at least one line of reference to be visible from every record.

3 Vertical card index

Small cards are kept upright in a metal cabinet, box or drawer, and are normally divided by guide cards. The index can be alphabetically or numerically arranged.

4 Strip index

Any office will need to have lists of names or numbers to give easy access to things like telephone numbers, account numbers, addresses, etc. The information is usually typed on a strip of card which can be easily fixed into a 'mount'. This mount could be a frame on the wall, consisting of a number of leaves, a free-standing construction, or pages in a book.

5 Rotary index

This is a card index system, but the cards are stored in a circular drum which can be rotated to bring each card into view in turn.

Maintaining the filing system

In normal filing systems it is important to implement certain support procedures to ensure efficient operation. For example, when a file is taken out, or a document removed from a file, an **outcard** or **outmarker** should be completed. This is put in the file in place of the document being used, and should indicate the *date* the document was removed, the *department* or *person* who borrowed it, the *date range* that the document refers to, the *subject* of the document, and an indication of when it will be *returned*.

As a system expands (or contracts) certain files become **dead files**. This could mean that they are either no longer required and can be destroyed, or that the original files have become so thick that certain information is removed and stored in a different place. In practical terms, for example, documents relating to the last six months might be kept in the current file, and anything before that would be transferred. Obviously, as soon as the retention date for the documents has expired they can be destroyed (usually **shredded** for security reasons).

People in business organisations

Within an organisation it might be desirable to store certain information in more than one place – for example, a copy of a letter querying an invoice might be required by the Sales Department and the Accounts Department. This can be done either by photocopying and storing the same document in two different places, or by **cross-referencing**, using a system by which all information would be kept in one file, but a reference to this main file would be placed in the files of all interested parties.

ASSIGNMENT: Appraisal of a filing system

For this assignment you will need to assess one filing system currently in use in either your own organisation, or in an organisation to which you have access. The idea is to select a system which can easily be observed in use, and which is not too complex in its function or design.

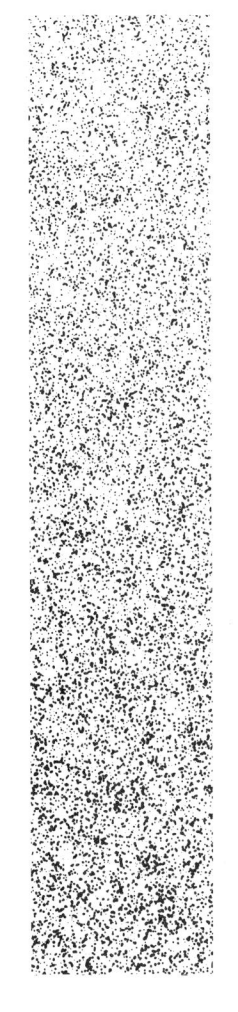

You are required to produce a **short formal report** (see 'Notes for guidance') for your immediate superior (or the Head of the Section in which your chosen system is operating). You should collate your information under the following headings, and then produce the report.

Report headings

- the location and purpose or function of the system
- physical storage methods
- classification system
- size (of each file, and of the whole system)
- users and usage
- outmarkers
- dead-filing
- conclusions: good and bad points
- recommendations for improvement

Notes for guidance: the short formal report

A report can be defined as a document designed to give the person(s) calling for the report information necessary for further action. To aid comprehension and easy identification of particular aspects, a schematic presentation is desirable, with appropriate headings, sub-headings and numbered points. Fig. 10.4 indicates the conventions of content and layout normally applied to this type of formal report. Remember, decisions might be made on the strength (or weakness) of your report, so research thoroughly, select carefully, convey information, conclusions and recommendations clearly, and stick closely to the conventions of structure and presentation.

Fig. 10.4 The layout of a short formal report.

For the attention of ....

Full and explanatory title

1 <u>TERMS OF REFERENCE</u>   ('Introduction' can be used)

   This should indicate the scope of the report, the background to the situation, any specific source material, and why the report is being submitted.

2 <u>Procedure</u>

   Explain accurately and concisely how the research was conducted — how the information was collected, who was interviewed etc.

3 <u>Findings</u>

   (a) <u>Sub-heading</u>
       (i)
       (ii)
       (iii)

   (b) <u>Sub-heading</u>
       (i)
       (ii)
       (iii)

   (c) <u>Sub-heading</u>
       (i)
       (ii)
       (iii)

   These should be presented schematically. The number of main sections, the number of sub-sections, and the extent of the individual comments will depend on the information you have available and the requirements of the recipient. Do *not* use note form. The sequence of sub-headings should be logical and, as far as possible, in rank order.

4 <u>Conclusions</u>

These can be presented as a narrative paragraph, or a number of points. In the latter case, accurate cross-referencing with main findings is desirable. A continuation of the schematic presentation can be used if appropriate.

5 <u>Recommendations</u>

See comments on 'Conclusions'.
Recommendations should not be included unless specifically asked for.

                    Signature: ....

                    Designation: ....

                    Date: ....

Microfilm and microfiche

The concept of microfilm or microfiche is simple. A photographic image of a document is produced in miniature on a continuous strip (microfilm), or on an A5 sheet (microfiche). A special 'reader' which magnifies the photographic images and shows them on a screen is required with either system, and it is quite expensive for an organisation to equip itself to photograph, process, store, view and reproduce documents. Each of the systems has its own advantages. The microfilm is really like a simple filmstrip, with each frame showing a different document. It is particularly useful if documents need to be viewed in sequence. Microfiche will have between 60 and 100 documents recorded on a single sheet (fig. 10.5) and has the advantage that documents can be viewed in any order, and can be selected quickly and easily.

*Fig. 10.5
A microfiche and reader.*

Technology, data handling and data transmission

The move towards more 'technological' systems of data storage leads us naturally into a consideration of computer-aided data handling and the integrated electronic office. Information technology is developing so fast that it is easy to get carried away with enthusiasm, and make claims such as 'the clerical function will cease to exist in five years' time', or 'in ten years none of us will be going to work because we shall work from home with our own micro-computers'. Even though development is very rapid, it is important to keep things in perspective. The technology is available to turn the office as we know it into a fully integrated information processing centre, but the implementation of such a concept requires careful planning, and we will not see a transformation of the face of business activity overnight. The introduction of such systems is often done a bit at a time, and integration is not always the result. However, let's consider the main areas in which information technology has made tremendous advances and discover to what extent *you* have experienced the change. You may not be able to complete the next activity until you have read the explanatory sections which follow it.

Information handling and transmission

ACTIVITY

Outlined below are the main areas in which information technology has facilitated the development of greater speed, efficiency, and access to data in the functional areas of the office. Figs. 10.6 (a) – (h) also indicate stages in the development of systems, some of which are very much out-of-date, but can still be found in offices (and colleges!) around the country. Draw out each table, completing all columns from your own observations, research or experience.

Note: Expand the tables to accommodate the information.

Fig. 10.6(a)

Computing	Organisation	Department	Specific uses	No. of users
accounting machines calculators (personal or desktop) mainframe computer mini-computers micro-computers				

Fig. 10.6(b)

Copying	Organisation	Department	Specific uses	No. of users
spirit duplicator ink duplicator photocopier facsimile production electronic transmission				

Fig. 10.6(c)

Dictating systems	Organisation	Department	Specific uses	No. of users

shorthand
   (person to person)
dictaphone
centralised dictation
   systems				

Fig. 10.6(d)

Information storage	Organisation	Department	Specific uses	No. of users

paper files
microfilm/microfiche
computer data store
   (tape)
computer data store
   (disk)				

Fig. 10.6(e)

Library systems	Organisation	Department	Specific uses	No. of users
reference books teletext viewdata (e.g. Prestel)				

People in business organisations

Fig. 10.6(f)

Mail	Organisation	Department	Specific uses	No. of users
public mail service private couriers internal systems inter-company systems electronic mail				

Fig. 10.6(g)

Telecommunications	Organisation	Department	Specific uses	No. of users
telephone telex teletext teleconferencing				

Fig. 10.6(h)

Writing systems	Organisation	Department	Specific uses	No. of users

hand-written form
   filling
typewriters (manual)
electric typewriters
electronic typewriters
word processing
   (micro-based)
word processing
   (dedicated)				

You will certainly be familiar with some of these systems, and it is obviously unnecessary to describe here the functions of such things as a telephone or a typewriter. In other areas, however, a brief explanation might be useful to help you to understand the extent of technological developments in information handling and transmission.

Telex

Telex works like the telephone, but sends written messages instead of the spoken word. The message is typed on the teleprinter, and sent to the recipient by dialling a special number. The public telex network then conveys the message to its destination, where it is printed out on another teleprinter. Systems have been developed from the electro-mechanical printers, which are bulky and noisy, to silicon chip-based technology, where the telex terminal resembles a word processor with a Visual Display Unit (VDU), and the text can be prepared on-screen. This allows for easier editing before transmission, and when it arrives (on screen) at the other end, the recipient can choose whether or not a print-out ('hard copy') is required. Modern systems allow two choices – a 'dedicated' telex machine, or a micro-computer with telex software. The latter version is more flexible, but more expensive.

Information handling and transmission

Teletex

This, like telex, uses the public network, but the quality of the service it gives is better. Based on an ordinary micro-computer or word processor, the presentation is clearer, the range of symbols it can transmit is much wider, and it is nearly six times as fast.

Telemessage

This is part of British Telecom's electronic mail service, and operates through the Prestel network. In days gone by we would send a very urgent message by telegram. We now send a telemessage which guarantees next day delivery and can be initiated from an ordinary telephone by dialling the operator.

Electronic mail

Sometimes referred to as 'mailboxing' or 'email', a system like this sends messages by electronic means, and in some circumstances can replace many standard communications such as memos, letters and telephone calls. The system can be used internally, or externally using the public telephone network. To use the system you have to be a subscriber, and this 'membership' means that you are allocated a certain space in a central computer's memory. This space is your 'mail box', and it has a number which people can dial into. Other subscribers can, therefore, send messages to your 'mail box', where they will be stored until you decide to read them. You can then reply directly through the computer, or take a print-out for further consideration. The limitation of this system is that it can only send text. The great advantages are that messages can be sent very quickly and it requires only a micro-computer, a **modem** (telephone link/adaptor) and access via a telephone line to the central computer base.

Linking different equipment

(See also later comments on **integrated software**).
As mentioned before, recent developments in office automation now mean that all items of electronic equipment such as word processors, micro-computers, the telephone system, and mainframe computers can be interconnected to form a total electronic communication system.

Private Automatic Branch Exchange (PABX)

Modern computerised PABXs not only route internal and external calls but offer a wide range of other telephone facilities. These include: automatic transfer of a call to other extensions, abbreviated dialling, conference calls (audio-conferencing – i.e. many extensions linked together at the same time), automatic call back, automatic return to operator for an outside caller if an extension fails to answer, queuing of incoming calls, and computerised directories. The PABX can become the centre of the office network of communication equipment, and the more advanced PABX can link different equipment over the telephone lines creating a network. All communication from all sources, both inside and outside the office, can be routed through the PABX to the central control unit, which, in turn, will electronically divert the messages to whichever destination is required.

Local Area Network (LAN)

Some large organisations have created LANs which make it easy for different items of electronic equipment to communicate with each other, and to share ancillary equipment like printers and files to prevent duplication.

Where an organisation has introduced office equipment a bit at a time – a word processor here, a personal computer there, a printer somewhere else ('stand-alone' systems) – the LAN allows them to be linked so that they can exchange information and share resources.

Viewdata

Viewdata is a general term used to describe public computerised or electronic information services. The basic characteristics are a central computer which is very large and houses a vast data-bank and a network of terminals, connected to the central computer through the telephone network.

An example of viewdata in operation is the **Prestel** system run by British Telecom which – at the time of writing – provides approximately 280,000 'pages' of information which are available to the user (on screen) at the touch of a button. This information is on a range of topics from current share prices, to weather reports, to vacancies in major hotels.

Teletext

Also referred to as videotext, this is a television-based information system whereby any viewer has access to a vast range of information provided free by the BBC (Ceefax) and ITV (Oracle), by simply using a television remote control which operates through a special adaptor in the television.

Facsimile

The transfer of images such as photographs or architects' plans from one place to another is more difficult than text, but can be done using telecommunications. Equipment such as telex cannot cope with this type of work, but specialist machines are in use for scanning the image, encoding it and transmitting the signals to a receiving machine which decodes them and prints the image on paper. This is known as facsimile transfer (fax).

Reprography

While we have facsimile transfer systems, which provide an exact replica of an original document or drawing, let's not forget the simpler world of copying and duplicating. The ever-reliable **carbon paper** is still in use for very limited copies, and **NCR paper** has already been discussed in the chapter on business documents. Many organisations now prefer to rent, lease or buy a **photocopier**, and there are many to choose from, ranging from desk-top models to very large, complex machines which will copy in colour, reduce, enlarge, copy both sides at once, feed in originals automatically, collate and staple documents, all in one process.

This doesn't mean that other methods of producing copies are no longer used, and machines including **spirit duplicators** and **offset litho duplicators** can still make their contribution to the business world. To bring copying right up to date, we have the **duplicator/copiers** which are described as intelligent copiers/printers. These electronic copiers are controlled by a micro-processor, which can accept input from other compatible equipment such as a word processor or computer, and will produce a master and then make and collate the required number of copies automatically.

ASSIGNMENT: Conveying information

1 Provide brief definitions and explanations of the following aspects of data handling and transmission which have not been dealt with in this chapter so far:

electronic typewriter
word processor
multi-bank dictation system
tandem dictation system
PMBX

call-connect system
video conferencing
datel
paging systems
closed circuit television

2 Working in pairs, choose any two of the topics in 1, and produce **visual aids** which could be used to describe and explain to a group of visiting business students what the system is and how it works. Assume that your visual aids will be produced as overhead-projector (OHP) transparencies, and design them accordingly. There is no limit on the number you produce, but remember that visual communication needs to be clear and simple if it is to be effective.

3 Using your group as the target audience, give a short talk about any one of the methods of communication you have dealt with in this assignment, using your own visual aids to demonstrate and explain which method you are talking about, how it works, and what its uses, advantages and disadvantages are in a business situation. Be prepared to answer questions.

Notes for guidance: oral presentations

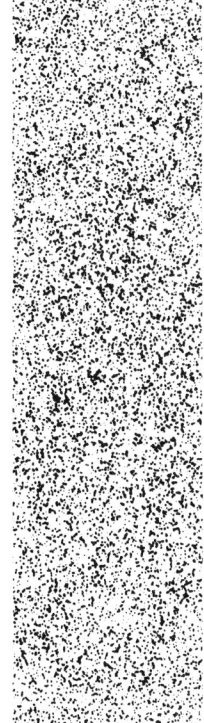

Oral presentations can range from the lengthy, formal lecture to a simple, informal demonstration or explanation of equipment or a procedure. With any oral work, *preparation* is all-important, and it takes time to prepare the topic so that the presentation will be effective. For this assignment you will already have researched the topic superficially, but you are now in the situation of having not only to explain and describe what you are talking about, but also to answer questions. Do you have enough information?

1. Research – make sure you have enough material and that it is comprehensive enough to answer any general questions. Try to anticipate what questions might be asked.
2. Structure your information so that you can present it in a logical sequence which will be easy for the audience to follow and understand.
3. Identify specific aspects of the topics which could benefit from the use of visual aids, and determine (for this assignment) at what points you are going to show them. Remember, each visual aid should have a specific function. Ask yourself 'What will it do for the audience?' Demonstrate? Explain? Clarify? Confuse?
4. Check your facts – there is nothing worse than giving your talk and then being faced with some 'know-all' who points out to you that your information is out of date, or who claims to have seen some statistics which prove you wrong!

Note: It is not a good idea to write out the complete talk and simply read it to your audience.

However, it is certainly a good idea to have some notes in front of you when you stand up to speak. Not only will they guide you through in the correct sequence, but they can be used to prompt you when a visual aid, or change of OHP transparency is required.

This is another situation in which a schematic presentation can be useful, but, obviously, you should restrict the amount of information you write out and concentrate on **key** words or ideas which you can simply glance at to refresh your memory. The aim is to talk as naturally as possible, and this will not happen if you try to read lengthy passages from a sheet in front of you. Fig. 10.7 shows in diagrammatic form how a set of notes for a demonstration of office equipment could be set out.

Fig. 10.7

```
                    NOTES

For:

(Full explanatory title saying where, when, to whom and on
what topic the talk will be given.)

Sources of information:

(This is really for your own sake so that you can demonstrate
the validity of what you are saying.)

Introduction:

(This will summarise the purpose for which the equipment is
used and indicate its general usefulness in given
situations.)

Operation/implementation:

    Stage 1    visual aid (specify)
               (i)
               (ii)
```

Stage 2
    (i)
    (ii)

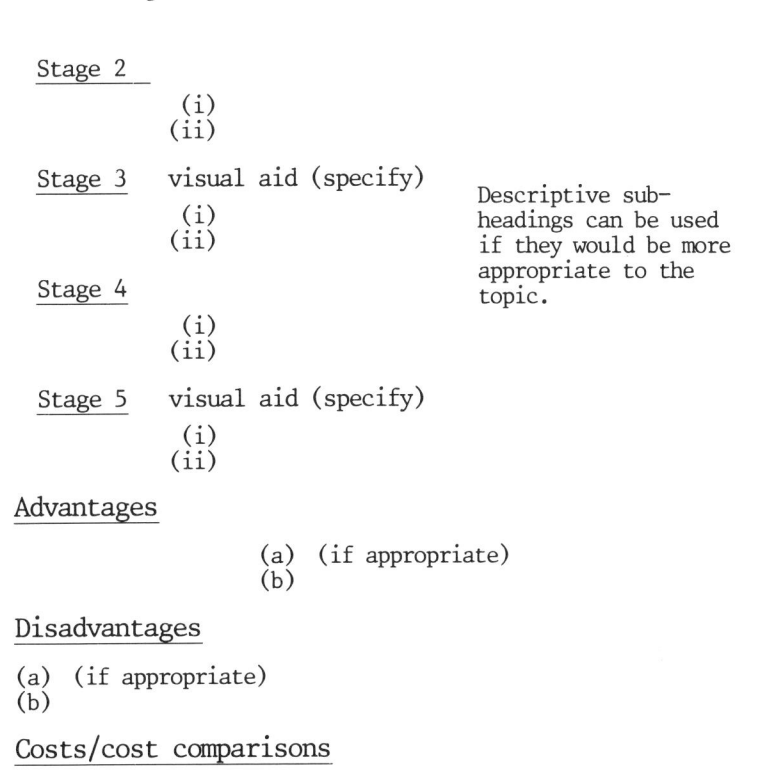

Stage 3   visual aid (specify)
    (i)   Descriptive sub-
    (ii)   headings can be used
                                     if they would be more
Stage 4   appropriate to the
    (i)   topic.
    (ii)

Stage 5   visual aid (specify)
    (i)
    (ii)

Advantages

    (a) (if appropriate)
    (b)

Disadvantages

(a) (if appropriate)
(b)

Costs/cost comparisons

(if appropriate)

Conclusions

(If appropriate — these could possibly specify or reinforce the application in given business situations.)

Recommendations

(if appropriate)

Having worked through the various stages of preparation, you actually have to *deliver* the talk. Nothing will take away the nervousness you will experience but you should feel a little more confident if you have prepared your materials well. Don't be afraid to refer to your notes, because there is nothing worse than a speaker who 'dries up' or starts talking nonsense. Remember these principles:

try to maintain eye-contact with your audience;

don't stare at one person – move your eyes around the room and try to gauge how they are responding to you;

concentrate on *how* you talk – don't gabble, mumble or whisper, and try to modulate the tone and pitch of your voice so that it is not unnaturally high;

don't try to adopt a 'forced' speaking voice or accent – the chances are you will make yourself sound foolish;

pronounce all your words clearly (don't 'clip' the endings) so that everyone can hear clearly what you are saying.

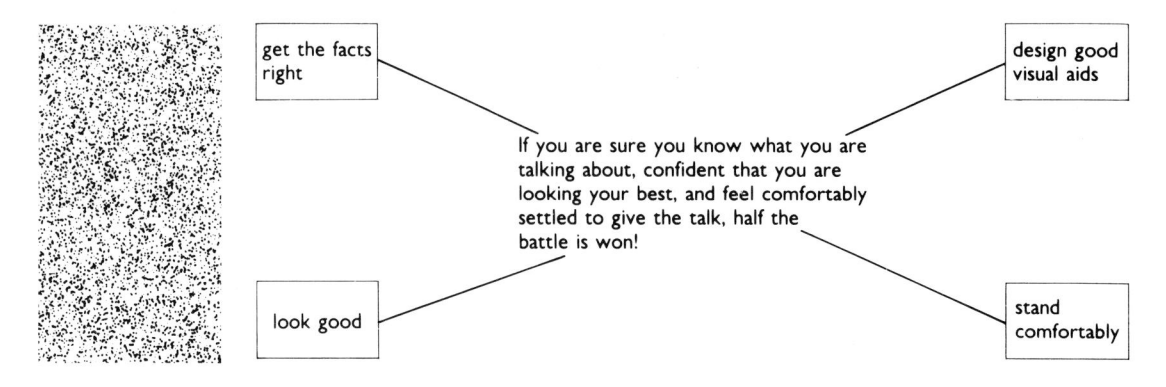

```
get the facts          design good
right                  visual aids
         \            /
          If you are sure you know what you are
          talking about, confident that you are
          looking your best, and feel comfortably
          settled to give the talk, half the
          battle is won!
         /            \
look good              stand
                       comfortably
```

The computer

We have already considered in general terms some aspects of computer-aided data handling, and the role of information technology in the modern office, but now let's look at the computer itself, and some other ways in which it is applied to business life.

Automatic data processing is not a new thing, and the use of systems such as 'punched card' date back to the Industrial Revolution (e.g. 'programming' weaving looms). Such cards have a sequence of coded holes punched in them, and have been developed to automate a range of

Fig. 10.8 Some peripheral devices used with computers.

Input	Output
punched cards ⎫ limited use perforated paper tape ⎭ nowadays	
magnetic ink character readers e.g. on cheques, statements, etc.	printer (impact, daisy wheel, dot-matrix, etc.)
optical character readers (recognised by shape)	
mark readers (e.g. indicating answers to multiple choice questions)	visual display unit (VDU)
document readers	
remote input units	computer output microfilm (COM)
magnetic tape encoder	
on-line terminal (usually a VDU and keyboard)	
key-to-disk (intermediate storage of information on magnetic disk)	storage media (back-up storage on disk or tape)
light pens	
electronic light pens	photo-typesetting devices
hand-held or telephone key pads	intelligent copiers
voice input	

activities in both industry and commerce. In particular, the system has served administrators very well as a means of speedy sorting and retrieval of information. However, use of the punched card system has declined as the computer has come into its own, because such systems cannot compete with the computer's arithmetic and logic unit which can search, sort, collate and calculate almost instantaneously. We are now in the era of electronic data processing.

The computer, however, is not superhuman in its capabilities – only in its speed of operation. It cannot do anything the human brain cannot do, and it cannot operate without human involvement at some stage. In fact, it is the human involvement which causes most of the problems! Computer systems can range from simple micro-computers (stand-alone) to a complex network of linked mainframe computers and peripheral devices in various parts of the world. Peripheral devices fall into two general categories (see fig. 10.8).

Computer applications

All the **hardware** described in fig. 10.8 is only any use if appropriate **programs** are used. The programs contain the basic data and instructions which enable the computer to operate in a particular way. Programs are written for a variety of applications, and enable data to be input, stored, manipulated, retrieved and output for many specific aspects of business, such as:

order processing	sales billing/invoicing
credit control	stock records and control
production control	pay-roll
pensions	sales/purchase/nominal ledgers
typesetting	personnel training records
bulk mailing	access control by magnetic card or voice
filing	word processing

In the management area, there are other applications, including sales forecasting, analysis of data, staff planning and constructing 'models', and complex **databases** can be built up to provide relevant information for decision making.

Filing

To give you a little more insight into computer applications, it might be useful to consider some specific examples and general concepts. Let's start with something we looked at earlier in this chapter – **filing**. If traditional filing methods are to be replaced with electronic ones, the same basic principles must be applied. Information needs to be easily and readily accessible, and careful thought must be given to the nature of the system, its volume, lifespan, classification, and cost.

Modern electronic filing is dependent upon 'database management systems' – bought as software packages and used in conjunction with a micro-computer or computer terminal – which are designed for creating, updating and manipulating information (files). Such systems allow users to construct their own format for records in a file, and to vary formats as required. In many packages there are limitations associated with the number of headings that can be used and the amount of information that can be stored. However, the benefits are numerous, as once users have set up the records by deciding what information to store and how to store it, they can then:

- add new records, update existing ones and amend them instantly;
- perform mathematical calculations based on the stored information;
- conduct complex searches for particular types of information;
- sort and order records according to a range of criteria, e.g. alphabetical, age, date of birth, etc;
- display the records on a VDU;
- print out information as required;
- link up with other functions through **integrated software packages** (see below).

Word processing

In the general area of text production, **word processing** application packages are designed to enable the user to use a computer terminal and printer as a sophisticated typewriter. A well-written program enables the user to store and retrieve text as required, to move text around the screen, to add to it or delete from it and generally to manipulate the structure and appearance of the finished product. Text can be **justified**, i.e. the words spread throughout the line so that the margins at each side are straight. Automatic centering is also a common facility. A built-in spelling checker queries words spelt differently from those held in store, and key words or phrases can be searched for throughout a document if required. One of the problems with older types of packages (which, however, are still in common use) is that, because some VDU screens are able to display only forty characters in a line, the user is not able to compose documents on the screen in the way that they will be printed out – the printer typically having a maximum line of eighty characters.

The database

The word **database** has been used a number of times in talking about computer applications, and describes a collection of records holding information which can be accessed by computer. Such records may have something in common with each other (e.g. a personnel database would most likely contain names, addresses, dates of birth, payroll numbers, departments, career histories, qualifications, etc.) or they may have a common subject (e.g. Lawtel, a database used by the legal profession and accessed via Prestel, which provides information about decided cases, statutes, precedents, and current and impending legislation).

The database is kept up-to-date by those authorised to do so, by adding, deleting, or changing records. Users can search for individual records or select a group of records based upon characteristics of their choice.

Since the same information may be required by a number of different departments, the idea of a database is that it should be as comprehensive as possible, include all the information that anyone is likely to want, and should be immediately available to anyone authorised to have access to it. Thus, a database can be stored and updated on a central computer, while people with terminals can have access to it. One of the largest databases in the United Kingdom is Prestel, which we have already mentioned, but even this is dwarfed by many in the USA, where there are over 20,000.

The spreadsheet

Another term you will come across is **spreadsheet**. This is an application program which presents the user at a VDU screen with a grid representing rows and columns. Each row and column is numbered or lettered so that each location can be identified by its co-ordinates, e.g. A1 would be at the top of the first column, B1 at the top of the second column, and so on.

The actual size of the spreadsheet is usually much larger than can be viewed at once on the screen, so the user, by using the appropriate keys on the keyboard, can move around the spreadsheet at will, the screen acting as a sort of window on to the spreadsheet beneath.

The spreadsheet can be 'headed up' with whatever column or row descriptions the user requires, and figures or formulae can then be entered in the appropriate locations. For example, figures which the user wishes to be added together can be entered in two locations and a formula which identifies and adds together the contents of the two locations can be entered in a third, e.g. in location A3 insert +A1+A2. Whatever figures are then inserted in A1 and A2 will always be added together and the answer put in A3. Such a facility enables users to vary figures as required to see what effect such changes have upon the final outcome without having to make all the intermediate calculations involved themselves.

The spreadsheet can be used for financial modelling, or as a simulation technique, and is widely used by decision makers, who can see the expected results from different alternatives before they actually make the final decision.

Integrated software

Integrated software is the term used to describe a situation where spreadsheets, databases and word processing, possibly with the addition of graphics, are used together in a computing system, and it is possible to move from one such program to another and back again, making use of each facility, to produce the finished work. This can only be done if the different software packages are integrated. It should be possible, for example, to start with a spreadsheet, call up information held on a database, and incorporate the results in a document using the word processing and graphics functions.

The data processing function

Some organisations are big enough to have separate Data Processing Departments which might contain analysts, programmers, data preparation personnel, controllers and operators. A simple organisation chart for such a department might look like the one shown in fig. 10.9.

Fig. 10.9 The organisation of a typical data processing department.

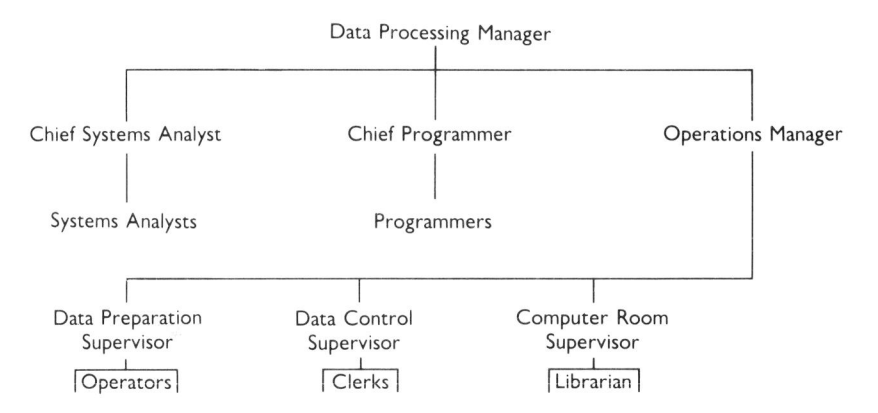

```
                        Data Processing Manager
                                 |
        ------------------------------------------------
        |                        |                      |
Chief Systems Analyst    Chief Programmer      Operations Manager
        |                        |                      |
Systems Analysts           Programmers                  |
                                                        |
                    ------------------------------------------
                    |                   |                    |
            Data Preparation     Data Control         Computer Room
               Supervisor          Supervisor           Supervisor
                    |                   |                    |
              [Operators]           [Clerks]            [Librarian]
```

Programming the computer

Systems analysts act as a link between the users and the programmers. They carry out feasibility studies by asking questions of the users and thoroughly familiarise themselves with exactly what each user expects the computer to do for him or her. Using their knowledge and experience the systems analysts should be able to suggest ideas that would help the users get more benefit from the computerised system. The systems analyst then prepares a systems specification including flow-charts which describe in great detail exactly what the computer will need for input and what it will produce as output. Once this is agreed as final by the user, the systems analyst passes the specification over to the programmers, who convert the various flow-charts and routines into computer code. A most important stage is the testing of the program. This is done first by the programmers, to see that it behaves in the way they expect it to. It is then tested by the systems analysts, and finally by the users. Their object should be to 'break' the program by testing it with extremes of data, or a combination of exceptional situations. The users should also satisfy themselves that the program is going to provide them with exactly what was agreed in the specification. A common problem is that once users see what can be done by computer, it triggers off new ideas and they then want to start making changes. This is one reason why it is so important that the systems analyst explores all such possibilities before the final specification is agreed.

Computer operations

The operations side is concerned with the day to day running of the computer.

Data preparation consists of inputting data to the computer from source documents.

The data control supervisor ensures that all the input is ready when it is needed, and that it has been properly 'ordered' before being used to update the master files.

The computer operators are responsible for loading the computer, for running the various jobs and for taking 'saves' (copies of the master files) at regular intervals, so that if something goes wrong they can reconstruct the files without too much trouble.

The librarian is responsible for looking after all the tapes and disks containing the master files, the transactions files and the programs. This is a very responsible job, and its importance should not be under-rated, although it is often given to the most junior member of staff. If the wrong tape or disk is loaded, wiped clean, or overwritten, or if the disks 'go missing', the consequences can be disastrous.

Protection of information

Integrity, security and confidentiality of information is vital. Even if the information produced by the computer is not confidential, it is still essential that it should be **secure**, i.e. protected from accidental or deliberate destruction. This is usually done by always having more than one copy of every program, master file and transaction file. Such extra copies should be kept in a safe place, outside the computing area. It is common for firms with computers to hold copies of each other's work. Sometimes the tapes are lodged with the companies' bankers for safe keeping. Since the files are constantly being updated, a regular routine of replacing the old tapes with new ones should be set up.

In computing, **integrity** means that all data being input to the computer is correct. For example, the date '31 September' is obviously wrong, and any program should prevent such a date from being accepted at the time data is being prepared for input. The programmers should write in as many checks as they can to ensure that all dates of birth in an employees' file show that all employees are at least 16 years old, and less than 65. In an invoicing routine they could provide range checks so that a particular quantity was always more than 100 but less than 1000, and in multiples of 10. They could also provide for all serial numbers to be validated by check digits so that errors in transposition were almost eliminated. Errors in transposition (e.g. keying in 12345 as 12435, or some other combination) are the most common faults in data preparation. A check digit is simply another number which has a unique mathematical relationship with the serial number to which it is attached. This means that if any of the digits in the serial number are transposed, the check digit will no longer have that unique relationship, and the operator can be informed that something is wrong which has to be corrected before further data can be input. Any such check is designed to ensure that, as far as possible, only valid data is input to the computer.

Confidentiality is important to ensure that only authorised people can obtain access to information held on a computer, and it is usual for a series of passwords to be used. Only a person using the correct password, which is allocated to the individual and changed at intervals, can then obtain access to privileged information. It is also common to identify individual terminals, so that only people using the correct password at an authorised terminal can obtain access. Passwords and terminals may also have limits so that only certain levels of information can be obtained. To go further would require additional passwords, or terminal access elsewhere. Despite these precautions it is never possible to be 100 per cent certain of confidentiality and, therefore, some firms make use of encryption, where a program converts all the information into a code, which has to be converted back to the recipient's program before it can be understood. This is of particular value when information has to be transmitted over telephone lines or via satellites.

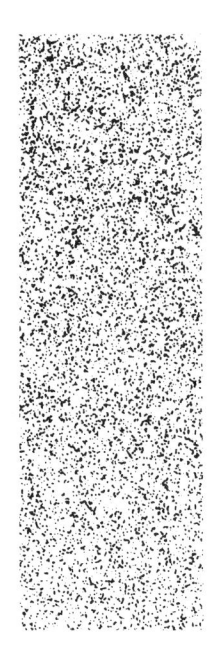

ASSIGNMENT: Directory enquiries

You work directly under the Data Processing Manager of Mardock Manufacturing, and he calls you into his office one morning for a briefing. As always, you know that such a briefing will mean a lot of extra work for you, so you listen carefully to what he says:

> For the last month or so I've been getting enquiries and requests for information from a number of Section Heads and Department Managers concerning the application of software packages to their particular work areas. As you know, most data is processed through our section, and I'm a little suspicious of their motives in wanting to investigate other methods of dealing with specialised functions. However, I can't appear to be paranoid about it, so I've agreed to draw up a directory of appropriate packages for the Accounts Department, Personnel, Stores, and the Typing Pool – sorry! 'Office Services' section!!
>
> I want you to look into this for me, and provide me with a run-down on what's available. Use the specialist mags., trade press, professional journals or whatever you can get hold of, and draw up as comprehensive a list as you can, giving a brief description of each package, what it does, what hardware it can be used with, and – if possible – an indication of cost.
>
> I need it by next week, and I'll be away until next Tuesday, so drop it on my desk with a covering memo, will you?

# SECTION 3

The working environment

CHAPTER 11

People, organisations, and change
Case study: Renaissance Kitchens

It is undeniable that the move towards the 'electronic office' will continue, with totally integrated systems becoming more and more desirable (essential!). Constant research and development means that new advances are being made almost every day, and the cost of appropriate hardware is becoming less and less significant in the light of benefits to be gained. Costs of electronic equipment in general have tended to fall as sophisticated techniques have been developed (for example, consider the drop in price of video recorders), and even recent innovations like the **videodisc** – using laser technology and electro-optics – might become less expensive as time goes on.

With constant advancement, and implementation of new methods of working, organisations must adapt to ensure that they can maintain their market positions or continue to provide the service the public wants in the most efficient way. 'Change' is a continuous process, but it does not only relate to ideas, concepts, systems and methods – it also relates to *people*. Organisations are people, and without them nothing will get done. In basic terms, if the people who are responsible for implementing and applying modern business procedures do not receive the necessary education, training, knowledge and support, the new systems cannot work effectively.

Pressure for change

As 'change' is inevitable in any organisation, it is worth considering what sources exert pressure for change, including the technological advances we have already looked at. Fig. 11.1 outlines some influences on change, and aspects of change, ranging from specific work-practices to general societal attitudes. This is not intended to be a comprehensive summary, but aims more to expand your general awareness, and encourage an overview of the way in which society, education, government, industry and commerce interact to create and affect our working environment.

Let's return now to the people – those who effect change, and those who are affected by it. The hardest battle to be fought will be over people's **attitudes**. It has been said that one person's attitude is another person's prejudice, but whatever we call this state of mind, it is obvious that it affects an individual's or a group's willingness or ability to respond. It is a

People in business organisations

belief, and therefore is very difficult to change or counteract – unless the right conditions are created to encourage change.

Fig. 11.1

New products/new technology

1 **Automation** affects job design, speed of operation, hours worked, etc.
2 **Different products** require different technology and different skills.
3 **New techniques** require new skills.

Competition

1 **Competitive markets** mean it is essential to be aware of what other companies offer.
2 **Keeping up** with competitors engenders constant change.
3 **Research and development** is often an ongoing process.

The workforce

1 **Improvements in education** mean that a workforce is likely to be more aware than in the past.
2 **Management styles** need to change to encourage the co-operation of a better educated workforce.
3 **Trade Union activity** can lead to changes in attitudes and work practices.

Changes in consumer wants

1 **Obsolescence** can often be brought about because of new products.
2 **Fashion** often demands rapid changing of products.
3 **Buying habits** have moved away from the corner shop to hypermarkets and, therefore, presentation/packaging of goods has changed.
4 **Rapid consumer change** can lead to decline for companies who haven't foreseen changes.

The government

1 **Legislation** relating to health and safety at work, equal pay, equal opportunities, etc. has brought about dramatic changes.
2 **Financial information** must now be made more widely available, and often presented in a particular way.
3 **Personnel** changes have been necessary to fulfil/implement requirements.
4 **Monopoly situations** are scrutinised very closely and take-overs controlled.

Society

Education, social values and attitudes during the past 40 years or so have undergone dramatic changes, and have led to legislation aimed to improve such things as the environment (ecology), conservation, the employment of disadvantaged people (e.g. disabled), advertising, facilities at work, etc.

People, organisations and change

How are attitudes formed?

Fig. 11.2

Fig 11.2 shows the three main formative influences on our attitudes.

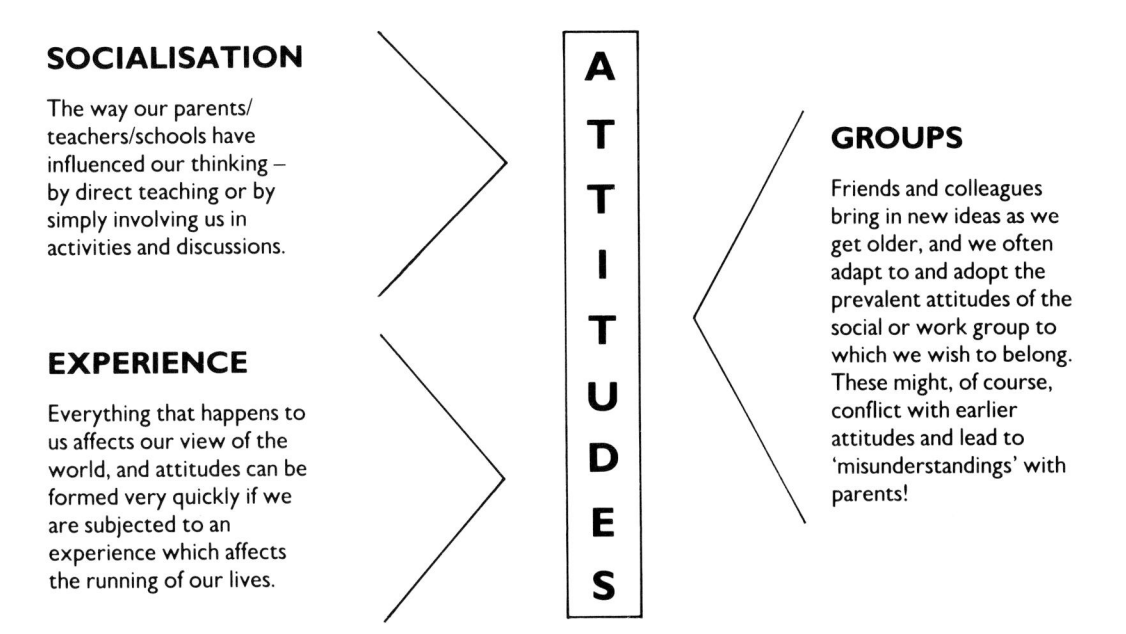

SOCIALISATION

The way our parents/teachers/schools have influenced our thinking – by direct teaching or by simply involving us in activities and discussions.

EXPERIENCE

Everything that happens to us affects our view of the world, and attitudes can be formed very quickly if we are subjected to an experience which affects the running of our lives.

ATTITUDES

GROUPS

Friends and colleagues bring in new ideas as we get older, and we often adapt to and adopt the prevalent attitudes of the social or work group to which we wish to belong. These might, of course, conflict with earlier attitudes and lead to 'misunderstandings' with parents!

In any of these situations, the right conditions have been presented to form or change our attitudes, and very often a change of attitude is simply the formation of a new one in place of an old one.

This simplistic explanation might make it sound as if it is easy to persuade someone to change their attitude, but nothing could be further from the truth. The reason for this is that (as you can see from fig. 11.2) our attitudes are usually influenced and reinforced by people for whom we have respect, love, or admiration, and by experiences which have directly affected the way in which we run our lives. Our attitudes have often brought us 'rewards', such as social approval, acceptance by a group, admiration, respect, congratulations, even promotion. Nobody wants to change when things are going well!

In the work environment, a manager often comes up against entrenched attitudes (prejudices!) and ideas when he or she wants to introduce a new working practice or change long-standing procedures; and if such changes are imposed, it is often the people at **supervisory** level who have to bear the brunt of any reaction.

Why do people react against, or fear, change?

If we think about an office environment, and consider how dramatic the changes caused by the introduction of modern technology might be, it is easy to identify general concerns which influence people's reactions.

Economic factors

The most basic concern is usually **economic**. Is the introduction of new equipment going to result in job losses, cuts in hours, or the closing of complete sections/departments? Nobody wants to be made redundant, or have their economic stability threatened, and unless employees can be convinced that they will not 'lose out', there is likely to be opposition, or at least non co-operation.

Social factors

Another important consideration revolves around each individual's perceived **social** position. Even basic office re-organisation (changing desks around) can be seen as a threat to established social relationships.

'I've always worked well with Shirley.'
'I don't want to work with him.'
'Who am I going to have to sit next to?'
'I know how he thinks.'
'We've got this job well organised.'

The problem of having to form new working relationships, or even join a new 'group' can be upsetting and quite daunting to many people.

If a functional area of an organisation is being completely restructured, with consequent transfers, promotions, new supervisors or managers, the problems are magnified.

Personal factors

Another area of concern is often the individual's **personal fears**. Will they have to learn a new skill? Do they have the ability to learn a new skill? Will they be able to cope with the different work? What will this do to their health? The range of personal fears is enormous, and even though they are sometimes founded on lack of understanding, they are very *real*, and affect people's response to change.

The results of all these fears and concerns can, of course, affect the running of the organisation, and might be manifested in a number of ways (see fig. 11.3).

As you can see, the managers and the supervisors could have a difficult task on their hands in some organisations, and it is the recognition of this that is likely to lead to a greater appreciation of the **human relations** aspects of introducing change. If consideration is shown for *people*, then those people are more likely to show a willingness to listen and, hopefully, co-operate. The principles listed in fig. 11.4 give some basic guidelines for the implementation of change.

People, organisations and change 113

Fig. 11.3

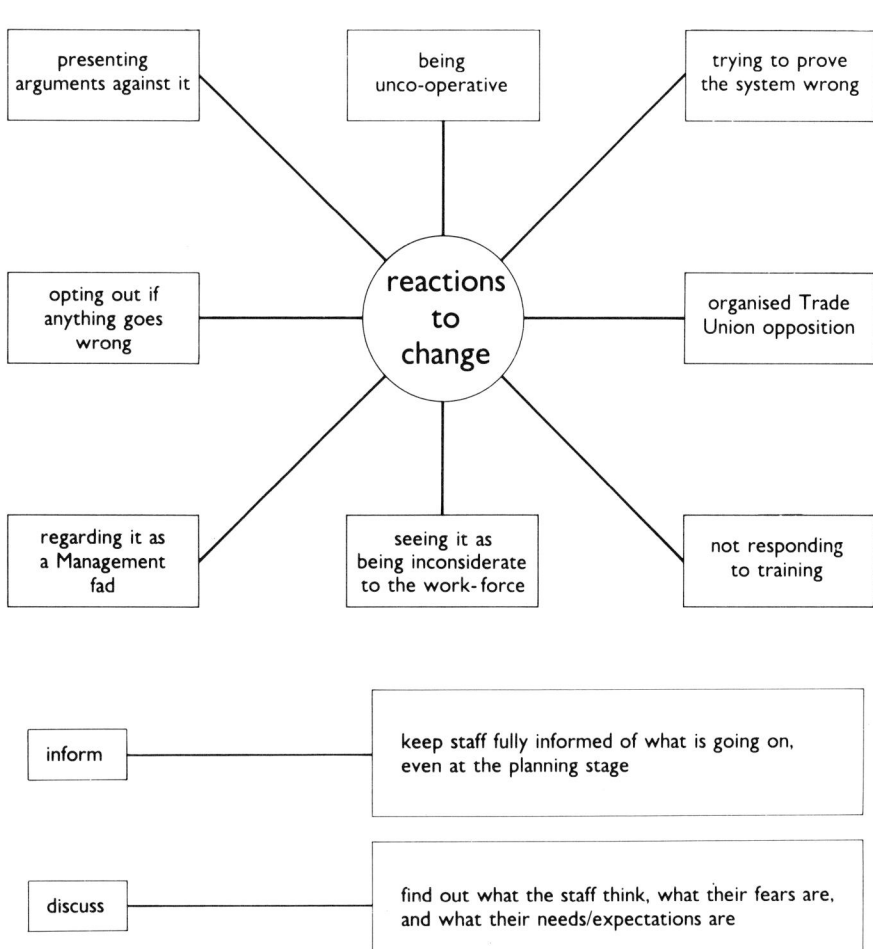

Reactions to change:
- presenting arguments against it
- being unco-operative
- trying to prove the system wrong
- opting out if anything goes wrong
- organised Trade Union opposition
- regarding it as a Management fad
- seeing it as being inconsiderate to the work-force
- not responding to training

Fig. 11.4

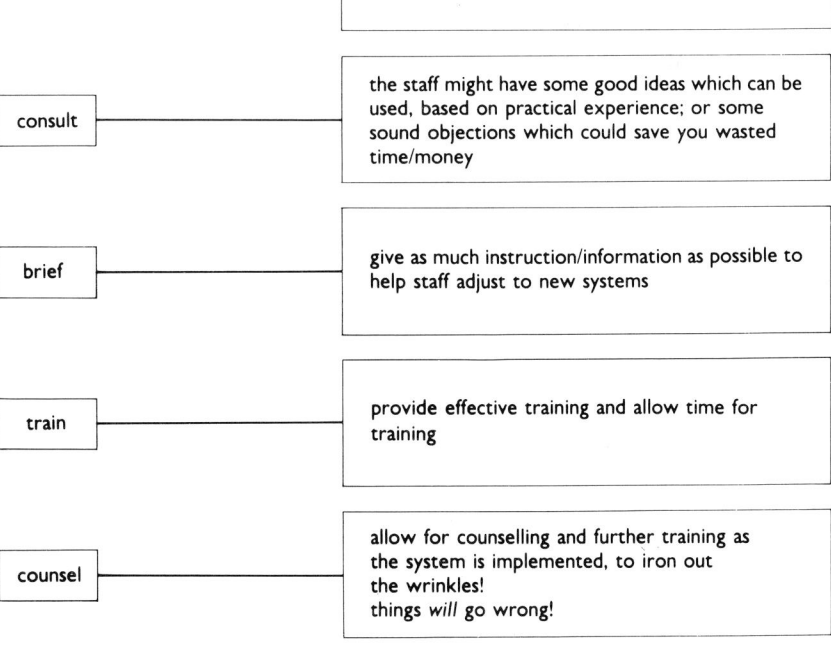

inform	keep staff fully informed of what is going on, even at the planning stage
discuss	find out what the staff think, what their fears are, and what their needs/expectations are
consult	the staff might have some good ideas which can be used, based on practical experience; or some sound objections which could save you wasted time/money
brief	give as much instruction/information as possible to help staff adjust to new systems
train	provide effective training and allow time for training
counsel	allow for counselling and further training as the system is implemented, to iron out the wrinkles! things *will* go wrong!

ASSIGNMENT: Small Change?

For the last twelve months you have been working as assistant to the Training Officer of the Albatross Insurance Group, and during that time you have both been involved in designing and implementing in-house training programmes for staff from various branches, who have had to cope with the introduction of integrated communications and data handling systems to their offices. This has been a massive task, and you have learned a lot from your experiences about how people react; and what kind of approach is required to make such a changeover as smooth as possible.

Word has got round that your Group has been particularly successful in encouraging positive attitudes towards change, and you are approached by the Editor of *Training Monthly* to write an article for the next month's edition. He explains:

> What we really want is a general article of up to 750 words, simply aiming to make training officers in all areas of industry and commerce realise that 'change' is not something that happens to other people – it is an essential part of progress and it *will* happen to them soon! There needs to be something on why organisations have to change, what the major problems are, the human relations aspects, and how the whole business needs to be approached.
>
> I thought a suitable title might be 'Are you on the change?' or something like that. On second thoughts, that might be misinterpreted by some people, so I'll leave it up to you.
>
> By the way, you will get a small fee for this!

Write the article *after* reading through the Notes for guidance which give you some information on the techniques of article writing, and include an activity which asks you to analyse an article of your choice.

Notes for guidance: writing an article

Articles can be written for a whole range of publications, including newspapers, magazines, in-house publications, pamphlets and specialist journals, and from the writer's point of view the most difficult task is to produce something which is perfectly suited to the intended audience. Unfortunately, any audience is made up of individuals, each of whom will respond (or react) in a different way, and it is, therefore, likely to be impossible to please all of the people all of the time.

Experienced writers will be able to adapt their style and approach to suit any chosen audience; but those of us who are inexperienced need some guidelines to help us identify how an audience can be approached, and to recognise some basic writing techniques.

The first thing to be aware of is that any article will be written for a *special* audience, who will have their own characteristics, interests and ideas. It is essential to **identify** this audience, and **identify with** them. To do this you need to consider the 'reader profile'. This, together with your knowledge of the type of publication you are writing for, should give you a reasonable indication of what approach you can take and what style you can adopt.

For example, if you were writing an article on micro-computers for *Computer Weekly*, your approach would probably lean towards a technical appraisal, emphasising capability, compatibility, special functions, etc; if, however, you were writing the same article for *Good Housekeeping* or some other general magazine, your approach might be much less specialist, with emphasis being placed on user-friendliness, the benefits to ordinary people, interesting software packages, applications in the home, etc.

Therefore, the style, the language, and even the content might need to be adjusted to suit the needs of any particular audience. Fig. 11.5 shows how a writer has to think carefully around the publication, the audience and the subject before embarking on the task of producing an article.

Fig. 11.5

Appropriate treatment: specialist language, layperson's language, style, content, tone, reader interest, conciseness, accurate information, reader identification, sound argument, balanced view, readability, relevant material

Reader profile: interests, specific jobs, attitudes, expectations, educational background, sex distribution, social background, age range

Publication: pamphlet, other specialist, brochure, house journal, newspaper, magazine, newsletter

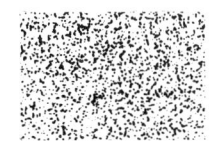

the idea or topic

The major problem that the inexperienced writer encounters is in trying to avoid writing an *essay*. Most of us have spent much of our education and training being forced to write essays, and it is difficult to get out of the habit of presenting ideas in an abstract and academic style. The following activity should give you the opportunity to see how other writers avoid this problem.

ACTIVITY

Select an article of your choice from any type of publication and try to decide in your own mind why you have chosen it. The reason doesn't really matter, as long as you are honest with yourself, and bear the reason in mind when you look more closely at the article. (**Note:** take a photocopy so that your tutor can assess your work effectively.)

Write an analysis of the article, commenting upon the following aspects:

> ### The medium
>
> What is the publication? Classify it. (Specialist, general, professional journal, etc.) What is its function? What sort of circulation does it have?
>
> ### The audience
>
> a   Identify the general audience of the publication.
> b   Identify the specific audience of the particular article. Is the audience specialist? Ordinary people? Predominantly male/female? What is their educational and social background? Will they have jobs? What are their expectations/aspirations? Do you think they would demonstrate any particular attitudes or prejudices?
>
> ### The article
>
> a   **What does it aim to do?**   Entertain? Inform? Persuade? Provoke?
> b   **The content topic.**   Is it appropriate to the intended audience? Is it interesting? Is it topical? specialist? general? contentious? Is it a suitable topic in relation to the aim?
> c   **Style approach.**   Is it written in a way which will appeal to the audience? Will they understand it? Is the tone suitable for the topic?

Some of the following techniques can be identified in many published articles.

- **The heading:** this should be interesting and eye-catching to 'grab' the attention of your reader. Keep it short, and don't try to be too clever.
- **The first paragraph:** this should not be too long and should introduce something in which the readers are interested. Ideally they should also be able to recognise and identify with the situation you are talking about.
- **Reader involvement:** to help the readers feel involved, you can adopt a 'personalised' style – i.e. talk directly *to* each individual. Use the words 'you' and 'we' to create a 'group' or 'membership' feeling.
- **Anecdotes, analogies and quotations:** very useful techniques to employ in trying to get your point home. If the readers can recognise something they know they are much more likely to respond to it.
- **Remember:** at all times keep the **aim** of the article in mind. What do you want to achieve? What response would you like?

ACTIVITY

> Read a variety of articles, and see if you can identify any of these techniques – or any others! Consider how effective they are and how *you* respond to them. This activity can be done in your own time, at home, or you can devote about an hour to it in your college library.

Now return to the assignment: Small Change?

People, organisations and change

Case study: Renaissance Kitchens

The background

When Peter Wandell first formulated the idea for his business, he was working as Marketing Director for a large international laminate manufacturer, and was, consequently, heavily involved in the fitted kitchen market.

His idea was based on the realisation that when someone makes the decision to replace a kitchen, their main aim is to give the kitchen a new fresh look. If it were possible to achieve this prime objective at a fraction of the anticipated cost, then the volume potential would be enormous for the manufacturing company. Existing suppliers of fitted kitchens invariably ripped out the existing kitchen and started rebuilding from scratch, thus wasting what was often a perfectly good structural framework, and consequently increasing costs. The question that Peter started asking was: 'Why buy a whole new kitchen when it is possible to refurbish the existing "skeleton" and still produce a whole new look?'

He devised a plan to sell, direct to the public, kitchen component parts to fit existing kitchen structures. By this means, not only could the customer have a brand new kitchen at a much reduced price, but the work could be completed by the average DIY enthusiast with the minimum of fuss and upheaval.

The product offer

Peter's aim was to manufacture and sell kitchen doors, drawer fronts and working surfaces, together with accessories including hingeing systems, handles and worktop joining extrusions, and sell them direct to the public nationwide. All the vertical surfaces, doors and drawer fronts would be offered in square edge Formica laminate and melamine-faced chipboard, both balanced with white on the reverse side, cut to any size. This service would allow replacement facings for imperial or metric units, or a mixture of both. There would be a choice of four handle trims from which the customer could choose. As with doors, worktops could be ordered from any one of sixteen designs and cut to any size, width or length (metric or imperial). Flat-pack frame units (floor-standing or wall-mounted) would also be available in five standard sizes (in case a customer wanted to extend or change part of the existing kitchen layout).

Starting up

Having resigned his post as Marketing Director, Peter spent three months **planning** as many aspects of his business as he could. His assets at this stage were £11,000 in cash (raised by selling his boat and changing his four-bedroomed detached house for a more modest one), and 20 years of industrial experience (mainly in marketing). The 'planning on paper' completed, Peter sought factory premises. Devon was chosen as an appropriate location because it was a long way from the main manufacturing centres of the kitchen furniture industry and would, therefore, provide an ideal test marketing base from which to assess the feasibility of the service.

Stage 1: the pilot year

Phase 1   September to January
Production

Peter decided to produce worktops only initially, so that he could minimise risk and assess the demand for drawers and drawer fronts. He bought the following equipment:

1 radial arm saw
1 jig-saw
1 edge trimmer
a quantity of blank post-formed worktops in two- and three-metre lengths

A skilled machinist was also hired to operate the radial saw. With these resources the firm went into production, cutting worktops to size, edging them with laminate, and selling them direct to the public.

Marketing

Prices were determined in terms of a specified mark-up on costs, because the product was new and there was, therefore, no means of comparison, and no precedent for any particular market price.

Advertising

Advertisements were placed for six weeks in two local newspapers, promoting the concept of a **replacement service** as opposed to **new** kitchens.

Administration

Peter set up a limited company, Renaissance Kitchens, Ltd, and registered for VAT. He opened a bank account in which he deposited his £11,000 and set up a basic book-keeping system, comprising:

sales day book
cash journal – to control bankings
wages book

Procedures such as stock control and purchase control were done on a day-to-day basis through visual checks, and Peter took care of all administration as well as assisting in production.

Phase 2 January to September

The order book was full. The idea appeared to work, and Peter decided to launch the full service to include doors and drawer fronts in the spring.

Production

Expansion of production required the following additions to equipment and materials:

1 scribing saw
additional machine tools
a quantity of double-sided board material for doors and drawer fronts

Peter also hired an additional machinist, two wood-workers, and a sales clerk to do the book-keeping, deal with telephone orders, and take orders from visitors to the factory. He could now spend more of his time on the marketing function as well as managing the business.

The new components were priced per square metre on a 'mark-up on cost' basis.

Advertising

The January and February advertisements in the two local papers were 'flashed' with an announcement of 'doors coming March'.

In March a series of twenty- and thirty-second advertisements were broadcast on local radio to announce the new service.

Administration

More formal procedures of order processing, purchasing and stock control were adopted to control the resources of the expanding business. Peter no longer assisted in production but concentrated all his efforts on the planning, co-ordination and control of the business, and on the marketing function.

Stage 2: September to date

By the end of the first year's trading, it was clear that the service was accepted and that the potential share of the market was significant. Indeed, such an innovative idea could lead to 'growing' (i.e. extending) the overall market. The time had come to research the idea of expanding the service nationally.

This painstaking process of investigation, assessment and planning took Peter six months of concentrated effort. He anticipated that he would require at least £75,000 to 'go national', and he finally managed to raise this money from an Investment Broker who had access to substantial 'risk capital'.

Production

From September onwards production expanded enormously, necessitating additions to staff and equipment, and a change of premises.

The new organisation

The firm is organised as follows.
Managing Director: Peter Wandell – still responsible for marketing and design.
Sales Director: responsible for a local sales manager, who in turn is in charge of two local agents paid on a 'commission only' basis. The Sales Director is also responsible for six national agents based in Edinburgh, Leeds, Cambridge, Bristol and London (2), who are also paid on a 'commission only' basis.
Works Director: with overall responsibility for production, assisted by a Works Manager. The works manager controls the day to day running of the factory and is in charge of a Quality Inspector, a 'Carcass' (framework) Manager, and a Woodworking Supervisor.
Quality Inspector: in addition to his own work, supervises three packers. The Carcass Manager is in charge of two frame-makers who produce the necessary structures for any additional units the customer may require. The senior Woodworking Supervisor oversees the manufacture of the replacement units. Answerable to him are two more supervisors; one is responsible for eight machinists; the other supervises one handler (an operative who attaches handles to doors), two hinge drillers, and three edgers (operatives who trim raw edges of board with laminate strip).
Commercial/Purchasing Director: (previously the sales clerk) is responsible mainly for controlling money. She undertakes the purchasing herself, and is responsible for an Office Manager and a Customer Service Manager. The Office Manager supervises a production planner, a telephonist, a purchase ledger clerk and a sales ledger clerk. The Customer Services Manager deals with customers who may visit the factory, and with agents. He supervises a clerk who assists with order processing.

Marketing

The Launch

Peter decided to use a public relations launch as a major frontal attack on the market. He had insufficient capital to advertise nationwide to obtain 'leads', and, since his idea was innovatory, there was much to be gained from a public relations exercise.

Realising that he needed an equally innovatory approach to the PR exercise itself, Peter sent invitations written on some of his replacement doors to the women's magazine press, and women's/home editors of the national daily newspapers. The invitations requested their presence at a champagne launch for a new concept in fitted kitchens to be held at the Hilton Hotel in London. The result of this PR exercise was free editorial comment in some of the daily newspapers and many women's magazines during the following six months.

The customers who enquired about Renaissance Kichens replacement units were sent a brochure and order form. Orders were made up at the factory in Devon and delivered to the customers by a road haulage firm within three weeks. Orders are still taken direct from customers as well as through the agents.

Administration

Administrative procedures have become much more complex as the company has expanded, and it is evident that documentation needs to be rationalised.

Stage 3: the future

Peter is now researching the possibility of selling his products through quality retail outlets by setting up demonstration 'tableaux' in selected stores, and producing point-of-sale advertising material for customers to take away with them. A consultant would be on hand to discuss plans and give advice.

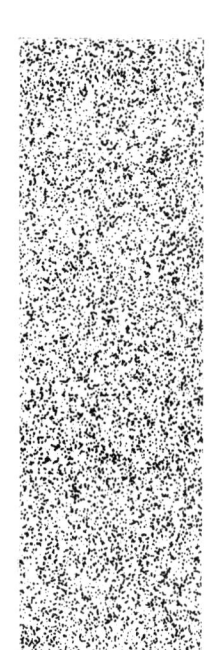

ASSIGNMENT: Progress

Renaissance Kitchens, Ltd. has developed into a more complex organisation. Peter Wandell (MD) recognises the need for employees to be aware of the overall structure/lines of authority, and feels that it would be useful to produce an organisation chart which could be made available to them, and also help him clarify his own ideas for continuing rationalisation and expansion.

Task

Using the information given in the case study, construct a vertical-type organisation chart for the company.

At times, during the development of the company (particularly in the early days when much of the administration was done on a day-to-day basis) there were instances of confusion and lack of co-ordination and planning which sometimes led to a shortage of materials, miscalculation of production schedules, delay of urgent orders, etc. With the establishment of more formal 'departments' and areas of responsibility, things have improved and are running fairly smoothly. However, it is important to ensure that the systems are effectively co-ordinated and integrated to enable the company to progress with maximum efficiency, and it is decided to make an analysis of possible problems that could arise from a failure to co-ordinate activities within and between the functional departments. With many possible problems identified in advance, development planning can be more effective.

People in business organisations

Task

Looking closely at the structure of the various departments in the company, and considering their functions, prepare a report for Mr Wandell identifying as many possible results of such failure to co-ordinate activities as you can. There is no requirement for you to suggest how these can be avoided, or make any recommendations – simply outline potential problems.

Notes: a Use a memo-report format.
 b Discussion with colleagues is an essential part of identifying and clarifying problems of this kind.

ASSIGNMENT: 'Integrated Business Systems'

As indicated in the case study, there is some concern over administrative procedures.

You are a member of a small team at 'Integrated Business Systems', and you specialise in designing business documents to meet the specific needs of companies who are starting up, expanding or rationalising their operations. As Renaissance Kitchens is a local company, you are aware of their plans for the future, and are one of three firms who have been approached by the management team to design a range of documents to meet their needs. The instructions below indicate what is required, and you should pay particular attention to the presentation of your work in a business-like format. The following points should be considered carefully, and you should remember that you have been asked for *draft* documents which the company will assess and use as a basis for their decision.

1 Your completed submission will comprise a folder of work containing all necessary information. The folder will be provided, together with a treasury tag and a quantity of paper. All materials should be held in the folder by means of a simple hole in the top left hand corner.
2 All forms should be drafted on unlined paper, and must be as realistic as possible. (Note: different colours may be used if these are available.)
3 Additional information (as required) can be presented on normal lined A4 paper. (These requirements are given at the end of this assignment.)
4 The forms and supportive information should be presented in a logical order, with some method of classification.
5 The customer should be able to identify each type of form immediately, and extract/select/refer to it with ease.
6 The whole presentation should be preceded by a covering letter which will reflect the situation your firm is in, i.e. competing for business and trying to impress the customer with your efficiency, design quality, flexibility, helpfulness, and ability to produce the goods.
7 As part of the covering letter, which should be written on unlined paper, design and incorporate a company **logo** for your own firm.
8 Design a logo for Renaissance and, if appropriate, incorporate this in the form design.

Requirements

At this stage you are submitting a range of sample draft forms, and need not attempt to produce every document or form which might be associated with such a company. Obviously, it is important to cover the major operations, as outlined in this summary of what happens in the Renaissance organisation.

Many customers will order direct by post, after making initial enquiries, and will be sent a **postal order form**. If it is necessary for someone to visit the customer to advise

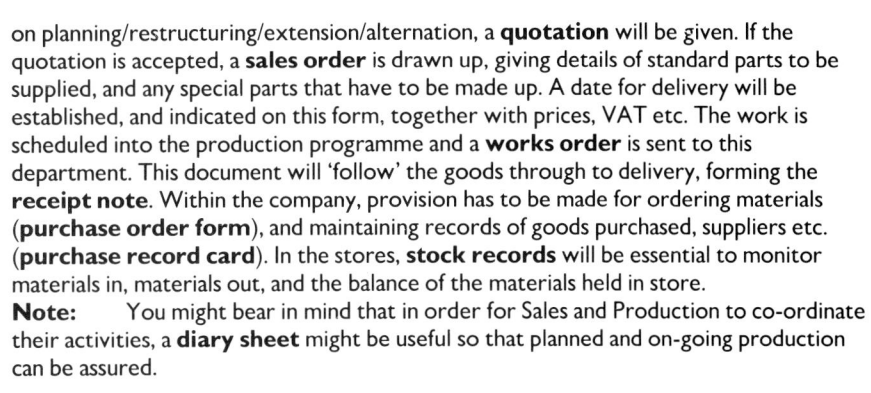

People, organisations and change

on planning/restructuring/extension/alternation, a **quotation** will be given. If the quotation is accepted, a **sales order** is drawn up, giving details of standard parts to be supplied, and any special parts that have to be made up. A date for delivery will be established, and indicated on this form, together with prices, VAT etc. The work is scheduled into the production programme and a **works order** is sent to this department. This document will 'follow' the goods through to delivery, forming the **receipt note**. Within the company, provision has to be made for ordering materials (**purchase order form**), and maintaining records of goods purchased, suppliers etc. (**purchase record card**). In the stores, **stock records** will be essential to monitor materials in, materials out, and the balance of the materials held in store.

Note: You might bear in mind that in order for Sales and Production to co-ordinate their activities, a **diary sheet** might be useful so that planned and on-going production can be assured.

When the goods have been delivered to the customer, an **invoice** will be sent out, requesting settlement of the account. As much information is duplicated on a number of these forms, they could be produced as multi-sets, using NCR paper. Some forms which could be 'combined' in this way are the sales order, works order, receipt note and invoice, and you might need to indicate to the customer that multi-sets can be extended to meet further identified needs as the company expands. Remember that not *all* information needs to be copied through on to each form, and, therefore, selective carboning or blanking-out might be necessary.

To summarise, for this assignment you have to:

1 Design the forms and other documents required.

2 State the purpose of any item of data to be entered on each form which isn't self-explanatory.

3 State the filing method and system of classification you would recommend for each form, if it is to be kept. For example, the stock record cards could be stored in a visible card index in part-number order.

4 Put together the complete package (including covering letter), paying attention to the guidelines given earlier.

Note: You may wish to revise Chapters 9 and 10 before starting this assignment.

CHAPTER 12
Practical communication skills (2)

The telephone

In Chapter 5 you dealt with a whole range of communication methods, many of them much more sophisticated than the telephone. However, the importance of this well-established business tool must not be underestimated. It is convenient, easy to use, and efficient, both as an internal and external means of getting in direct contact with people.

Because it is so familiar to us, we tend to forget that actually using the telephone is a skill in itself. It can quickly convey an impression of the efficiency or otherwise of any person or organisation, and bad telephone habits can seriously damage the reputation of a company in the eyes of the public.

An earlier assignment gave you some practice in making a telephone call, and emphasised good preparation and back-up notes for reference. Receiving a call, and dealing with it effectively is an even greater skill, and one in which all members of an organisation should be given basic instruction. When you take a call, you immediately reflect the quality and efficiency of your organisation, and your responses can influence the attitude and opinion of the caller. As with any verbal communication, the desirable qualities for dealing with people on the telephone are clear speech and expression, courtesy, helpfulness, tact, accuracy, and positive approach.

If you adopt the following techniques, at least the caller's first impression of you and your organisation will be reasonable! Assuming the caller is from outside:

1 Say 'Good morning' or 'Good afternoon'.
2 Give the name of your organisation or department (or your telephone/extension number), followed by your own name. For example, 'Good afternoon. Sales Department. Sheila Jones speaking.'
3 'Can I help you?' is often useful at this point.

You might now find that you need to make a few notes, so make sure there is a note-pad handy at all times.

4 Listen carefully to the caller's request, and decide whether or not you can deal with it.
If you can satisfactorily deal with the call yourself, do so.
If you need to transfer the call to another person, make the transfer as quickly and efficiently as possible.

Practical communication skills (2)

If you need to go and find certain items of information, either ask the caller to 'hold the line' and tell her or him what you are doing, or take the name and number and call back.

If you cannot answer the query and nobody else is available to do it, apologise, take the name and number, and assure the caller that you will get somebody to call back as soon as possible.

It might be necessary for you to pass a message to another member of your organisation, and – if you are lucky – there will be a special telephone message pad to use. All organisations will have their own ideas about the design of telephone message sheets, but whatever they look like, certain essential information must appear so that the recipient can answer the following questions:

Who is the message from? (i.e. who was the caller?)
What company is he/she from?
When (date and time) was the call received:
Who took the call and sent the message?
What is the message?
Do I have to take any particular action? (e.g. ring back, write, call.)
Is there a contact number?

In addition, the message sheet should indicate to whom the message is being sent, his/her department or section, and whether or not it is urgent.

ACTIVITY

When you got back into the office after lunch yesterday, you took a call from a client who had been trying to get hold of you all the morning, and who was extremely angry because you had not called him back, despite the fact that he had specifically asked for messages to be passed to you.

You apologised profusely, and explained that you had been out at a meeting until 11.00 am, but that the message(s) should have got to you before lunch. This seemed to irritate him even more, because he had been trying to telephone the company during the lunch hour, and nobody had answered the telephone at all between 12.30 and 1.30 pm. You managed to pacify the client eventually, and deal satisfactorily with his query, but you feel that something really ought to be done about the poor basic communications arrangements in your office. It's obvious that a proper telephone message form should be in use, and that something should be done to ensure that such messages are distributed quickly. In addition, it isn't a very good advertisement for the company when no-one can make an incoming call during the lunch hour.

Think carefully about the implications of this situation, and write a memo to your Office Manager, Mary Watveare, explaining the problems and suggesting a realistic solution. You should attach a suggested design for a telephone message sheet to the memo for her consideration.

Remember that this is a self-initiated communication, and you must approach the situation very carefully – you don't want her to think you are criticising her or trying to tell her how to do her job! Be tactful and diplomatic.

Circular letters

Circular letters are used by organisations when they need to contact a large number of people, and when the contents can be standardised. In industry, commerce and public administration, such standard communications are often used, and can usually be classified under one of the following categories.

Conveying routine information

Government departments such as the Department of Social Security, and utilities such as the Gas, Water and Electricity providers, regularly issue circular letters to customers on a whole range of topics from new tariffs, to methods of payments, to better services.

Asking for support

Many voluntary organisations use a circular letter to try to persuade people to come to the Christmas Fayre, support their Jumble Sale, join their activities, etc.

Appeals

Some charities and some voluntary organisations try to raise funds by contacting members of the public 'in their own homes', through the post. Although – as I am sure you know – many people simply throw such unsolicited material away, it must still be worth the organisation sending them or else they wouldn't bother!

Advertising/sales

Advertising and sales literature can take many forms, and circular letters constitute only a small proportion of the 'paper' that thuds on to our doormats. One of the market leaders in this field is *The Reader's Digest*, where sophisticated productions and regular mailing techniques are highly successful.

ACTIVITY

Try to acquire an example of each of the above types of circular letter, and analyse the functions, aims, techniques, styles and formats in a tutor-led, classroom discussion, trying to identify and establish common approaches. Some pointers are given in fig. 12.1.

These ideas might not mean anything to you immediately, but think them through and apply them to any examples that you have found. Look at any part of the letters and ask yourself 'why?'

Fig. 12.1

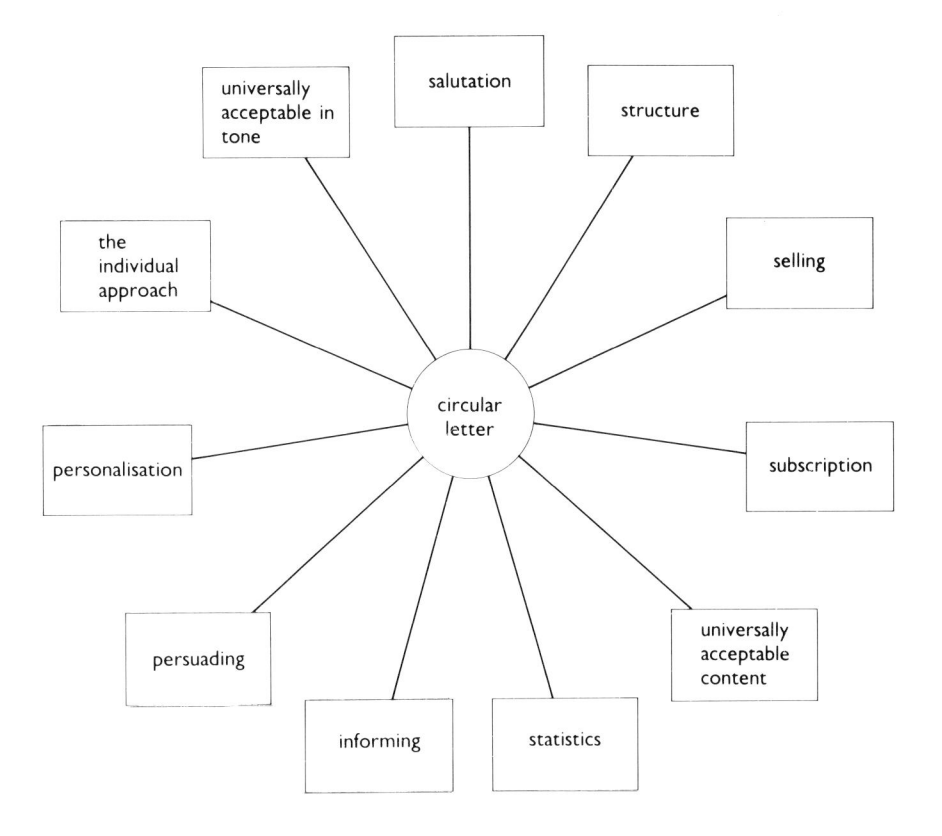

Practical communication skills (2)

```
                    salutation
    universally
    acceptable in              structure
    tone

    the
    individual                    selling
    approach

                    circular
                    letter
    personalisation               subscription


                                  universally
                                  acceptable
    persuading                    content

              informing  statistics
```

The writing of circular letters is a specialist task, particularly if they fall in the advertising/sales category. However, there are certain principles which even the experienced writer cannot entirely ignore.

1 Bearing in mind that the public can be suspicious when something unexpected comes through the post, the first task of the writer must be to arouse the reader's interest, allay any suspicion the readers might have that they are being 'conned', or state briefly the purpose of the letter.

2 The next move might be to encourage participation, persuade the readers to want to gain the benefits offered, or to move into the detail of the information being conveyed.

3 It might be advisable at this point to reassure the readers even further, and convince them of the credibility of your organisation, or the quality of your product or service – i.e. your own reputation.

4 Finally there must be the encouragement to take action. It is no good spending money trying to persuade or convince people if there is no follow-up. There must be a point or method of contact, for example a return-slip, name and telephone number, prepaid card, or prepaid envelope.

Can you identify any of the techniques in your examples?

ACTIVITY

> Bearing in mind the principles and techniques discussed so far, write a circular letter to residents of your town from a national organisation which hopes to open a superstore in the area. Many people are concerned about the effects this will have on a major residential area, and there has been substantial opposition from local shopkeepers.
>
> You should aim to drum up support for the superstore development from the local population, by outlining the merits of your scheme, and persuading them to attend a public meeting to show their support.

Circular letters are not exclusively used to contact people outside the organisation, but can be used **internally**. The function can still be easily identified, for example to persuade, support company policy, invite people to participate. This technique can be used to involve employees' families as well as the workforce, and will usually – in these circumstances – offer some kind of benefit as the major point of persuasion.

ASSIGNMENT: The Move

Stanhall Manufacturing is an engineering firm which is expanding its production capability and plans to open a new manufacturing unit on the Churchmead Industrial Estate, situated just outside Wanningford, about 50 miles away from the main factory in West Didworthy. Wanningford is a thriving town established in the 1960s, and has been referred to as 'the South West's Milton Keynes!'.

The main problem for the company is that their research indicates a lack of highly trained engineers in the Wanningford area, and it is essential that they persuade key skilled staff from the 'home' factory to move to the new area and help set up the operation there. Obviously, it is not easy to persuade people to uproot and move their homes and families, and despite the generous financial and 'support' inducements the company has offered, there hasn't been a very enthusiastic response.

The Personnel Manager decides that some positive steps must be taken, and decides to organise a day trip especially for the spouses, so that they can see for themselves what the new environment has to offer.

He calls you into his office and says:

> *We're going to send a letter out to all the families of our key staff, inviting them on this trip. We've got all their names and addresses on disk, so if we get the appropriate letter set up on the word processor, then we can send an 'individual' one to each person. They all know roughly what the situation is, but it wouldn't do any harm to reinforce what the benefits will be – particularly the financial ones. Point out that the trip will be free, and lunch will be provided at the Leat House Hotel – that should encourage them. We'll aim to leave here at 08.45 and should get back by 3.30 – in time for them to pick the kids up from school. I've got to go over to Wanningford for a couple of days, so I'll leave the letter in your hands – OK?*

First of all, consider the situation carefully, and discuss in detail the implications. Establish exactly what the incentives and financial 'support' inducements might be; decide whether there are any problems to be anticipated in organising a trip like this. What day of the week will it be on? How will they travel? What about those with young children?

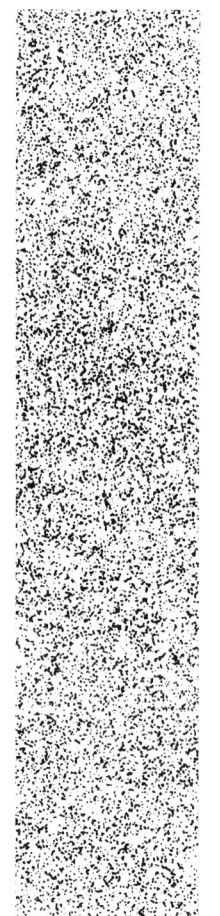

Do they all have to get to your factory by 08.45? What will happen during the day? How long will the actual journey take? How long will they spend in Wanningford? What will they see? Will anyone travel with them? etc. etc.

Then draft the letter, making sure you don't adopt a 'holiday brochure' approach.

Leaflets and pamphlets

ACTIVITY

Collect some examples of leaflets and pamphlets for analysis. If you visit a Post Office, you will find that there is a range of them available free, dealing with a wide variety of topics. Don't grab handfuls of them, as this is likely to antagonise the staff and result in complaints to your college! Another source is the college itself, where course leaflets and brochures are usually available from individual departments. A third possibility is to keep your eyes open when you are shopping, and pick up any advertising material you come across; and a further possibility is that you might receive something suitable through the post at home.

Whatever the source(s), you should aim to acquire at least five examples to help you with the following work.

Producing advertising material

Marketing and selling through printed material can be done at point-of-sale, through the Press, through the post, or by door-to-door distribution. We have looked at circular letters as a method of contacting the public, but much wider use is made of leaflets and pamphlets by many organisations.

The preparation of this material is a specialist task, usually performed by a Public Relations Department or an external advertising agency, and it can take many forms, ranging from a single printed sheet to a glossy, multi-page brochure. Obviously, different methods of advertising are aimed at different sections of the market, and the decision as to which is most appropriate will depend on the selling 'situation', and – of course – the cost.

There are many aspects of producing appropriate advertising material that must be left to experts (e.g. quality of paper, photographic material, graphics, etc.) but, in the first instance, it is often essential for a company – particularly a small one – to produce a **draft** or outline of how they think the material should be arranged/designed.

Drafting techniques for pamphlets and leaflets

In producing drafts which are going to be subject to amendment, there are basic skills and techniques that can be applied in order to indicate the intended visual effect. Study the following examples and see if you can identify any of them in the pamphlets you have collected.

Paragraphing

a   The paragraphing should reflect the correct function of a paragraph, i.e. deal with a single topic.
b   Paragraphs should be kept short to avoid visual boredom, and to aid comprehension.

Indentation/Insetting

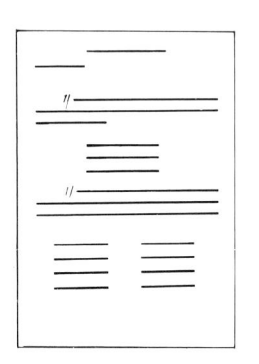

a   A variety of visual effects will help maintain reader interest.
b   Such techniques can be used to emphasise important information.

Underlining

a   Headings and sub-headings can be emphasised in this way.
b   Important words, information or instructions can be made to 'stand out'.
c   The technique should be used sparingly, as it can lose its effect.

Variety of print

a   **BOLD CAPITALS**
b   ORDINARY CAPITALS
c   S P A C E D   C A P I T A L S
d   ordinary writing

Note: There are many more varieties of print available to the professionals, but in a hand-written draft, it is difficult and time-consuming to go beyond this.

Enumeration and visual focus points

a Enumeration, or sequential numbering, is usually more appropriate for information such as instructions, where the *sequence* might be important.
b Visual focus points are useful for emphasising benefits or advantages.

Question and answer

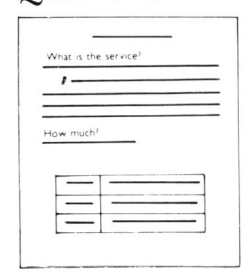

a This technique should be used sparingly, and not throughout a leaflet.
b It is useful for anticipating problems and queries.

Diagrams and graphics (not photographs)

a Simple graphs
b Simple bar charts
c Basic tabular material
d Artists' impressions
e Cartoons
f If photographs are required, the position and subject of these can be indicated.

Personalisation

a It is important to speak *to* the customer.
b Don't be afraid to use the word 'you'.

Emphasise benefits

a Negative information should be kept to a minimum.
b Make use of the 'small print' technique. For example, hide any legal exclusions or restrictive conditions at the bottom of the back page!

Contact point or advice for action

a Follow-up is essential, and therefore you must persuade the recipient to *act*.
b Make sure there is a method of contact, for example prepaid card, freefone, telephone number, individual's name, address.

Instructions

a These must be clear in meaning, and stand out on the page.
b The style of any instructions is flexible, but often the easiest is the **imperative**. This can, however, be a little impersonal.

Colour

a This can be indicated or actually used.

ACTIVITY

Choose one of your specimen leaflets, and analyse it carefully in the light of the techniques outlined above, and any others you can identify.

Specify each technique as you identify it, and comment upon its use in the context of the type of information being presented. Say whether or not you think it is effective, and explain why.

Submit the pamphlet with your commentary.

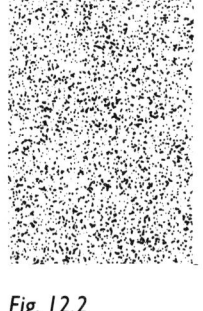

ASSIGNMENT: Marketing for Renaissance Kitchens, Ltd.

You will need to recap on the case study in Chapter 11 before attempting this.

With the expansion of Renaissance Kitchens, the mail-order business is running quite smoothly, with advertising in the national press and the 'free' papers in certain areas. The local trade and the 'tableaux'/consultant approach are ticking over quite well, but Peter Wandell feels they would benefit from a re-vamped marketing strategy, and it is decided to produce two types of literature.

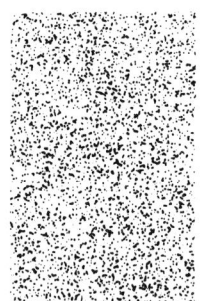

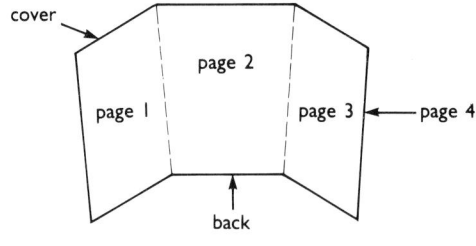

Fig. 12.2 Format for a brochure.

1. For the tableaux/consultants in quality retail outlets, a new glossy brochure is planned as a point-of-sale handout. In order to keep the cost as low as possible it is decided to adopt a simple format based on a single A4 sheet, divided into three by folding laterally. This will give six 'pages', which will include photographs and written material (see fig. 12.2).
2. For the local trade, it is decided to distribute simple leaflets, printed on A5 paper on one side only, on a door-to-door basis, with specific area saturation at monthly intervals.

Design and draft appropriate marketing material to meet these requirements.

CHAPTER 13

The workplace and the law

Office design

The creation of a new office is a task which demands close analysis of how the work space is to be used, thorough planning, and careful, closely-monitored implementation. Even the re-design of an existing office can be a traumatic experience, both for management and for those workers affected by any changes. However, such design is a very important element of the general work environment, and must be considered from a number of points of view, for example, personal, aesthetic, efficiency, comfort, social, company image, practical use, cost.

A major aim is to provide working conditions in which people are happy and can enjoy their job, but the personal needs of individuals must be balanced against the practicalities of performing the work, and the requirements of relevant government legislation in this area. Some general influences on office design are shown in fig. 13.1.

Fig. 13.1 Influences on office design.

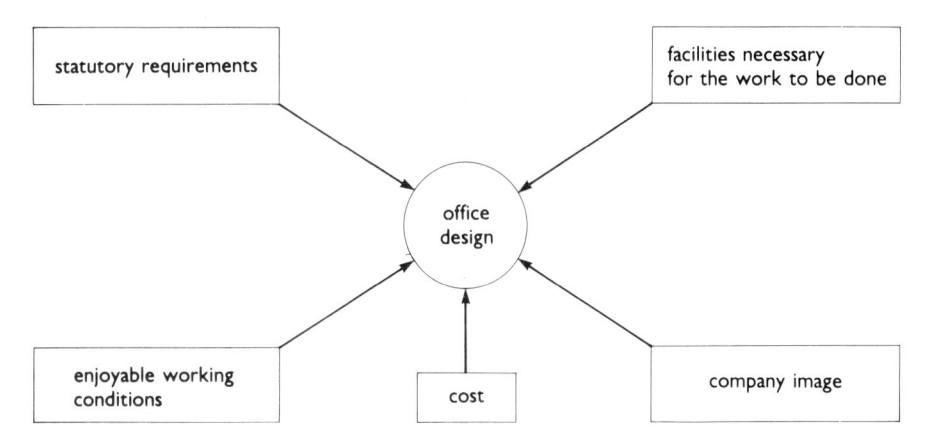

The law

It is fairly clear that the legal requirements relating to conditions in offices need to be borne in mind at all stages of planning and design. Since the early 1960s a number of Acts of Parliament have been passed which specify minimum standards, and an indication of the general requirements of these is given in figs. 13.2 – 13.5.

Fig. 13.2

1963
Offices, Shops and Railway Premises Act

Main concern: physical conditions.

Specific considerations: space per person, cleanliness, lighting, ventilation, sanitary arrangements, heating, temperature, washing facilities, drinking water, first aid, fire precautions, lifting of heavy weights, accidents, notification of accidents, noise.

Fig. 13.3

1969
Employers' Liability (Compulsory Insurance) Act

Main concern: insurance of employees.

Specific considerations: cover must be provided through authorised insurers to insure employees against injury and disease resulting from their employment. It is the employer's responsibility to provide this. A valid Certificate of Insurance should be on permanent display.

Fig. 13.4

1971
Fire Precautions Act

Main concern: precautions against fire.

Specific considerations: certain premises must have a current fire certificate, which confirms that adequate arrangements have been made, and precautions taken.

Note: Many small businesses are not covered under this Act, but are still required to take fire precautions under the Fire Precautions (non-certificated Factory, Office, Shop and Railway Premises) Regulations, 1976.

Fig. 13.5

1974
Health and Safety at Work Act (HASAWA)

Main concern: to supplement the 1963 Act – Safety and Health.

Specific considerations: provision of safe working conditions, free from health hazards; employers have an obligation to provide adequate information, training, instruction, and supervision for all health and safety matters; employers must ensure (as far as is practicable) that safety practices are followed and that employees do not endanger themselves or colleagues.

The workplace and the law 135

ACTIVITY

Write a *brief* commentary in answer to each of the following questions, explaining what the relevant Act(s) of Parliament include in their regulations. Don't attempt to write too much on each. Concentrate on the essential, basic or minimum requirements, and state which Act the information has come from.

1. What space should be allocated to each employee in the work environment?
2. What are the basic regulations concerning provision of lavatories and washing facilities?
3. What is the recommended minimum temperature for an office after the first working hour of the day?
4. Do any of the acts specify what procedures should be followed in case of accident?
5. Is there any regulation which would apply to a piece of office equipment such as a guillotine for cutting paper?
6. What determines whether or not business premises require a fire certificate?
7. Specify three precautions which are recommended for business premises which *do not* require a fire certificate.
8. What happens if an employer does not comply with the 1969 Act?
9. What reference(s) to noise levels are made in the Health & Safety at Work Act (HASAWA) and the Offices, Shops & Railway Premises Act?
10. Under HASAWA the employer is expected to provide 'supervision'. Suggest how this can be done.

Health and safety policy

Such an important aspect of working life as health and safety requires a national policy, and enforcement of the various acts is monitored and executed through three special bodies (fig. 13.6).

Fig. 13.6
The hierarchy of enforcement bodies.

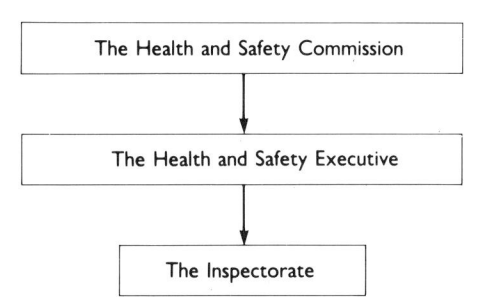

The Health and Safety Commission
↓
The Health and Safety Executive
↓
The Inspectorate

The Health and Safety Commission is appointed by the Secretary of State for Employment, and consists of representatives from employers' and employees' organisations, and local authorities. It aims to ensure that adequate advice and information on health and safety matters are available, together with appropriate research and training. New regulations are introduced as and when they are necessary, and Approved Codes of Practice established. The Health and Safety Executive has the responsibility of enforcing the Acts through the Inspectorate, has to undertake any work required of it by the Commission, and provides an advisory service. The

Inspectors have quite wide powers, which give them the right to enter premises at any reasonable time, conduct investigations, inspect relevant records, and instigate proceedings if they think an offence is being committed under the Acts.

Physical conditions

In basic terms, the requirements in an office for satisfactory conditions can be looked at under the general headings of **lighting**, **heating**, **noise** and **ventilation**. Cleanliness is also quite important and cleaning is usually done on a regular basis by cleaning staff, caretakers, or specialist contractors. Good conditions or bad conditions in the other areas can, however, have direct effects on the way in which people work, as indicated in figs. 13.7 – 13.10.

Fig. 13.7

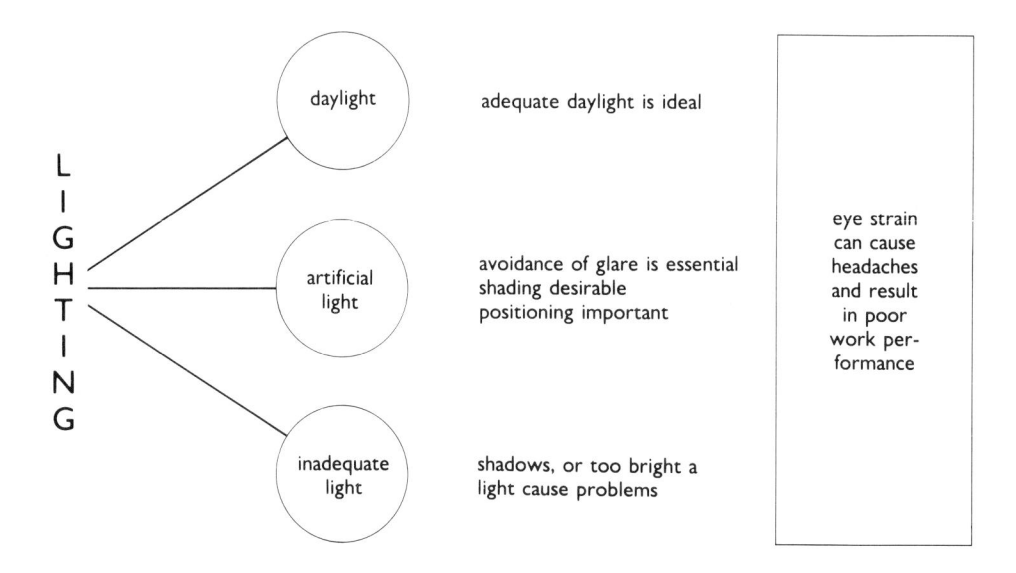

LIGHTING

- daylight — adequate daylight is ideal
- artificial light — avoidance of glare is essential; shading desirable; positioning important
- inadequate light — shadows, or too bright a light cause problems

eye strain can cause headaches and result in poor work performance

Fig. 13.8

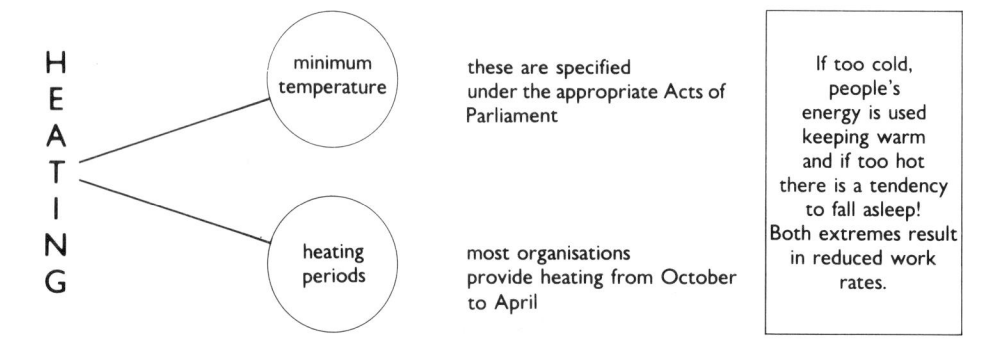

HEATING

- minimum temperature — these are specified under the appropriate Acts of Parliament
- heating periods — most organisations provide heating from October to April

If too cold, people's energy is used keeping warm and if too hot there is a tendency to fall asleep! Both extremes result in reduced work rates.

Fig. 13.9

NOISE

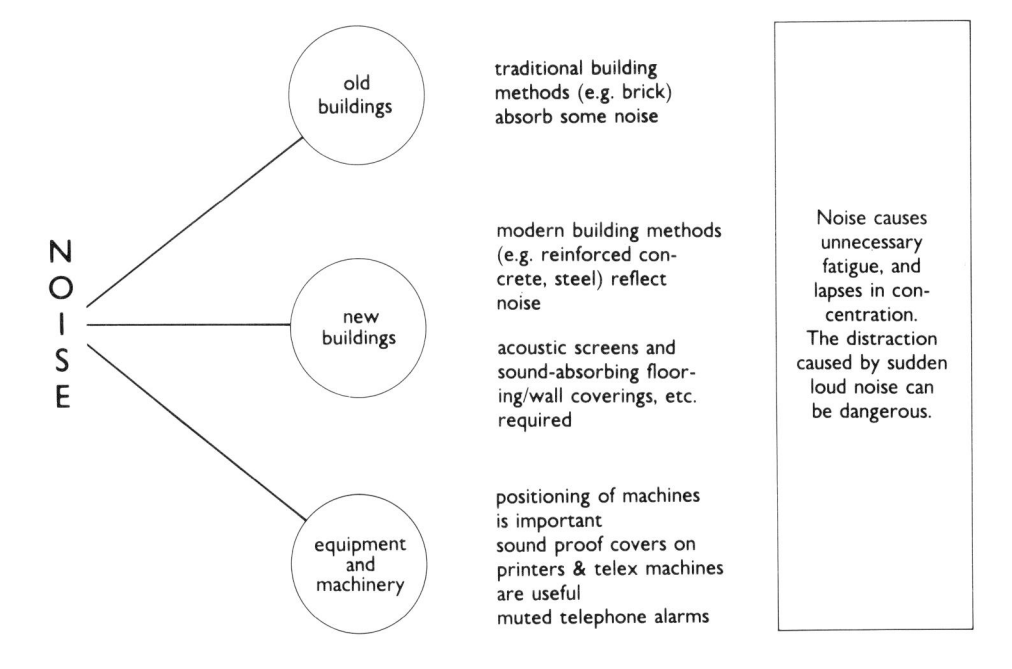

- old buildings — traditional building methods (e.g. brick) absorb some noise
- new buildings — modern building methods (e.g. reinforced concrete, steel) reflect noise; acoustic screens and sound-absorbing flooring/wall coverings, etc. required
- equipment and machinery — positioning of machines is important; sound proof covers on printers & telex machines are useful; muted telephone alarms

Noise causes unnecessary fatigue, and lapses in concentration. The distraction caused by sudden loud noise can be dangerous.

Fig. 13.10

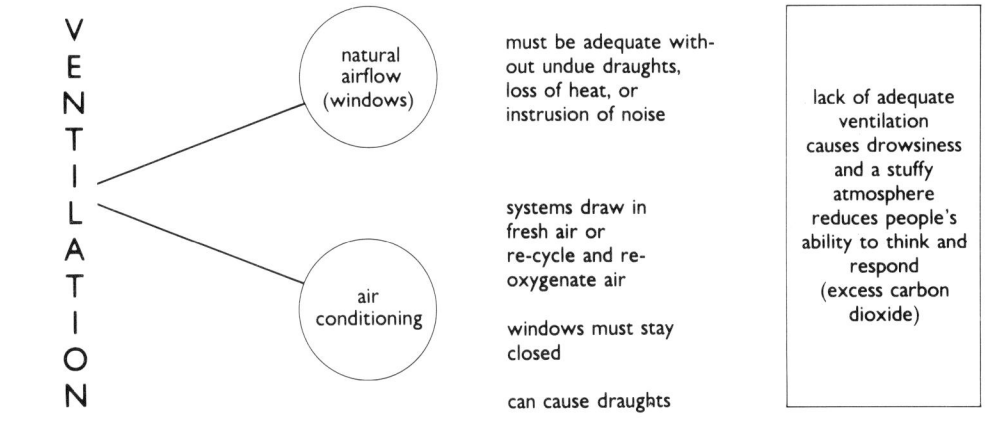

VENTILATION

- natural airflow (windows) — must be adequate without undue draughts, loss of heat, or instrusion of noise
- air conditioning — systems draw in fresh air or re-cycle and re-oxygenate air; windows must stay closed; can cause draughts

lack of adequate ventilation causes drowsiness and a stuffy atmosphere reduces people's ability to think and respond (excess carbon dioxide)

Types of office layout

In older office blocks, or business premises which have been in use for many years, it is still quite common to find a **traditional layout**, with staff working in a number of small rooms linked by a corridor or interconnecting doors (fig. 13.11).

There are arguments for and against this traditional type of layout, which you might like to consider.

Fig. 13.11 Traditional floor plan.

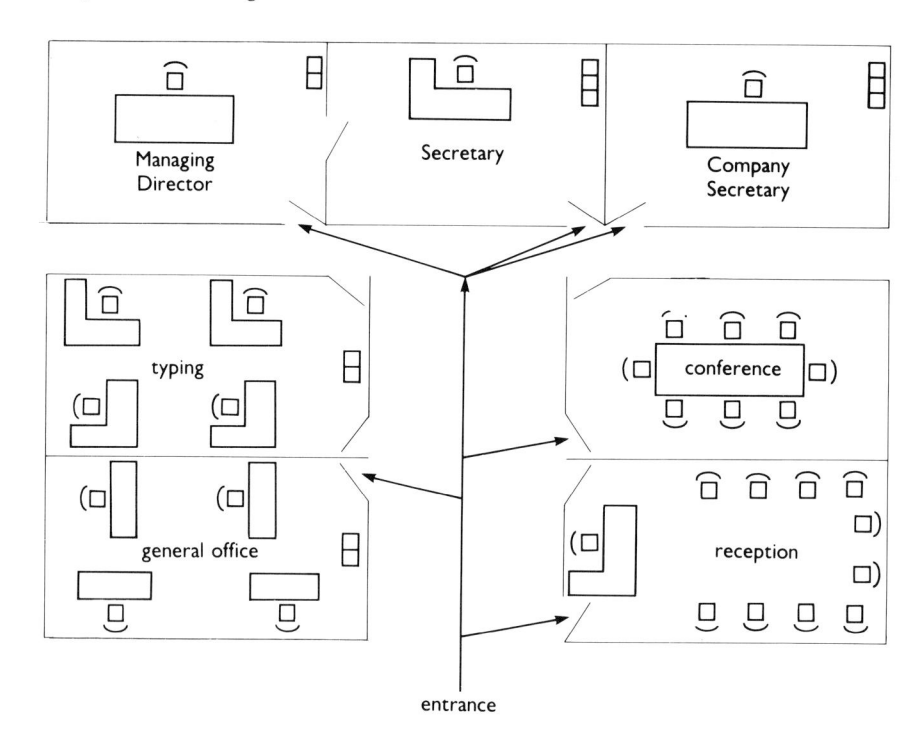

For	Against
privacy	supervision more difficult
security	distribution of documents takes longer
confidentiality	
quiet	greater distances to walk
reflects status	consulation with colleagues more difficult
allows for personal decor	
allows for personal furniture arrangement	
allows for individual preferences regarding lighting, heating, ventilation, smoking, etc.	

The alternative to the traditional layout is an **open-plan** floor arrangement, where a great number of staff work in one office, albeit a very large one! There can be a number of sections, or even departments, all working together in a general work area. Obviously, this could be chaotic, but with the effective use of **office-landscaping** techniques, satisfactory working conditions can be achieved. Such landscaping can include the use of plant arrangements, the linking of furniture and equipment in work-groups, and the use of acoustic screens or even filing cabinets to create a certain amount of privacy. Fig. 13.12 shows how such arrangements can be made.

As with a traditional layout, there are various arguments to think about in relation to an open-plan layout.

*Fig. 13.12
Open-plan office.*

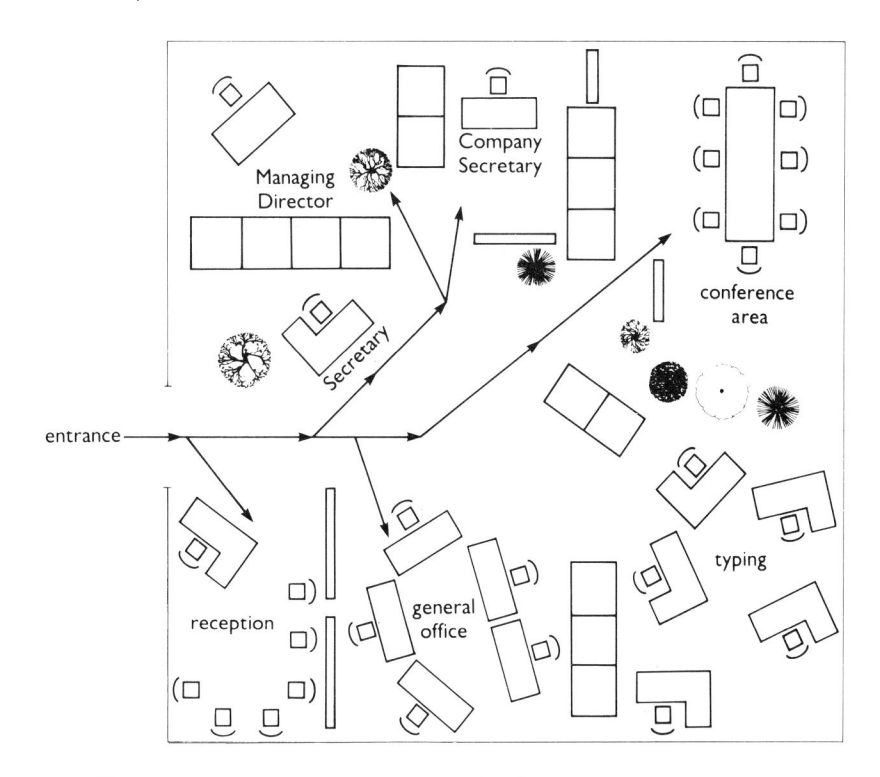

For	Against
more economic use of space	lack of privacy
more effective work-flow	difficulty of maintaining confidentiality
easier supervision	noise
cheaper lighting and heating	more difficult security for cash, etc.
	inability to cater for individual preferences

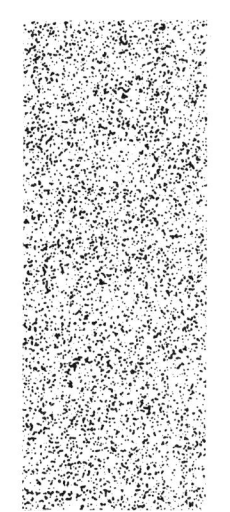

ASSIGNMENT: Office design at Renaissance Kitchens

In order to improve the co-ordination of activities at Renaissance, Peter Wandell has decided that the whole system would work better if as many of the administrative activities as possible could be performed in one area, in an open-plan office. It is your task to analyse the situation, and come up with a proposed office layout. Although a scale is indicated, you are not concerned with scale drawings at this stage, only a practical layout design for the various administrative activities. The following procedure will help you make the necessary decisions.

1. Read through the Renaissance case study in Chapter 11, and gather together all the information you produced in answer to the assignments 'Progress' and 'Integrated Business Systems'.
2. Consider carefully the organisation chart you produced for Renaissance and list the people who (a) are involved in administrative duties, and (b) could practically work in a general administration centre.

140   People in business organisations

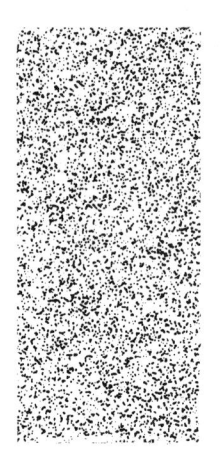

3 Divide up the list into groups of people who perform related duties. To do this, study the functions to be carried out in the office, and group together those who work together on each stage of the administrative process. You should use the background information given to you in 'Integrated Business Systems' to help you establish the range of activities performed, and the information flow between groups or individuals.

4 Decide what furniture and equipment each group or individual is likely to need, and make a note of these requirements. Think this through carefully as you will need to incorporate much of the 'hardware' into your plan.

5 Consider the two possible sites proposed by Peter Wandell, shown in figs. 13.13 and 13.14, both of which have roughly the same floor area, and design an appropriate office layout to meet the requirements of Renaissance Kitchens. Produce one design for each site, using plain white A4 paper, and drawing your floor areas according to the shape and dimensions specified. Some landscaping techniques are shown in fig. 13.12.

Fig. 13.13
Site 1

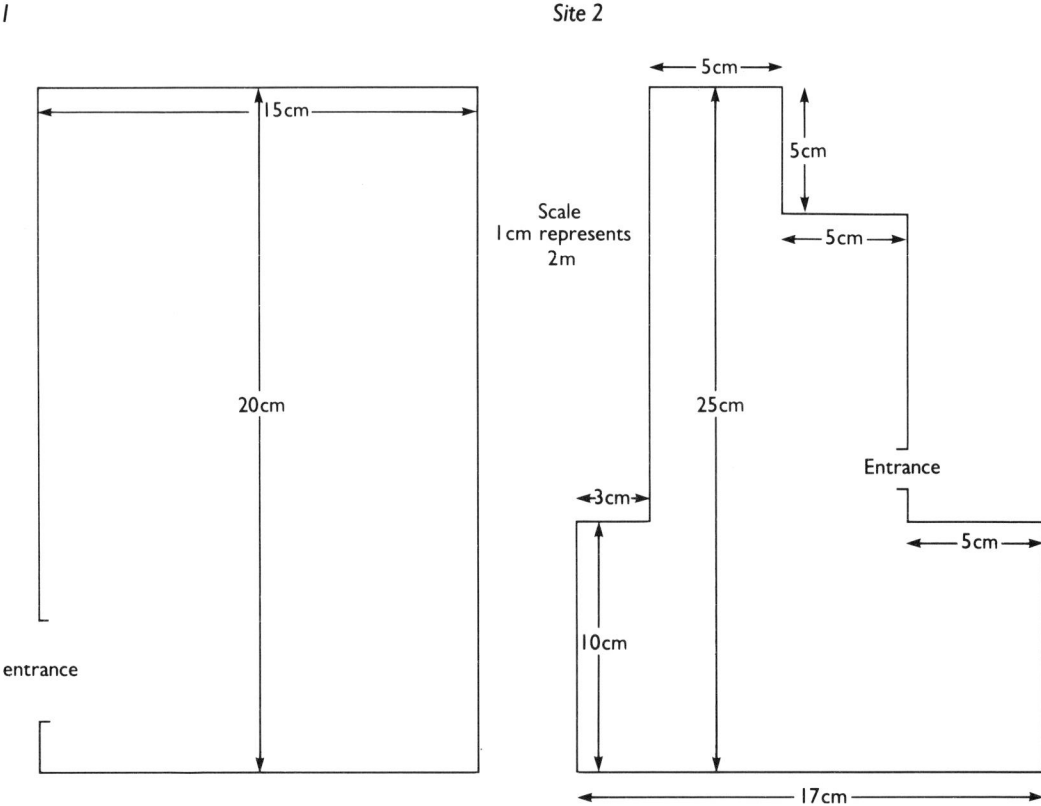

Fig. 13.14
Site 2

Scale
1 cm represents 2m

Information flow

It is quite likely that your first attempts at planning the Renaissance office will not have given full consideration to the **workflow** or **information flow**. The main concern will have been to get everything in, and use the space efficiently. However, another principle of office design is to reduce the amount of 'travelling' that documents or individuals have to do.

Fig. 13.15 Information flow diagrams.

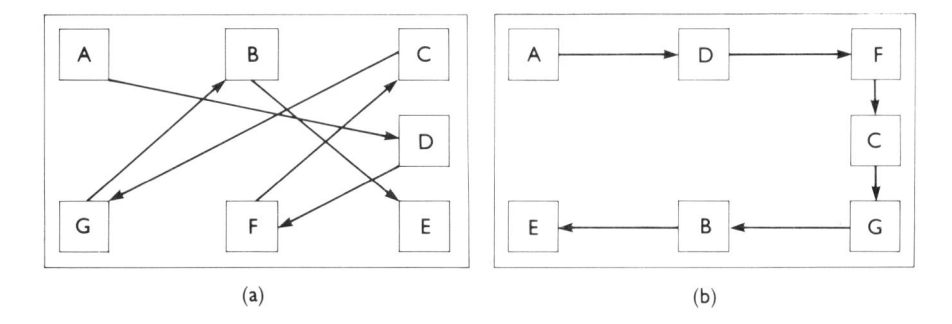

The two simplistic diagrams in fig. 13.15 show how the routeing of a document could be made more efficient by placing the functional personnel in an appropriate sequential arrangement in the office. Obviously, most offices with a variety of documents passing through them and activities going on, cannot be so simply organised, but the principle of using information flow as one of the criteria for design is important, and you can reduce time, effort, distance, congestion and costs.

ACTIVITY

Exchange the plans you have drawn up in the preceding assignment with others in your group. Ideally, you should end up with two different plans (for Site 1 and Site 2) from two different people.

Analyse each of these plans in the light of what you know about the workflow and information flow in Renaissance Kitchens, and write a commentary on each one explaining why you think the layout would be effective or ineffective for the functional activities you know have to be carried out. Consider all aspects of the administrative procedures, and decide how well you think the office would work!

More design considerations

In addition to considering the relative merits of traditional or open-plan arrangements, and general layout/design, thought has to be given to more basic things such as wall-coverings (painted or papered?), floor coverings (carpets, tiles, or some other material?), window blinds (or curtaining?), and how these might affect the general physical environment from the point of view of noise, light, heating etc.

Colour schemes have to be worked out with decisions being made on whether bright colours should be used, or pastel shades. Some colours are restful, some cause eye strain, and some combinations can have a disturbing effect on individuals. Obviously, it is important to consult those who will be working in the office, and make decisions based on their preferences, and the type and size of room that is being used.

Office furniture is another area in which it is easy to make mistakes. The main considerations should be:

What will it be used for?

People in business organisations

What size is required for efficient operation?
What specialist furniture is required?
What is the best height of desk for people to work at?
What design of chair is most suitable for each task/operation?

If any of these things are wrong, individuals may suffer specific physical effects (e.g. backache, eye-strain, headaches) with a consequent drop in productivity and efficiency.

ACTIVITY

Under the HASAWA every employer has a general responsibility to ensure the health, safety and welfare at work of all employees, so far as is reasonably practicable. Within the general statement there are a number of specified areas which are particularly referred to, and there is also a clear indication that the *employee* has a duty while at work to contribute towards the general safety of the environment. Using a tabular format as shown in fig. 13.16, outline the employer's responsibilities and the employee's responsibilities in relation to the general conditions in the workplace.

Employer's responsibilities	Employee's responsibilities
(a)	(a)
(b)	(b)

Fig. 13.16

CHAPTER 14
Management, human relations and conflict

In Chapter 4 we considered the distribution of authority in an organisation, and discussed organisation charts as an attempt to illustrate the formal relationships in an organisation, the main lines of communication, and the flow of authority and responsibility through the various levels of management. What we didn't do was look at 'management' as a concept, and think about the different interpretations that can be applied to such a commonly used word.

How often have you heard (or made) statements like:

'It's a management decision.'
'They went bust because of poor management.'
'It's management's responsibility to deal with that problem.'

In general terms, 'management' refers to a collection of people who are responsible for running a business on behalf of the owners: that is, they establish and implement policy, and aim to ensure profitability. In a practical business situation, all sorts of terms are used to describe people at different levels who are considered to have management responsibilities, the most common areas being **executive**, **administrator**, **supervisor**, **director**, and, of course, **manager**. These terms are often used very loosely,

Fig. 14.1 Personnel distribution in a medium-to-large organisation.

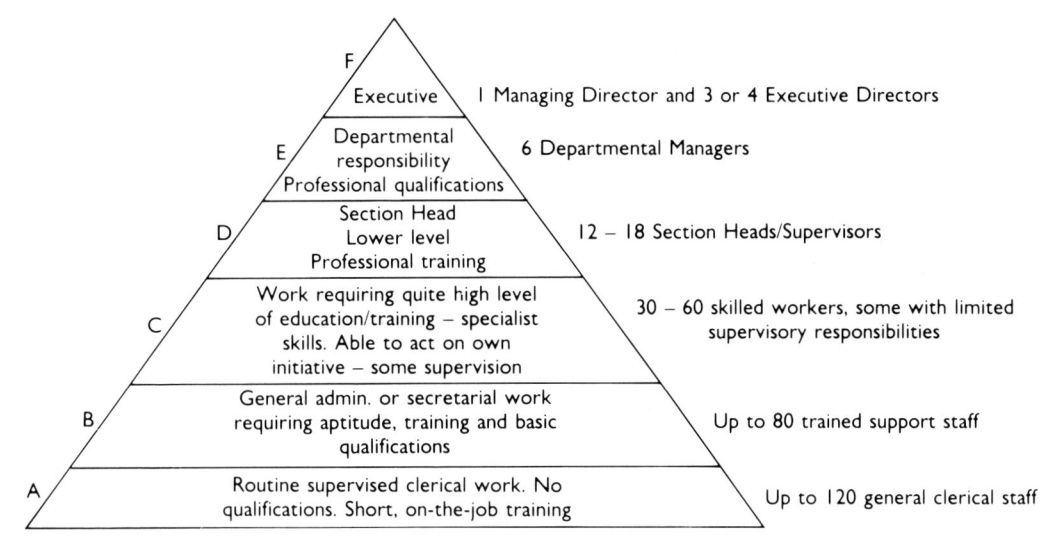

Level	Description	Staff
F	Executive	1 Managing Director and 3 or 4 Executive Directors
E	Departmental responsibility / Professional qualifications	6 Departmental Managers
D	Section Head / Lower level / Professional training	12 – 18 Section Heads/Supervisors
C	Work requiring quite high level of education/training – specialist skills. Able to act on own initiative – some supervision	30 – 60 skilled workers, some with limited supervisory responsibilities
B	General admin. or secretarial work requiring aptitude, training and basic qualifications	Up to 80 trained support staff
A	Routine supervised clerical work. No qualifications. Short, on-the-job training	Up to 120 general clerical staff

with the functions and responsibilities associated with a particular title differing from organisation to organisation.

Office work is often particularly difficult to classify and define, so, to get some idea of where any individual could fit into the hierarchy, it can be useful to construct a pyramid diagram showing what skills and qualifications might be required at particular levels (fig. 14.1). This pyramid structure also indicates that the higher up the 'ladder' you go, the fewer people there are holding those responsibilities. In fig. 14.1 an indication is given of the number of staff who might be working at each level in a hypothetical medium-to-large company.

ACTIVITY

Produce written answers to the following questions:

1 If you were starting work, or if you are in work at the present time, at what level would you place yourself? Why?
2 Specify what sort of training or qualifications you might need to acquire in order to progress to the next level.
3 At what level will you feel qualified to work when you have achieved your BTEC National Certificate or Diploma?
4 Identify someone you know (in any organisation) who could be classified in Sections D, E or F. Describe their job, responsibilities, qualifications and experience.
5 Identify someone you know (in any organisation) who could be classified in Sections A, B or C. Describe their job, responsibilities, qualifications and experience.

Management styles

Having thought about the levels of authority outlined in the pyramid diagram, and which you identified in the last activity, you should be able to demonstrate fairly clearly what *you* think a manager is. The next stage is to look at how managers work. How do they deal with people? How do they solve problems? How do they get things done? What styles of management do they employ?

Obviously, each individual will react to situations in different ways, and a manager is no different. However, there are some broad classifications we can use to show how different approaches can be adopted and identified as styles of management. They are **authoritarian**, **democratic**, and **laissez-faire**. Figs. 14.2, 14.3 and 14.4 show some of the characteristics of these styles.

The conclusion most people will come to when considering these styles is that the democratic approach is best. But is this really the case? If an emergency arose at work, would you expect your manager to take decisive action to solve the problem, or would you prefer him or her to call a meeting to discuss it? Very often, immediate decisions and action are essential, and democratic consultation might not be appropriate.

Management, human relations and conflict

Fig. 14.2

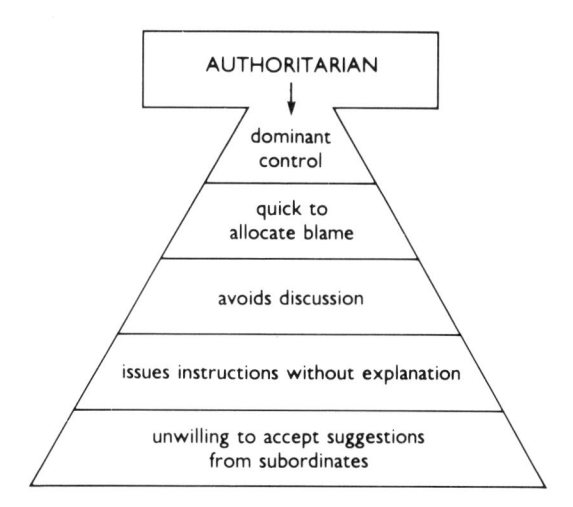

```
               AUTHORITARIAN
                     ↓
                 dominant
                  control
              quick to
            allocate blame
           avoids discussion
      issues instructions without explanation
     unwilling to accept suggestions
            from subordinates
```

Fig. 14.3

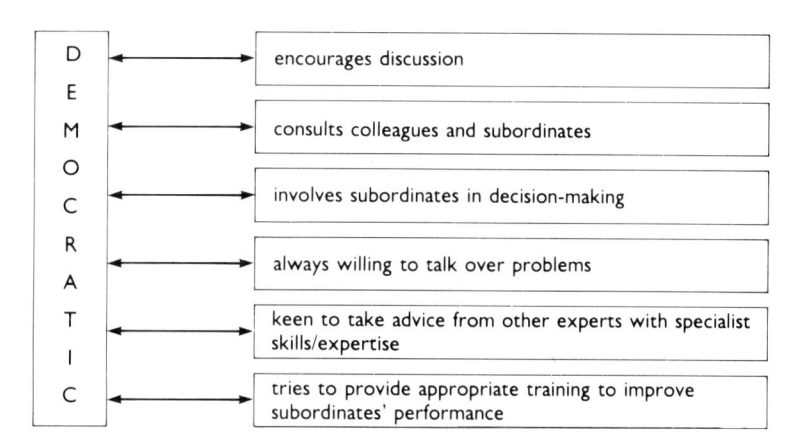

D ↔ encourages discussion
E
M ↔ consults colleagues and subordinates
O
C ↔ involves subordinates in decision-making
R
A ↔ always willing to talk over problems
T
I ↔ keen to take advice from other experts with specialist skills/expertise
C ↔ tries to provide appropriate training to improve subordinates' performance

Fig. 14.4

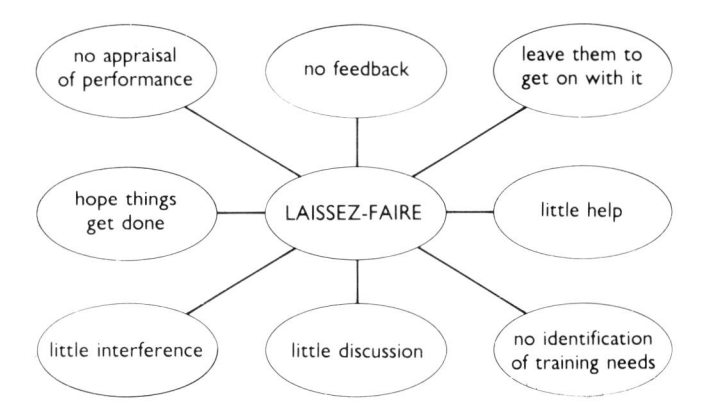

LAISSEZ-FAIRE
- no appraisal of performance
- no feedback
- leave them to get on with it
- hope things get done
- little help
- little interference
- little discussion
- no identification of training needs

The manager

When trying to identify the personal qualities we would associate with someone in a management position, it is likely that most of us would expect intelligence, a sound knowledge of the business, good general and professional qualifications, proven expertise in their specialist area, effective communication skills, an ability to get on with people, and the confidence to make decisions. A manager with such personal qualities should have no need to adopt one particular style of management, because he or she will recognise that every situation will require a different approach: sometimes the work will get done more effectively if people are left to get on with it; sometimes, in a crisis, it will be necessary to override normal consultative procedures and implement an immediate course of action.

The skill of management is to read a situation accurately, and adopt an approach which is most appropriate in the circumstances, and will achieve the best results. In achieving these results, the manager has to rely on the staff, and accept responsibility for the quality of their work. Obviously it is in any manager's best interests to ensure that the people under him or her are working as well as they can, and performing their jobs effectively. In order to monitor these aspects of a department, some system of appraisal is essential, whereby each individual can be made aware of his, or her, performance and progress. One method of doing this is by implementing a policy of **Management by Objectives** (M b O).

How M b O works

The essence of this system is that the organisation has to identify and establish exactly what it intends to achieve over the next 'period'. (The period can be six months, twelve months or sometimes longer.) These overall objectives will require a particular approach if they are to be achieved, and within an organisation a forward-planning team needs to establish how the various departments have to work to help achieve the objectives, and what specific contribution each can make to the overall plan. This process should involve consultation with department managers and result in the establishment of a set of departmental objectives for each functional area.

Logically, this process can be continued down through the organisation so that the various sub-sections within each department can be examined to see how they can help the department meet its objectives, and individuals in responsible positions can (through discussion and consultation, participation and involvement) establish with their superiors an appropriate and feasible range of personal objectives. This may involve analysis and re-drafting of job-descriptions and highlight a need for specialist training.

One thing to bear in mind about an M b O approach is that at the individual level, the objectives identified will most likely be quite specific in their requirements. As you move up through the organisation to identify departmental objectives, branch objectives and corporate objectives, they will be formulated in much more general terms, with overall policy statements indicating broad plans of action rather than specifying particular achievement or training criteria for individual employees.

However, it is at the individual level that the work has to be done, and the principles of M b O imply a regular system of consultation and appraisal for all employees. Implemented effectively, M b O can lead to the motivation and development of individuals through regular and systematic reviews of performance, the identification of training needs, the co-ordination of effort, and (hopefully!) the achievement of the organisation's goals. However, effective implementation needs to be based on a participative approach rather than an authoritarian one, and consultation, performance-review and appraisal can be very time-consuming for a busy manager.

ACTIVITY

Consider this conversation between two senior managers concerning the introduction of a formal system of appraisal into their company. John Reaper is the Production Manager, and Angela Dunsford is the Personnel Manager.

J. R.: I don't see the point of introducing these appraisal procedures if we know our staff well, and know what they can do. It's a waste of time and money!

A. D.: The main point is, John, that it would benefit the company as well as the individual. It's not a one-sided thing and it can lead to a much more effective use of our main resource – people!

J. R.: Sounds like a lot of nonsense to me. All *my* people are interested in is how much they can take home at the end of the week.

A. D.: I agree that salary is certainly an important element, and this would be considered as part of any appraisal system. The aim, however, would be to make sure staff are aware of the *basis* for awarding salaries, and to establish a direct link between performance and reward. It's much better that people know where they stand – but salary isn't the most important thing . . .

J. R.: You try and tell my staff that!

A. D.: O.K.! Let's look at it from the production point of view. If your staff were paid according to the quantity or quality of work they produced in any period, what would their reaction be if they suddenly found that their wages were £20 less than normal one week?

J. R.: They'd be knocking on my door for an explanation.

A. D.: Exactly! They would want to know what had gone wrong, or where *they* had gone wrong. This is a basic function of formal appraisal schemes – to identify strengths and weaknesses. Then, if anybody has a particular talent, it can be exploited; or if the employee has shown that he or she is weak in any particular area, appropriate guidance or training programmes can be designed to remedy this. The company *and* the worker benefit by making the worker more efficient.

J. R.: Well, it sounds all right in theory, but you've used a rather extreme example...

A. D.: All right, let's think of another situation. What if someone on the production line came up with an idea for improving the process and saving time and materials in making a particular component?

J. R.: They'd probably tell the chief engineer, who'd discuss it with me, and if it proved practical we might implement it. If it *did* work, the 'inventor' would get the standard £50 bonus.

A. D.: That's all right in the production area, but how do you identify 'potential' in other areas such as clerical or administrative or executive?

J. R.: I hadn't really thought about it.

A. D.: One of the ways is to have regular discussions with people and encourage progressive thought by openly discussing how jobs are done and what the problems are. Individuals can be assessed in this way, and given tasks to do which allow them to develop their own skills and potential. It's not so cut and dried as your production solution, but often the only way to get the best out of people is to give them a little more responsibility, provide incentives, and enable them to take on more challenging work so that they can prove their abilities. The appraisal interview can be the springboard for this sort of action.

J. R.: Well, that certainly seems to make sense, and I suppose it's one way of getting to know your staff a bit better. In fact, it could be a useful two-way communication exercise, giving the staff the chance to talk about any worries or complaints that they might have as well as trying to assess their strengths, weaknesses and potential.

A. D.: Now you're talking! That's exactly the way I would hope an appraisal system would work...

J. R.: You hold on a minute. I didn't say I accepted the whole idea, just that I could see some useful possibilities...

A. D.: Well, let me put some other ideas to you. You know we all work to the M b O system of setting goals or targets for each six months? The appraisal system can be integrated with that and used as a means of discussing and establishing individual and departmental goals for the next period. This would then tie-in very nicely with the overall staff planning policy, and we could ensure that everybody is – as far as possible – being employed in the most efficient and cost-effective way.

J. R.: Some of this seems a bit airy-fairy to me, but I can certainly see the usefulness of some aspects of a formal appraisal system. I'll have to think about it a bit more. Let's have another chat before Friday's Board Meeting.

Task

Taking the preceding conversation as the springboard for your ideas, use a tabular format (see fig. 14.5) to outline the **aims** and **benefits** of an effective appraisal scheme. You can make use of any other source material you can find, but don't be

Management, human relations and conflict 149

tempted to give lengthy descriptions of various methods of appraisal – concentrate on the general aims and benefits.

There are certain areas you should ensure that you cover, including staff, planning, performance assessment and target setting.

Fig. 14.5

Aims	Benefits
Performance assessment	(Comments)
Staff planning	

ASSIGNMENT: Waterlane College of Higher Education (1)

General introduction

In any organisation 'human relations' is an important concept. A fundamental explanation of this term is that it involves the behaviour of both individuals and groups, and, in the context of a working situation, the way in which individuals, factions or departments react to or interact with each other.

Obviously, this interaction can have a dramatic influence upon the effective operation of any organisation. Bad human relations can cause delays, lack of co-operation, dissatisfaction and work of a poor standard. The organisational structure of a company is important, and lines of communication and authority need careful planning and consideration. In your work on organisation charts in Section 1 you will have appreciated how complex the establishment and analysis of effective organisational structures can be.

However, no matter how well planned and structured an organisation might be, there are no short cuts to effective human relations. When dealing with people's feelings, their status, their sense of security, their personal fears, wants and needs, it is impossible to draw up a set of regulations which will solve all problems that might arise. People are individuals, and their problems are individual ones which need delicate handling and a sensitive approach. In many circumstances, things can go wrong even when a manager feels every effort has been made to ensure that things run smoothly – as you can see by what happened at Waterlane College of Higher Education.

The background

Within the College, a centralised Office Services section has been established to deal with all the general typing and reprographic requirements of the ten departments. The section has been in existence for twelve months, and was formed by bringing together the old typing-pool and duplicating section. The person who ran the duplicating section retired, and the responsibility for reprography was brought into Office Services under the section leadership of Katherine Syrett.

Miss Syrett had 'worked her way up' in the College. She had started in the typing pool at the age of eighteen and had proved to be competent and well-liked. After five years she applied for the post of Personal Assistant to the Vice-Principal, Mr W. Farmer, and was chosen from a number of strong applicants. She did the job well and gained valuable general experience of the working of the College and the inter-relationships of the various departments. During her ten years as the Vice-Principal's PA, Miss Syrett undertook a number of part-time study courses which not only enabled her to improve her skills, but also gave her more formal qualifications in office and administrative management. When she was 33 she successfully applied for the post of Supervisor of the typing-pool, and after another few years she became Section Head of Office Services when the section was formed.

She had responsibility for fifteen typists and clerk-typists, who were also trained to use the reprographic machinery inherited from the duplicating section. Her main duty was to allocate and supervise work, ensuring that high standards were maintained. Her staff enjoyed working under her, regarding her as firm but fair, and the general efficiency and quality of work was highly regarded throughout the College.

During the last five or six years, Miss Syrett took on the responsibility of ordering all stationery and supplies for her section, and was given authority to assess new products in the office machinery range, which included seeing representatives and demonstrators herself, and subsequently making a report and recommendations to Michael Drysdale, the Chief Administrative Officer. Her recommendations were invariably agreed, and found to be sound in the light of experience.

The first signs of trouble in the section came when the Chief Administrative Officer decided that the reprographic facilities were out of date, and wanted to purchase a sophisticated copying machine which could copy both sides of a sheet of paper at once, collate, staple and virtually operate unattended. He had seen the advertisement for the machine in *Professional Administration*, and had contacted the Tamshi company to arrange for a demonstration. When John Davey, the Tamshi representative, came to the College he convinced Michael Drysdale that the Tamshi Copyfast was ideal for the heavy copying load of the College. They discussed all aspects of the machine, including servicing, contracts, costs (installation and per copy), flexibility, performance and reliability. When Drysdale was certain that this was the right machine, he called Miss Syrett in to talk to the representative. He asked her if she had any queries about the working of the machine, or any general points she wanted to raise. Miss Syrett was surprisingly quiet and asked few questions and seemed not to be interested in the whole business. She did comment, however, that if Mr Drysdale was satisfied then she was sure the machine would be all right.

Putting aside his thoughts about Miss Syrett's rather off-hand attitude, Michael Drysdale was able to negotiate very favourable terms with Tamshi, and arranged for the new machine to be installed in three weeks' time. He informed Miss Syrett of his decision, and she agreed that she would be present when the Tamshi representative and service engineer came to demonstrate the machine and give her staff basic training in its use. On the appointed day, however, she made it clear that the work-load in Office Services was such that she was unable to take time off for the demonstration, and that she could only release seven of her staff for training. She asked her deputy – Joan Waters – to attend in her place. Her general attitude was expressed clearly when she said to Joan,

> 'All the staff have plenty of experience in reprography, so make sure that not too much time is wasted. All these photocopying machines are very similar, so this training is not really necessary. I certainly hope the machine turns out to be as good as Mr Drysdale thinks it is, otherwise a lot of time and money will have been wasted.'

Management, human relations and conflict 151

The demonstration went ahead, and the machine came into service. Within a couple of weeks problems started to occur. First of all there were some uncharacteristic complaints from departments that work was not being done quickly enough, and in some cases the quality of the copies was not up to standard. Miss Syrett explained this away by saying that the machine kept breaking down, and that her staff were finding it difficult to operate. The paper jammed frequently and the toning controls seemed to be ineffective.

When Michael Drysdale heard of the difficulties, he immediately contacted Tamshi and asked for the engineer to call and check the machine. When the engineer came, she found that the basic operation of the machine was quite satisfactory, but that there was evidence of incorrect handling. Paper was being loaded incorrectly, and the automatic controls were being over-ridden manually, thus causing poor copies. In discussion with Miss Syrett she mentioned this, but Miss Syrett insisted that the fault was with the machine, and that it was certainly not her staff who were to blame. The engineer reported her findings to the CAO, and left, confident that all would now run smoothly. Michael Drysdale decided to have a chat with Miss Syrett about the situation. He was surprised when he went into her office to hear grumblings and apparent dissatisfaction among the staff, and the general atmosphere was very 'unsettled'. His chat with Miss Syrett did not go the way he wanted it to, because she immediately became very defensive and pointed out that neither she nor her staff could be blamed for the malfunction of a machine. She made it clear that there had never been any trouble with the old machines, and implied that she felt he had made a hasty and unwise decision in dealing with Tamshi. The CAO decided to leave things as they were, and, after ensuring that the photocopier was working satisfactorily, said that he was sure there would be no further problems.

Things ran smoothly for the next two weeks, but then the complaints started to come in again. Drysdale was very annoyed about this, and accepted Miss Syrett's assertion that the machine was malfunctioning again. He rang Tamshi, and insisted that the problem was corrected.

This time, the service engineer and John Davey, the representative, came along and checked the machine through. John Davey was very puzzled at the problems Miss Syrett's section had experienced, but was annoyed to find that there had been further interference with the automatic controls, and that the paper carrier was being over-filled, causing two or more sheets to be taken into the machine and resulting in a 'jam'. The machine was thoroughly serviced, and all the staff were called in to be given individual training in the basics of using it. Many of them seemed to resent being taken away from their 'important' work in order to be shown how to use a machine which was 'not as good as the old equipment'.

In discussion with Michael Drysdale afterwards, John Davey made it quite clear that there was nothing wrong with the machine as long as it was used according to instructions. He felt that the staff were 'anti' the machine because of Miss Syrett's general attitude, and were making little effort to master the relatively simple processes involved in using it. His impression was that Miss Syrett's original lack of interest and subsequent reactions had affected the whole section, and jeopardised a good working relationship between the College and Tamshi.

The CAO was determined to sort the problem out, and summoned Miss Syrett to a meeting in his office the next day.

Task

Consider the problems outlined below, and discuss as a group the possible explanations/solutions.

I   The people who work in Office Services are obviously going through an uncharacteristically bad time. They are getting complaints about their work on the one hand, and being criticised for their general attitude on the other. This obviously

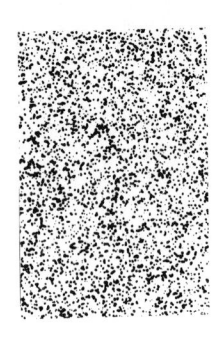

leads to low morale, and the situation seems to be going from bad to worse. Why do you think they have found themselves in this difficult situation?
2 Katherine Syrett's relationship with Management has always been very good in the past. Why does she seem to be in conflict with Michael Drysdale over this issue?
3 To what extent do you think Miss Syrett can be blamed for the problems her staff have experienced with the new machine?
4 What do you think about the CAO's role in this situation?
5 If you were Michael Drysdale, how would you approach the meeting with Miss Syrett? What would you hope to achieve? How would you deal with her apparent antagonism?

CHAPTER 15

Motivation, working in groups, and practical appraisal

Most people regard themselves as individuals first, and as members of particular human groups (e.g. family, work group, social group, etc.) after that – some of the groups changing regularly according to current interests and occupations.

In this chapter we are concerned with the individual at work, and how groups can affect the working environment. Most people go to work for a number of reasons, ranging from satisfaction of basic needs to fulfilment of personal ambitions and achievement of 'wants'. The interaction of these driving forces is complex, but determines each person's attitude and approach to working as part of an organisation.

Motivation theory

How many of the motivating factors listed here would you associate with your own approach to work?

satisfaction	friendship	somewhere to live
security	challenge	authority
food	status	creativity
protection from 'want'	pride	power
ambition	clothes	providing for family
'belonging'	self-expression	improved standard of living
using skills	economic	self-improvement

ACTIVITY

Put the motivating factors listed above into three groups, under the headings **Primary**, **Social** and **Personal**. Discuss as a group what you understand by each, and why it should be classified under its particular heading.

These motivating factors, and others, have been discussed, analysed and explained by management theorists for many years, and one of the main reasons for devoting so much time and talent to this sort of study is a perceived benefit in establishing a universal 'Theory of Management' which would enable all business organisations to be managed in an efficient and effective manner. However, this 'ideal' situation is unlikely to be achieved as long as organisations are made up of a collection of individuals, because everyone reacts differently to different stimuli, and (as we discussed in Chapter 14) an effective management style needs to be flexible and constantly adaptable.

Many ideas put forward by the theorists are valid as ideas, but don't necessarily stand up to analysis when applied to real business situations; and it is generally accepted that there has been a lack of uniformity of study methods, and even some confusion over what 'management' is! Contributors to the management debate have come from a variety of backgrounds, including practising managers, sociologists, psychologists, industrial psychologists, mathematicians, organisation theorists and even biologists. It is no wonder that ideas differ and theories abound.

Despite the confusing background to the science of management, it is useful to have an awareness of some of the 'big names' in management thought, and, in the context of this chapter, some knowledge of their ideas on **motivation**. The following assignment will give you an insight into the work of some of these.

ASSIGNMENT: a students' guide to motivation theory

In his essay 'The Motivational Basis of Organisational Behaviour' (1964), D. Katz said that an organisation could only function properly and effectively if the following three basic types of behaviour could be identified:

1. People must be induced to enter and remain within the system. High labour turnover and excessive absenteeism adversely affect the functioning of the organisation, but the mere fact that people *attend* work is not enough.
2. People must perform their appointed jobs in a dependable fashion, because if an organisation is to function at all there must be an on-going, stable pattern of activities and relationships.
3. In addition to the basic requirements in **1** and **2**, people must at times (assuming that the job allows it) demonstrate initiative, spontaneous activity and innovative approaches to achieving organisational objectives above and beyond that which is normally expected of them.

Most people would accept these points at face value as they establish a basis for organisational operation, but within this framework a whole range of motivation theory can be considered. As a student you will know the difficulties of ploughing through endless textbooks trying to sort out different people's opinions of various theoretical concepts. Wouldn't it be useful if someone provided you with an information sheet summarising the main avenues of thought on each topic, and providing references so that you could follow up each idea if you wanted to?

Task

Produce such an information sheet summarising the ideas of some of the main motivation theorists.

There are some general notes for guidance on the presentation of **information sheets** at the end of this assignment, but bear in mind the statement made in the first paragraph about 'flexibility'. The specimen layout includes *all* components that are likely to be required, and you must adjust this to suit your purpose.

In putting together your information, a schematic layout will be ideal, with the section heading being the name of the theorist, and the sub-headings dealing with the aspects such as Main Theories (or Main Ideas), Comments (in which you can outline arguments for and against the ideas), and References (in which you give specific source references for further reading). Within each sub-section, numbered points can be used if you think this would be useful.

You should aim to summarise the ideas of the following leading theorists:

Chris Argyris: American; first degree in psychology; has held position of Professor of Industrial Administration at Yale University.

Abraham H. Maslow: died 1970; psychologist of Brandeis University; known particularly for his 'Hierarchy of Needs'.

Douglas McGregor: died 1964; social scientist; American; Professor of Management at Massachusetts Institute of Technology.

Frederick Herzberg: concerned with how human needs can be satisfied at work; the Motivation–Hygiene Theory.

There is much source material available, and you will find that your college library or your local reference library will have a range of books which include information on motivation theory. You should not only consider books which are classified under 'Management', but also be prepared to explore other areas, including Business Administration, Secretarial Studies, Office Administration and Supervisory Studies. In fact, many general Business Studies texts will include chapters or sections on this important aspect of working life.

Remember: You are concerned with motivation – not general management theory.

Notes for guidance: the presentation of information sheets

Although it is a **formal** method of communication, the **information sheet** is highly flexible and can be structured to meet the specific needs of any particular situation or organisation. However, there are certain basic principles that can be applied, as outlined below.

1 Use an **attention line** to indicate clearly at whom the information is aimed. This could be:

> For the attention of Mr Sampson.
> For the attention of the Personnel Manager.
> For the attention of all staff.

If more than one person is to be circulated (but not all staff) the sheet should be marked 'For the attention of . . . (the senior person)' and a circulation list incorporated.

An indication of who is issuing the sheet should be given, together with date of issue.

2 The heading **information sheet** should be used, and written on a line of its own.
3 An appropriate title, indicating the subject/content, should be prominently placed after the heading.
4 A brief introductory paragraph can be a useful 'lead-in' to the information.
5 The main body of information should be classified and presented under appropriate

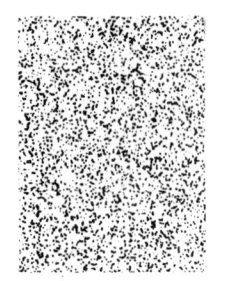

section headings and sub-headings. Beyond this, the material can be given as numbered points or as normal paragraphs. A schematic layout can aid comprehension.

Note: A good narrative style should be used – *not note form*

6 If any diagrammatic material is necessary, this can be incorporated into the normal format (if it is not too big) *or* can be attached as an appendix (appropriately numbered and referenced).
7 A concluding section or paragraph might be desirable.
8 Visual effect is important in any written communication. Fig. 15.1 shows how an information sheet could be presented.

Fig. 15.1 Layout for information sheet

For the attention of ....

From ....

Date ....

c.c. ....
....
....
....

INFORMATION SHEET
Title indicating subject/content

Brief introductory paragraph

Section heading

  (a) Sub-heading

  (b) Sub-heading

Section heading

  (a) Sub-heading
    (i)

```
                    (ii)    _____
                            _____
                            _____

         (b)  Sub-heading
                    (i)     _____
                            _____
                            _____
                    (ii)    _____
                            _____
                            _____

    _____
                        Concluding section
    _____
    _____
```

Groups – formal and informal

Motivation, of course, is not always simply an individual reaction or response – it can be dramatically affected by group influences. In Chapter 11 we considered in general terms some of the groups which are likely to have socialised us throughout our lives, resulting in the formation, consolidation, change or reinforcement of our attitudes (and prejudices!).

At work you are likely to be a member of a formal group, which has been established by management to perform a particular task or fulfil a particular role in the working of the organisation. This might be a department, or a section, or a small sub-group of specialists. As well as this formal grouping, you can probably identify a number of people with whom you like to spend your break-times or lunch-times, and who can loosely be described as a group of friends. These informal groups are equally important to you as an individual, and can have a positive function in the life of the organisation, ensuring cross-fertilisation of ideas, speedy communication and rapid feedback.

Whatever the group, most members have joined it voluntarily, and it stands to reason that each individual is deriving benefit from membership. Hopefully, the group is benefiting from the contribution made by each individual, and the organisation is benefiting from having a well-integrated workforce. It's pretty obvious that the interaction between the individual and the various groups to which he or she belongs is of great importance.

Groups are a fact of life, but why do people join them? It's unlikely that any of us have sat down and thoroughly analysed our reasons for working in the Accounts Section, or joining the darts team, or representing our colleagues on the Social Committee, so fig. 15.2 gives some general indications of why people choose to get together.

Fig. 15.2

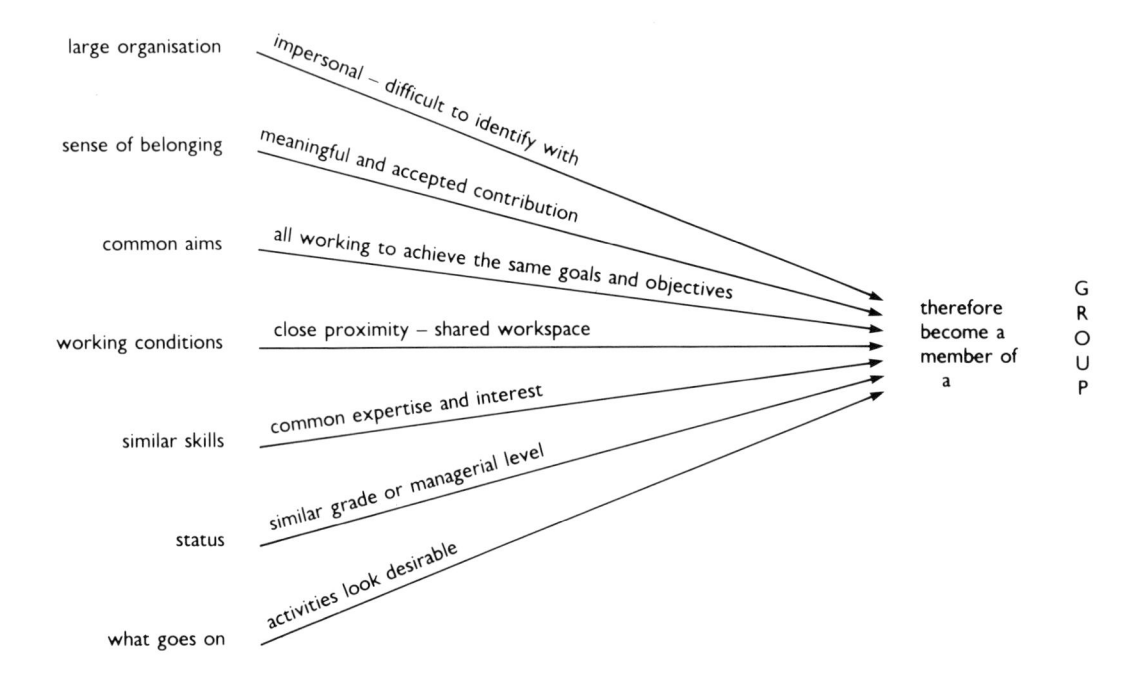

large organisation	impersonal – difficult to identify with	
sense of belonging	meaningful and accepted contribution	
common aims	all working to achieve the same goals and objectives	therefore become a member of a GROUP
working conditions	close proximity – shared workspace	
similar skills	common expertise and interest	
status	similar grade or managerial level	
what goes on	activities look desirable	

ACTIVITY

As stated at the beginning of this chapter, most people prefer to think of themselves as individuals rather than as members of a group or organisation, and you might be one of them! However, as you will have realised from the preceding comments, it is virtually impossible for anyone to exist as a total isolationist and, in any case, being a member of a group does not mean that you are obliged to forfeit your individualism or become a clone.

Think carefully about this very general definition of a group:

> '... a recognisable collection of people, organised formally or informally, whose inter-relationships are based on a range of identifiable characteristics.'

Is such a definition accurate? Does it have any drawbacks?

Task

Produce your own definition of a group (maximum 50 words), bearing in mind the ideas and explanations given in this chapter and your own knowledge of how groups affect your life.

The 'identifiable characteristics' mentioned in the definition given above are outlined in fig. 15.3. Consider the instructions and questions posed in the 'Tasks' column, and produce written commentaries based on your own experiences at work, at college, or in social groups. You should aim to include at least one work-based and one social group, and in your commentaries you should give a balanced picture by discussing a range of formal and informal groups.

Fig. 15.3 Group characteristics

Characteristics

Tasks

IDENTITY — Recognised by members and usually identifiable by outsiders.

1.1 List five groups of which you are or have been a member.
1.2 Classify each group as formal/informal, official/unofficial, organised/unorganised.

CONFORMITY — Members are expected to accept and reflect the group's attitudes, activities and behaviour.

Select one group.
2.1 Do you or did you agree with everything the group does?
2.2 Have you ever *not* participated in group activities? Why?

UNITY — Members are encouraged to present a united front to outsiders, i.e. solidarity.

Select one group.
3.1 Have you ever had to explain why you are/were a member of a particular group?
3.2 Have you ever had to defend/argue in support of a group's activities or behaviour?

PURPOSE — The reason for its existence is either clearly defined, or clearly understood by members, and all activities are geared to this.

Select one group.
4.1 What is/was the main purpose of the group?
4.2 Why did you join?
4.3 What satisfaction do you get out of being a member?
4.4 Are there any secondary activities that the group organises?

CONTROL — Admission to membership and/or expulsion is governed by the members.

Comment on all groups.
5.1 Did you apply to join each group?
5.2 Were you invited to join?
5.3 Have you left any of the groups?
5.4 How formal was the procedure for leaving?
5.5 Why did you leave?

EVOLUTION — Change is constant in response to circumstances and external pressures.

Select one group.
6.1 How many new members of the group have there been in the last six months?
6.2 Have any changes in main activities occurred?
6.3 Have people lost interest in the group? Why?

| | HIERARCHY | Leadership and influence may be formally established or informally recognised, but a hierarchy invariably emerges. |

Comment on all groups

7.1 Who exerts the most influence in any group?

7.2 Is there an elected or appointed leader or committee?

7.3 What is your own 'position'?

7.4 Would you like to hold any other 'position' in the group?

How groups function

In attempting the previous activity you will probably have touched on some of the points dealt with in the following summary, and this should help you relate the theory to your own experience.

It is a fact that large groups tend to split themselves up into smaller groups in which communication and interaction between individuals is easier. The smaller group allows for the quieter and rather shy person to be drawn in to activities or discussions, and for all members to make a useful contribution. But does this mean that a large group is ineffective? Obviously, it depends on the situation, because in some circumstances 'many hands make light work', and in others 'too many cooks spoil the broth'.

In the work situation, it is likely that any group will be subject to certain requirements such as co-ordination, common aims, agreed strategies, etc. Studies have shown that in such circumstances it appears that the larger the group, the greater the degree of co-ordination and control is needed, and this can lead to individual dissatisfaction, an increase in absenteeism and labour turnover, low motivation levels, and greater frequency of error. It is the unenviable task of management to identify optimum group size and help create an efficient working environment.

Within any group, the individuals, their interests and characteristics will help determine its effectiveness. If attitudes, ideas and motivations are similar, stability is relatively easy to maintain; if there is a wide variety of beliefs and approaches, there will be disagreements and possibly conflict, needing a high degree of co-ordination and organisation to create a positive working environment. The formation of group 'norms' will be recognised by all members and they may be informally 'understood' or written down in formal regulations governing activities and behaviour. It is the wish to be accepted which helps to hold the group together, and even the most informal of group requirements is likely to be adhered to because most people need to feel a sense of belonging and do not wish to be seen as being different. The pressure to conform is very strong. Each individual decides the extent to which he or she needs to adapt to fit in with group norms, and, therefore, we all change a little when we join a group. We are influenced by, and in turn influence, others.

Group decision-making

One of the most important (and indefinable) processes in business is that of decision-making. A decision can be made by an individual or a group, but that made by a group is normally more important and more binding than that made by an individual. If *you* make a decision to do something, it is quite easy to change your mind if nobody else is involved. If, however, you are a member of a committee which decides on a course of action, it is not quite so easy to get things changed.

Another aspect of group decision-making is that a number of people acting together are more likely to make high-risk decisions than an individual. The spread of responsibility makes people feel that there is 'safety in numbers' and, therefore, they feel confident that they cannot be blamed personally if anything goes wrong. The dangers of group decision-making stem from the influence that some individuals can exert on others, and from the pressure to conform.

Bearing in mind some of the comments made in this section, it would be quite easy to accept a sweeping generalisation which claimed that a work group which is of optimum operational size, and in which all the members are happy and satisfied, will be highly productive and efficient. However, we have to be realistic, and accept that it is likely to be a rare occurrence that such a 'perfect' group is created. There will usually be strong characters who pull the group in one direction or another, and influential members who persuade others towards particular courses of action. There are always likely to be some points of disagreement, and this in turn can lead to conflict and dissatisfaction if management does not identify the problems and work towards establishing harmonious working relationships. If a strong leader can be identified, who recognises and supports management/group/section objectives, then half the battle is won, and a thorough and sensitive approach to consultation and appraisal can often prevent minor dissatisfactions and disagreements turning into major conflicts.

ACTIVITY

> From the summary of group concepts you have just read, select one area in which you recognise something that has happened to you – at work, in recreational activities, or socially.
>
> Describe your experience, relating it specifically to the ideas dealt with in this part of the chapter, and explaining how it supports or contradicts the basic theories.

Appraisal methods

In Chapter 14, the general reasons for, and benefits of, appraisal schemes were discussed, so at this point, it would be useful to have some idea of how such schemes work. How is appraisal carried out? Practical appraisal means determining when and how the appraisal will be implemented (planning), establishing methods of recording the results (appraisal forms), and conducting an effective face-to-face interview.

There are a number of quite different methods of appraisal, and in the following sections the basic principles, advantages and disadvantages of each are outlined.

The narrative report

The manager/supervisor is asked to write a free-ranging, unstructured 'portrait' of each member of staff, in essay style.

For

The manager has complete freedom.

The manager can decide what to include, what to omit, what to emphasise.

Against

The effectiveness of the appraisal will depend to a certain extent on the communication skills of the manager.

Some managers do not feel competent to write such a report.

The report will be purely subjective and, therefore, open to abuse (likes and dislikes).

There will be a lack of consistency in appraisal reporting throughout the organisation.

Guideline assessment

This is a similar overall assessment, but the manager is asked a series of questions about each required characteristic.

For

Gives a degree of consistency throughout the organisation.

Allows the manager freedom to develop comments within the guidelines.

Against

In practice, the guidelines are often fairly vague, and therefore a thorough appraisal is not evident from the report.

There can be the same problems of subjectivity and communication skills as found with a narrative report.

Grading systems

These simplify the appraisal by listing required characteristics, and requiring the manager to appraise each person within a range of specified assessments. (See example in fig. 15.4.)

For

Appears to encourage consistency of approach throughout the organisation.

Quick to complete.

Requires little narrative comment.

Can accommodate varying degrees of complexity.

Against

Very general classifications.

Difficult to identify how standards have been established and therefore relies on subjective assessments.

Open to prejudice/bias.

Fig. 15.4 Example of a simple grading system.

```
                              2

                              (Tick the appropriate box)

    6  Punctuality         ☐   excellent
                           ☐   good
                           ☐   fair
                           ☐   unsatisfactory

    7  Dependability       ☐   excellent
                           ☐   good
                           ☐   fair
                           ☐   unsatisfactory
```

Merit rating

As with the grading system, this method aims to bring out employees' strengths and weaknesses by asking the manager to review their work in specific areas. Numerical values are often used so that ratings may be added up and employees ranked. (See example in fig. 15.5.)

For

Appears to encourage consistency of approach.

Quick to complete.

Requires little narrative comment.

Can accommodate varying degrees of complexity.

Can be used for ranking employees.

Against

Easy for appraiser to over-rate or under-rate any individual.

Very subjective.

Open to prejudice/bias.

The weak manager may be tempted to classify everybody as 'average'.

Fig. 15.5 Example of a simple merit rating system.

```
PRIVATE/CONFIDENTIAL

            STAFF ASSESSMENT FORM

Employee's name: ...............  Job: ...............
Age: ...................  Dept: ...................
```

	excellent 4	good 3	average 2	poor 1	comment
Performance					
Quantity of work produced			✓		
Quality of work produced	✓				
Technical knowledge		✓			
Knowledge of the job		✓			
Punctuality	✓				
Attendance	✓				
Attitudes					
to supervision		✓			
to fellow employees		✓			
initiative				✓	

Other appraisal techniques

There are variations on these basic systems, and each organisation will have its own requirements and approach. There might be a **forced choice rating system**, in which the simple categories of 'excellent', 'good', 'average', 'poor' are expanded into a series of statements, one of which the appraiser must select – a bit like multiple-choice examination questions! This method encourages the appraiser to think carefully about the person being assessed before making a judgement.

Another possibility is the **appraisal/review**, which can be a mixture of ratings, narrative and free-ranging views. The forms are often divided into sections with 'pointers' to guide the appraiser's thoughts and plenty of space for comments. In a system of this kind we should expect to emphasise such areas as:

- performance during appraisal period
- strengths and weaknesses
- successes and failures
- training requirements
- potential for promotion.

Whilst on the subject of appraisal, it is important to remind you of the Management by Objectives approach, which was discussed in Chapter 14, and which emphasises assessment of employees through their achievement, progress and accomplishments within a defined set of corporate, departmental or sectional objectives.

ACTIVITY

> Collect examples of as many different types of appraisal form as you can find. Obviously, it would be useful to include one from your own organisation, but see how many different examples you can find in text-books and reference books, and take a photocopy of each one to keep in your file.

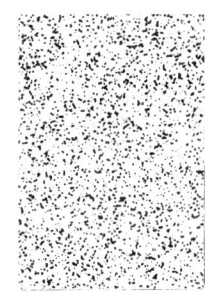

ASSIGNMENT: Waterlane College of Higher Education (2)

Analyse the range of forms you have acquired and, using them as essential reference material, draw up an assessment form which would be suitable for Mr Drysdale to use in his annual appraisal of Miss Syrett. The form should be as detailed as possible, and be designed to give a comprehensive assessment of the employee. Ideally it should be structured in such a way that it would be suitable for use in all appraisals of administrative staff at the Waterlane College of Higher Education.

Appraisal interviews

As you will have gathered, appraisal is an on-going process, and whatever methods are used it should be carried out regularly. Some organisations conduct formal appraisals once a year only; others do it half-yearly. Informal appraisal should take place as the need arises, particularly when targets and target dates have to be met.

In any of these circumstances, the most difficult and often the most crucial activity is the appraisal interview. Not all organisations are willing to discuss their appraisals openly with employees, but it is generally recognised that such an interview is often the best way of finding out not only what the abilities, potential and requirements of the individual are, but also what is wrong with aspects of the organisation's activities or procedures which only someone 'on the job' can identify.

The person conducting such an interview might be an employee's immediate superior/supervisor, or it might be someone even more senior in the organisation. Whoever does it, the interview can develop in a number of ways:

1 the interviewer might feel that the easiest approach is simply to tell the interviewee what assessments and comments have been made about him/her, and **inform** him/her what action is expected to be taken (involvement in courses, training, etc.).

2 a slightly better approach might be for the interviewer to tell the

interviewee what assessments and comments have been made, and then **persuade** him/her that a particular course of action would be beneficial to both the employee and the company.

3. by far the best approach is for the appraisal interview to be a two-way dialogue, in which the interviewee has the opportunity to **discuss** aspects of his/her assessment, put forward explanations, and hopefully identify any areas in which action needs to be taken. He/she should be **encouraged** to talk about the job, work objectives, procedures, frustrations, ambitions, required training needs, etc. A competent interviewer will **control and guide** the interview, **respond positively** to the interviewee's opinions, **stimulate and encourage constructive discussion**, and hopefully **bring the interviewee to a realisation of appropriate solutions** to his/her personal needs.

In an ideal situation, appraisal is most effective and valuable when both the interviewer and the interviewee have had time to think about and analyse the contents of the interviewee's appraisal form *before* the interview. This gives both sides the chance to think problems through and consider possible courses of action carefully. As a result of this approach, the interview should turn out to be constructive and beneficial, and will lead to a much more comprehensive and accurate appraisal report.

Attending an appraisal interview

You will almost certainly have to undergo an appraisal interview in your current job, or in your first job when you leave college, and it is important that you are adequately prepared for it. If you are given an indication beforehand of what people think of you, you can consider the implications and decide what points you want to raise. You might be asked to complete a self-appraisal form which will be designed to help you clarify your thoughts, and give your superiors some idea of how you feel you are performing in the job. If such preparation is not available to you, you would be well advised to make yourself aware of what type of information will be considered important.

First of all, make sure you know what the aim of the appraisal meeting/interview is.

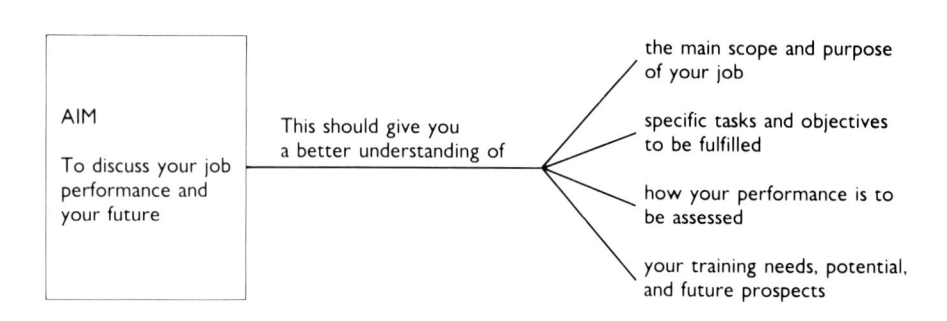

Fig. 15.6

AIM — To discuss your job performance and your future	This should give you a better understanding of	the main scope and purpose of your job
		specific tasks and objectives to be fulfilled
		how your performance is to be assessed
		your training needs, potential, and future prospects

Secondly, make sure that you are prepared to respond positively (not necessarily in the affirmative!) to basic questions such as:

Do you have a job-description which is up-to-date?
Do you understand all aspects of the job?
Are you fully aware of what is required of you?
Are you currently working to an agreed plan?
Have you discussed your progress with anyone recently?
Has there been any improvement in your performance since your last appraisal?

Remember, whether you answer 'yes or 'no' to any of these, you must be prepared to discuss, explain and justify your comments.

Finally, there are a number of areas in which you must be ready to make your feelings known, and about which you should be able to talk constructively. It is important, for example, to make sure your appraiser knows of any activities you have been involved in or any of your accomplishments which show that you have put effort into your job above and beyond the strict limits of the job-description. It is equally important to identify any areas in which you have experienced difficulties, aspects of the job you have performed particularly well, tasks you have *not* enjoyed, and to what degree you feel that the skills, knowledge and aptitudes you have are effectively utilised. It can also be useful to have thought about any particular training you feel you need, or courses you think would help improve your job-performance and prepare you for the next stage of your career.

Obviously, you can't walk into the appraisal interview and immediately 'take it over', but you will often find that it is necessary to guide the conversation, or lead the discussion into areas you think it is important to consider.

If you're lucky, you will be interviewed by a supervisor or manager who is experienced in conducting such appraisals, and who has developed a range of techniques which will ensure that the interview runs smoothly, with little or no conflict, and based on positive, constructive, two-way dialogue. You will, of course, present yourself punctually, and appropriately dressed (even if this does mean that you have to cut short your lunch time and wear less casual clothes than usual!). You might be able to recognise some of the approaches shown in fig. 15.7.

Fig. 15.7

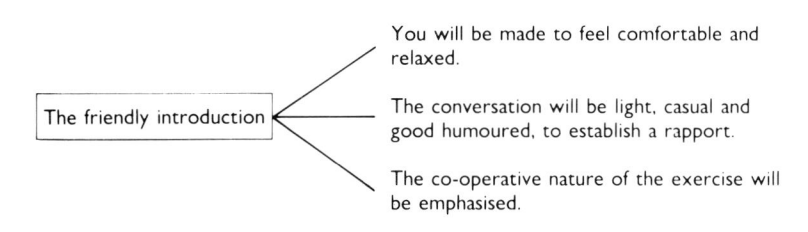

The friendly introduction
- You will be made to feel comfortable and relaxed.
- The conversation will be light, casual and good humoured, to establish a rapport.
- The co-operative nature of the exercise will be emphasised.

Establishing the aim

- The purpose of the meeting will be re-stated.
- The objectives of the exercise will be clarified.

The main discussion

- You might be asked to comment on the validity of your job description in the light of the job you are doing.
- You might be asked to identify any particular successes or failures you have had.
- You might notice that, although the interviewer is careful to give the management point of view, he/she does not directly contradict you or allow an argument to develop.
- You will be encouraged to speak openly, and the good interviewer will respond to your comments, noting down any important issues raised.
- You will be told what formal assessments have been made of you prior to the interview.
- You will discuss progress, receive acknowledgement of your good work, and have any weak areas identified.
- You will be given the opportunity to suggest any training/courses which would benefit you, particularly if specific areas of improvement or change are seen to be desirable. The interviewer might have definite recommendations to make and advice to give you.
- Your future prospects/career development will often be something you have to raise, but the good interviewer will be prepared to discuss this realistically.

The conclusion

- The interviewer will aim to end the meeting on a positive note, with a high degree of agreement between you.
- It will be important to establish goals and agree the timescale within which they should be achieved.
- You will be left in no doubt as to what the company thinks of you, what expectations you have for the future, and what you have to do to be successful.

The follow-up

- A final written appraisal (in whatever form is appropriate to your organisation) will be produced as a result of the interview.
- You will be given an opportunity to see the final result, raise any points that need clarification, and will be expected to sign the document.
- Any action discussed and agreed at the meeting relating to training/courses will be implemented as soon as practicable.

If these principles are followed, a manager or supervisor will be making a determined effort to perform this aspect of his/her job effectively, to the benefit of the employee and the organisation. If he/she is successful, good human (and industrial) relations will be encouraged, and a dynamic work environment can be created.

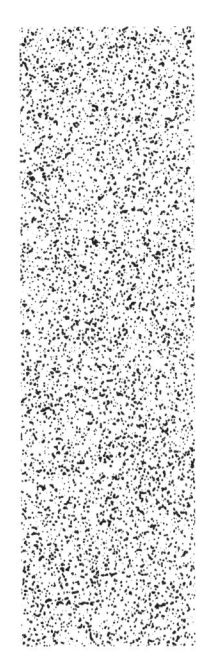

ASSIGNMENT: Waterlane College of Higher Education (3)

Task 1

In the light of the information you have dealt with in this chapter, you might have a clearer insight into some of the problems that arose in the Office Services section. Re-read the original case sketch and produce written answers to discussion points 1 and 5.

Task 2

Answer either 1 or 2.

1 If you were Miss Syrett, how would you prepare yourself for this interview? It is not a formal appraisal interview, but it would be advisable for you to be ready for anything, and be prepared to emphasise your own opinions on the situation, making sure that you try to show yourself in the best possible light.
2 Put yourself in the position of Mr Drysdale, having to interview Miss Syrett in the circumstances described. How would you want the interview to develop? Describe how you would handle the various stages: the first few minutes; introducing the problem; guiding the discussion; allowing fair time for responses; identifying solutions; concluding the interview.

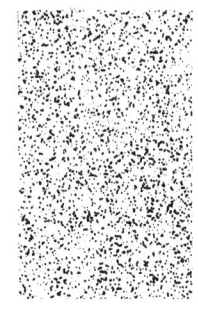

ASSIGNMENT: Waterlane College of Higher Education (4)

Within your course group, identify another member who has worked on a different section of Task 2 in the previous assignment, and conduct a simulated interview between Mr Drysdale and Miss Syrett. A ten-minute time limit should be put on the interview, and other members of the group should be encouraged to analyse and comment upon the performance in a tutor-led discussion. If facilities are available to make a video recording of the interview, this can be very useful in reinforcing discussion points and stimulating positive analysis.

SECTION 4

The job

CHAPTER 16

The job and the individual

In previous sections of this book you have been introduced to some ideas and activities relating to a range of business concepts which affect the performance of a job, including motivation, organisation and methods, management styles, group dynamics, appraisal systems and 'change'. Now we must look at the job itself, and it is not difficult to see that workers' perceptions of their jobs will influence their attitudes and behaviour. If a job is believed to be lacking in certain desirable attributes, the result can be feelings of dissatisfaction and, sometimes, disruptive behaviour. If a job is interesting, varied, and gives the performer a degree of responsibility and autonomy the results can be very different, encouraging a conscientious and committed approach to work. Therefore, the design of a job is very important and the implementation of ideas such as job rotation, job enlargement and job enrichment can move some way towards creating a feeling of job satisfaction.

In many working situations the main criterion for job design has usually been to minimise the immediate costs of performing the operation and increase productivity, with little consideration being given to the needs of the individual worker. It's no wonder that some organisations suffer from high absenteeism, high turnover of staff and consequent increases in operational costs. Obviously, it is good business practice to cut costs and increase output, but one of the bases for achieving this should ideally be through a better motivated and more satisfied workforce.

When change is necessary

The most difficult task for any organisation is to identify when changes are necessary, and it is a function of management to be sensitive to the tell-tale signs that things are not entirely satisfactory on the shop-floor, amongst the administrative staff, or even amongst supervisory staff and middle management. Regular consultation with employees and union representatives will usually reveal any undercurrents of dissatisfaction, but there may also be more general problems which point to the need for change. Fig. 16.1 suggests some of these.

When the need for change has been identified, there are certain principles that need to be borne in mind if any attempt to re-design or restructure work is to be made. These revolve around the ideal require-

Fig. 16.1

Symptoms shown in circle: low productivity, high staff turnover, requests for transfer, lateness, complaints from employees, poor quality of output, low morale, high absenteeism, difficulties in recruiting, breaks in production

ments of a well-designed job. Obviously, there are considerations relating to the general work environment (e.g. physical factors such as heating, lighting, decor, atmosphere, noise, etc.) and the inter-relationship of work groups, sections and departments, but the job itself is a primary influence on the individual worker and in a perfect situation should have as many of the characteristics shown in fig. 16.2 as possible.

Fig. 16.2

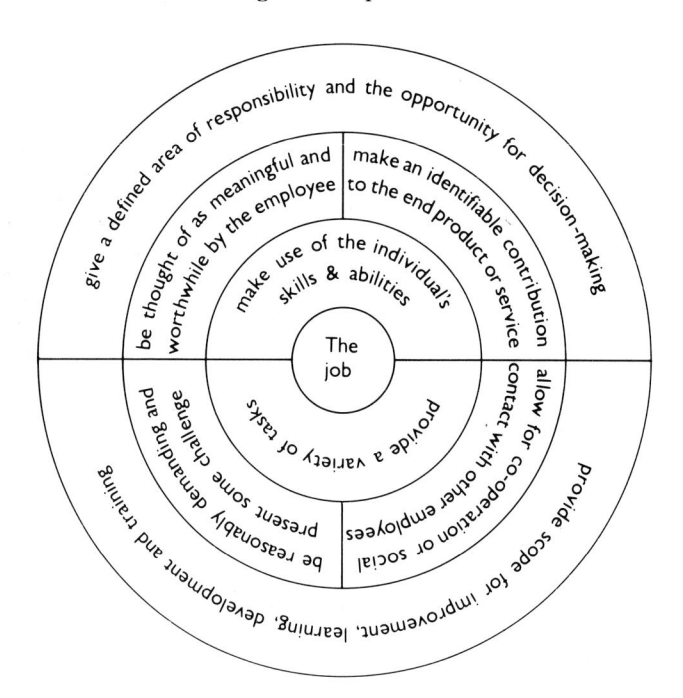

Characteristics of the job (shown around central circle "The job"): give a defined area of responsibility and the opportunity for decision-making; be thought of as meaningful and worthwhile by the employee; make an identifiable contribution to the end product or service; make use of the individual's skills & abilities; provide a variety of tasks; allow for co-operation or social contact with other employees; provide scope for improvement, learning, development and training; be reasonably demanding and present some challenge

Job rotation

One of the most common methods of giving employees more variety in work activity, and at the same time expanding the range of knowledge and skills they can offer, is **job rotation**. This 'job swapping' can bring a greater understanding of the range of operations in which an organisation is involved, and help employees recognise the importance of their jobs in the sequence of activities. From the company's point of view, other advantages are that the flexibility of the workforce is increased and a more efficient utilisation of staff is possible.

Despite the apparent benefits, job rotation has its limitations, because the basic level of work in which the employee is engaged remains the same, and there are difficulties of implementation where any 'demarcation' situation exists. Because of this, job rotation should be introduced with great care and forethought, after adequate consultation with the individuals concerned and union representatives.

Job enlargement

Another way of increasing interest and involvement is through **job enlargement**. Sometimes referred to as 'horizontal job-building', it involves expanding the scope of duties for which one person is responsible. In one sense, it is the opposite of extreme specialisation (e.g. where one clerk is responsible for opening letters; another extracts the contents; another identifies the recipient; and a fourth puts the contents into the appropriate tray!). Such enlargement encourages staff to perform a range of activities related to their main job and hopefully, avoids the boredom of constantly repeating the same task, and increases satisfaction by giving the employee more awareness of, and responsibility for, a broader span of achievement.

Job enrichment

Whereas job enlargement is a horizontal broadening process, **job enrichment** can be regarded as a vertical expansion of an individual's responsibilities. It need not necessarily involve an increase in the number of tasks an individual has to perform, but it does aim to involve the employee in decision-making and consultative processes, as well as introducing the principle of accountability. Such a development could mean the removal of constant supervisory control, more freedom in work practices, involvement in more complex procedures, more regular assessment/appraisal/review meetings, and more employee involvement in target setting, establishing objectives, and objective reviews of performance.

ACTIVITY

> You should be able to complete this activity if you are currently employed in a full-time or part-time job, or if you have access to someone who is willing to discuss their job in detail, including the tasks involved and the way in which their organisation works. Whichever of these situations you can identify with, the first task is to establish the main purpose of the job, and then suggest ways in which the work situation could be improved by job enlargement and job enrichment. The 'answers' to this activity can be presented as a commentary and a chart, and may be used as a basis for in-class discussion to determine the extent to which these concepts can be applied to different types of jobs and real work situations.
>
> Fig. 16.3 gives an indication of how your information can be structured, and guidelines are incorporated to give you some idea of contents.

Fig. 16.3

JOB TITLE ....

Main purpose of job

This should outline the main aim of the job and how it fits into the sequence of activities in the Section/Department/Organisation.

Role of the Supervisor/Section Head

What is he/she responsible for? What direct contact is there with the job holder? Who decides who shall do what? To whom is he/she responsible?

Extent of discussion/consultation between job holder and Supervisor/Section Head

Daily instructions? Direct supervision? Checking of work? Regular appraisal? Informal chats? Formal consultation/planning?

Required contact with others

Outline the extent to which co-operation with other staff, or reliance on other staff, affects the performance of the tasks involved in the job. For example, do you have to work in conjunction with someone else? Do you have to consult a Supervisor/Section Head? Is someone else waiting for your 'work' to be passed on to them? etc, etc.

THE JOB

Main tasks

Specify the range of tasks involved

_____
_____
_____
_____

Ways in which the job could be 'enlarged'

Suggest ways in which the job could be made more satisfying by incorporating a wider range of activities so that, for example, the job holder could complete a whole process rather than one part of it. Could the number of tasks be reduced, but the breadth of content increased? Make *specific* suggestions.

Ways in which the job could be enriched

Remember that 'enrichment' is vertical expansion, increasing responsibility and accountability, and involving the job holder in the decision-making process. Can you see how this can be done with the particular job you are analysing here?

The job and the individual 177

ASSIGNMENT: Agrimoor Fabrications, Ltd.

Note: This composite assignment draws on knowledge and skills from a number of areas dealt with in your course so far. It will be necessary to re-read and revise certain key areas.

Background information

Agrimoor Fabrications has been established for a number of years, and specialises in the manufacture of 'pattern' replacement parts for a comprehensive range of agricultural machinery. In addition, a profitable sideline has developed in manufacturing a limited range of small, specially designed, multi-function machines for the horticultural market.

The Managing Director has the role of Chief Executive, and, with the help of a Personal Assistant, is in charge of the day-to-day running of the whole organisation, which is based around five functional departments.

Each of these departments has a Director at its head, and the five areas covered are Personnel, Production, Finance, Legal and Administration, and Marketing. The head of the L & A department has a slightly different designation – 'Director and Secretary' – but has equal status with other Heads.

In the Marketing Department there are five sections dealing with Market Research, Publicity, Distribution, Export Sales, and Home Sales, and a sixth which is a general Sales Office. Each section has a Manager, and there are further divisions as follows: Market Research is sub-divided into Market Research and Customer Research; Publicity is sub-divided into Sales Promotions, Advertising and Public Relations; Export Sales is divided into three geographical Sales areas; the Distribution Section has Transport and Warehouse sub-sections; Home Sales is split geographically, with six areas; and the Sales Office has Statistics, Records, Order Processing and Customer Service. In the Marketing Department and the Production Department the sub-sections are headed by Assistant Managers, who all have the same status.

Situation

You have completed eighteen months of a two-year training period with Business Advisors, Ltd, a firm of Consultants who have been called in by Agrimoor to conduct a viability study for the expansion of their operation. As a preliminary to visiting the company, the Senior Consultant, Susan Johnson, calls you in and gives you the oral instructions in Task 1.

Task 1

'Look, I know we haven't got a complete run-down on the structure of Agrimoor, except for the Buying Division, but draw up an organisation chart to show what we have got, so that I have some idea of how the place works! Use our standard horizontal/lateral format, and make it as comprehensive as you can.'

Within a few days of starting the main study of Agrimoor, it becomes obvious that the general management is a little lax, and that in some areas the current administrative arrangements have developed in a fairly haphazard way as the company has grown. Most of the directors do not have extensive business experience and are largely unaware of how paperwork could be reduced by using multiple sets, for example. Susan Johnson feels that the first step is to produce a statement of how basic procedures could be performed more efficiently if multiple sets were used. The aim is to identify the major areas in which such a system would be beneficial, and outline the main advantages.

Task 2

Susan Johnson asks you to draft the statement, and suggests that a specimen invoice document should be designed and included as an appendix together with an explanation of what copies would be generated with this document, and the purpose of each. Put this information together as an **information sheet**, appropriately structured and presented.

Notes for guidance

An effective layout is essential to easy comprehension, and therefore you should make full use of the schematic or systematic method of presentation outlined in Chapter 15. The information sheet is initially for the attention of Ms Johnson.

Your investigations lead you into looking closely at Agrimoor's Purchasing system, and you conclude that the operation could be made much more efficient if modern techniques were introduced to streamline the procedures.

Task 3

Submit a memorandum to Ms Johnson stating your conclusions, and outlining the steps in designing an effective information system for Purchasing. You should consider and suggest ways in which a computer system could assist the purchasing function.

When Ms Johnson receives your memo it confirms her own opinion that there are a number of areas in which the Agrimoor operation could be made more efficient. She decides that it would be useful to conduct an O & M survey in certain sections, but believes that this could meet with opposition from some senior and supervisory staff. In order to avoid any confrontation, she plans to consult such staff individually, and then arrange a seminar during working hours at which she will give a short introductory talk on O & M, and allow them to raise any questions/concerns they might have.

Task 4

Draw up notes for the talk she will give, ensuring that you include the main aims of an O & M survey, and an outline of the main stages of such a survey. Indicate clearly any visual aids or supportive material she would need.

During your work on the Agrimoor consultation, you have noticed that there is some dissatisfaction amongst some sections of the workforce, and you feel that this is partly due to boredom, lack of variety and limited responsibility in their jobs. This gets you thinking about motivation in general, and you decide to submit an article to the magazine *Management in Action*, which is published quarterly by the Association of Professional Consultants.

Task 5

Write the article entitled 'There's no need for a job to be boring'. The main aim is to explain or demonstrate how job rotation, enrichment and enlargement techniques can increase motivation in a firm.

CHAPTER 17

Filling a vacancy

The recruitment and selection of staff is a complex and difficult task, and the main aim must always be to acquire an employee who will give the organisation what it wants from a particular job. Appointing the wrong person can have disastrous effects on the general team spirit and morale if conflicts and disagreements become the norm, or if the appointee's performance in-post is not up to standard. It is much easier to employ somebody than it is to get rid of them, so it is crucial that every step is taken to ensure that the appointment is necessary in the first place, and that the right person gets the job.

If a vacancy occurs because someone is leaving the organisation, the first thing a manager must do is find out why the person is leaving. A termination interview should not be an acrimonious 'mud-slinging' exercise but should be a positive move by the organisation to discover if there are any problems which have caused the employee to become dissatisfied with the job. Confidentiality must be guaranteed, frank discussion should be encouraged, and action should be taken as soon as possible to put right any identified faults in organisational structure or operation.

Job analysis

Whether the vacancy is for an established post, or whether it is a new post, it must be agreed that there *is* a vacancy, i.e. that there is a need for somone to carry out particular responsibilities. Once this is established, the best starting point is to go back to basics and decide what the job actually involves and requires. **Job analysis** is the total process of investigating and evaluating a job, and systematically recording the details. Fig. 17.1 shows the major considerations in such an analysis, but it should be borne in mind that the final result might indicate many more things, including similarity to other jobs, status, rewards, and worker-satisfaction levels.

In carrying out a job analysis, there is no required format for recording the information, but it is advisable to adopt a systematic approach and specifically identify the areas indicated in fig. 17.1. In addition there are some general questions that need to be asked, and it is a good idea to get the answers from the current job-holder *and* his/her supervisor or manager, so that a balanced view can be achieved.

Fig. 17.1 Aspects considered in job analysis.

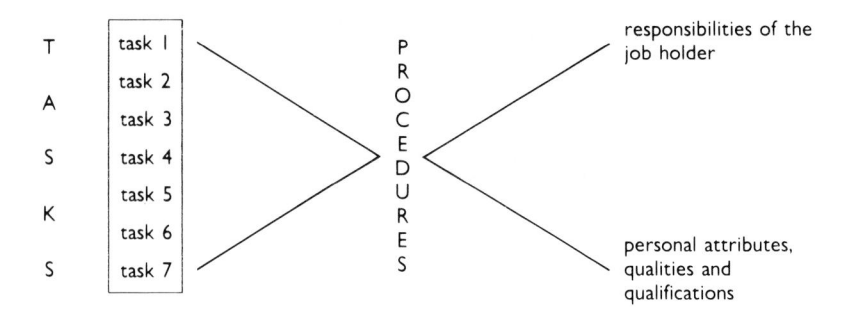

```
          task 1                              responsibilities of the
          task 2          P                   job holder
T         task 3          R
A                         O
S         task 4          C
K         task 5          E
S                         D
          task 6          U
          task 7          R
                          E                   personal attributes,
                          S                   qualities and
                                              qualifications
```

Questions

What is the exact job title?

In which Section/Department/Branch is the job based?

To whom will the job holder be responsible?

What is the overall purpose of the job?

Does the job holder have specific responsibilities for other staff, money, materials?

What are the consequences of his/her decisions in these areas?

What other people does the job holder work with?

What are the terms and conditions of the job – salary, hours, overtime, etc.?

What are the future career prospects for the holder of this job?

To give you an idea of some of the difficulties involved in producing an accurate job analysis, complete the following activity. If you are a full-time student, you can base your answers on any part-time job you have, *or* on the job of a friend with whom you have regular contact, and who will be willing to discuss work with you. If you are currently employed, the activity should pose no problem.

ACTIVITY

> Using your own job as the basis for your presentation, produce a detailed analysis of the **tasks** you are expected to perform as part of your normal duties. Produce your answer in tabular form (fig. 17.2), clarifying your thought further by indicating in Column 2 what specific procedure(s) the tasks are related to, and in Column 3 giving details of what tasks you think your Supervisor/Section Head/Manager expects of you. The aim is to see whether or not your concept of the job agrees with the way the organisation sees it.

Fig. 17.2

Tasks	General procedure	Management view of job
1		
2		
3		
4		

Job description

In any situation where a post has to be filled, the next step is to use the job analysis information as the basis for drawing up a **job specification**. For some reason, there is often confusion over what this phrase means, and people loosely use terms like 'job description', 'job definition', 'personnel specification', without being sure exactly what type of information they are talking about. For our purposes, the situation is easily clarified by referring to the following 'formula'.

$$JD + PS = JS$$

(job description)   (personnel specification)   (job specification)

A **job description** stresses job content, i.e. the duties and responsibilities involved in a job, sometimes extending to the skills and knowledge needed to perform the stated task. There are many different formats for job descriptions, and some are more detailed than others. The type of job description sent to an applicant for a post will usually be an 'outline', concentrating on the general areas of responsibility. Fig. 17.3 gives an example of this.

When someone has been appointed to a post, it might be desirable to give a little more detail of specific tasks in each of the general areas.

Fig. 17.4 gives an example of what can be referred to as 'detailed' job description and you will notice that a PIE (Performance is Effective) column is included to give the postholder an awareness of what has to be achieved to perform the job successfully. This type of job description would normally only be used *within* an organisation, and the example is based on the post of Group Buyer for a large Department Store chain.

Fig. 17.3 'Outline' job description.

PRIMTHORPE CITY COUNCIL

JOB DESCRIPTION

Job title and grade	:	Administrative Officer AO 2/3
Post no	:	12/03/702
Department	:	Entertainments
Division	:	Administration
Responsible to	:	City Entertainments Officer and Principal City Entertainments Officer
Responsible for	:	2 Clerical Assistants
Main purpose of job	:	Provision of administrative support services of a confidential nature to the specified Officers.

Duties and responsibilities

1. Prepare agenda items for committees and Chief Officer group meetings and take such follow up action as may be required.
2. Attend meetings.
3. Collate information for public inquiries personally conducted by the City Entertainments Officer.
4. Research information as required by Chief Officer, together with correspondence and enquiries.
5. Arrange accommodation, issuing rail warrants and preparing/processing claims for officers attending courses, etc.
6. Process documentation in connection with vacancies.

The postholder must undertake other duties appropriate to the grading of the post as required.

Fig. 17.4 'Detailed' job description.

British D & H Plc

Job description

Job title	:	Group Buyer
Division	:	Ladies' Fashion
Responsible to	:	Group Merchandise Controller
Responsible for	:	Deputy Group Buyer, 4 Store Buyers

Main purpose	: To select and buy merchandise of suitable quality at a competitive price, and in realistic quantity, to meet customer demand in Group stores; to ensure that this merchandise produces an acceptable stock-turn, thereby meeting the fulfilled gross profit targets set.

Main duties and responsibilities	Performance is effective
1 Knowledge of range, product and demand 1.1 To be aware of, and keep up to date with, relevant manufacturers' current and future merchandise ranges. 1.2 To be fully aware of sales patterns in the Stores, and other factors which assist in determining stock-buying requirements. 1.3 To liaise closely with store and departmental management about stock lines to meet customer demand — present and future. 1.4 To liaise closely with store and departmental management to keep them up-to-date with merchandise knowledge.	When knowledge of available merchandise is thorough and continuously updated; when this knowledge is communicated to store management; when a close liaison with store management and an analysis of sales figures promotes an awareness of — and insight into — present and future customer demand.
2 Sales 2.1 To liaise with Departmental Sales Managers and assist them in securing the highest possible stock-turn and sales growth. 2.2 To advise on the advertising of special 'promotions'. 2.3 To take appropriate action to 'dispose' of stocks which are giving an unacceptable stock-turn. 2.4 To visit each store regularly to discuss sales of merchandise with the Departmental Managers, and to advise on any display or merchandising techniques which would assist the departmental sales performance.	When sales of merchandise are maximised in every store, and an acceptable stock-turn produced throughout the range.

3 Buying	
3.1 To purchase the correct stock and secure the right stock-mix to meet customer demand, and the Group's stock-turn requirements, within the pre-determined budget.	When merchandise is purchased on the best terms and retailed at a competitive price. When financial purchasing limits are not exceeded and the required gross profit margin is achieved. When a suitable stock balance is maintained at all times.
3.2 To negotiate the most preferential buying prices.	
3.3 To buy only within the set 'open to buy' limits at all times.	
3.4 To keep suppliers to a minimum.	
3.5 To research new suppliers to seek improved terms or new merchandise ranges.	
4 Pricing	
4.1 To calculate and set selling prices in accordance with the required gross profit margin whilst remaining competitive with the retail market.	
5 Stock levels	
5.1 To ensure that stock is purchased proportionate to known sales statistics, and that stocks do not increase or decrease to unacceptable levels.	When each store is supplied with a realistic stock level to meet known sales demand.
6 Administration	
6.1 To draw up and process all orders for merchandise in accordance with Group Systems.	When all documentation concerned is completed legibly, correctly, and by the due date. When the Merchandising Controller receives the statistics required in good time.
6.2 To complete all relevant documentation in relation to the purchase, allocation, delivery (and, if necessary, return) of new stock.	
6.3 To complete all relevant documentation for the transfer of stock when required.	
6.4 To provide statistics on orders, purchases, stock-turn, gross profit, and sales, as required by the Merchandising Controller.	

Personnel specification

Another aspect of assessing prospective appointees to any post is to determine whether or not they have the necessary personal qualities to perform the duties effectively, and fit in with the existing workforce. A **personnel specification** is designed to identify what qualities are essential or desirable, and one common method of presentation is to base it around the 'Seven Point Plan' produced by Alec Rodger at the National Institute of Industrial Psychology. The seven points can be used to indicate the main areas of a personnel specification, as shown in the example in fig. 17.6. The information incorporated in each section comes from considering questions such as those in fig. 17.5.

Fig. 17.5 The seven point plan.

1 **Physical makeup**	2 **Attainments**
What does the job demand in the way of general health, physical strength, stamina, eyesight, hearing, speech, etc? Appearance? Age?	What general education, technical knowledge, specialised training and relevant experience are required?

4 **Special aptitudes**	3 **General intelligence**
What special aptitudes are required, such as mechanical skills, aptitude with figures, verbal expression, creative talents, clerical skills, manipulative skills?	What level of reasoning and learning ability is required?

	5 **Interests**
6 **Disposition**	Are there any general interests which are likely to affect the performance of the job or be relevant to job success – e.g. physical/outdoor activities, artistic expression, interest in constructing or repairing things?
To what extent is there a requirement to get on with people? Is initiative required? Will the job holder have to work alone? Accept responsibility? Work under pressure? Be persistent? Influence others?	7 **Circumstances**
	What domestic circumstances are relevant? What distances have to be travelled? Could overtime be worked? Is spouse's occupation relevant? Any brothers/sisters, etc?

When drawing up a personnel specification, it can be useful to incorporate a 'contra-indications' section to indicate anything particular which could exclude a person from being considered for the job. You will notice that in the example some of the headings are slightly different, but the information in each section is the same as in the seven point plan.

Fig. 17.6 Example of a personnel specification for a Personal Assistant.

Personnel specification

Qualities	Contra-indications

1 Physical characteristics

    (a) overall physical fitness
    (b) 25–30 years of age
    (c) smart appearance

any permanent debilitating illness; under 22/over 50

2 Qualifications/experience

    (a) preferably post-graduate Arts
    (b) certainly post 'A' level
    (c) Personal Secretary/Assistant qualification
    (d) typing stage III; Shorthand 120 wpm
    (e) previous administrative/supervisory experience

3 General intelligence

    (a) able to interpret information/instructions
    (b) able to make objective decisions
    (c) able to organise and work on own initiative
    (d) able to learn and implement established procedures

4 Special aptitudes

    (a) able to compose specialist communications
    (b) high degree of oral competence
    (c) tactful and diplomatic
    (d) able to drive

abrupt manner; poor speech quality

6 Special characteristics/personal qualities

    (a) ability to mix/get on well with all types of people
    (b) ability to work under pressure
    (c) persuasive/logical in argument
    (d) ability to delegate routine work

social isolate/loner

over-emotional; over-sensitive

remote

7 Circumstances

    (a) no excessive family commitments
    (b) free to travel
    (c) able to work flexible hours
    (d) lives within easy commuting distance of the office
    (e) not likely to have to move from the area
    (f) prepared to work overtime/extended hours when necessary

very young children

spouse mobile in job

lives too far from work

family commitments making overtime impossible

Another common format is the 'tabular' presentation illustrated in fig. 17.7.

The information is basically the same except that a distinction is made between 'desirable' and 'essential' qualities.

Legal note

When drawing up job descriptions and personnel specifications, the organisation must avoid **unfair** discrimination. It is obviously quite legal for an employer to discriminate in favour of the best candidate, but only in rare cases can it be specified in advance that – irrespective of qualifications – the job will go to a member of a particular sex, or race. There is also an Act of Parliament which aims to ensure that, where men and women do the same or similar work, they should be paid at the same rates.

Fig. 17.7 Tabular personnel specification.

PERSONNEL SPECIFICATION

Job title: Audio Typist

Attributes	Essential	Desirable	Contra-indictions
1 Physical	Over 20 years old. Good health; normal vision and hearing. Presentable in appearance.	Over 24 years old. Very good personal presentation and suitable for front-office work if required.	
2 Attainments	General education to GCSE standard. Specific audio-typing qualification.	GCSE – A, B or C grade pass in English. RSA 2 typing. RSA 2 Office Practice or similar.	
3 General intelligence	Average. Ability to comprehend and follow instructions. Show initiative and have the confidence to work without constant supervision.		
4 Special aptitudes	Typing speed 40 wpm. Accurate and generally well-presented work.	Typing speed 50 wpm. Immaculate presentation and high level of grammatical accuracy.	Inability to spell correctly.

5	Interests	Irrelevant as long as normal hours are not affected.	Some outside interests at least (indicates a balanced personality).	
6	Disposition	Able to get on well as a member of a team; conscientious; reliable; punctual.	Willing to train as word processor operator.	Introvert; a 'loner'.
7	Circumstances	Available to work a normal working day. Stable home background. Easy access to and from work.	Able to work overtime when required.	

ACTIVITY

> Employment law is a complex area, but there are certain established Acts of Parliament which relate to discrimination. Research this area and produce an **information sheet** outlining the main provisions of *three* major Acts, making sure you include such sensitive areas as race/religion, sex and pay.

Job specification

As shown in the 'formula' earlier in this chapter, a full job specification is a document which combines the job description with the personnel specification. They are simply put together to give a complete picture of the organisation's requirements in respect of a particular post, and to provide a sound basis for initial recruitment procedures and selection interviewing.

ASSIGNMENT: 'Headhunting' (1)

Note: This assignment will be assessed in conjunction with 'Headhunting' (2) at the end of the chapter.

A senior manager in your organisation is losing his Personal Secretary in the near future, and is very concerned about getting a replacement who will be as competent and efficient, and on whom he can rely to run his office effectively when he is away. He knows who he would like for the post, but she currently works for the Personnel Manager of another company in the area. The problem is, how to get her to apply for the job, and how to make sure that the job details are presented in such a way that she would be an ideal applicant. He comes up with the idea of using you as an intermediary, and suggests

Filling a vacancy

that you should arrange a meeting with her, preferably over lunch, and find out exactly what her present job involves, so that you can draw up a job specification which not only meets his needs, but also embodies duties and responsibilities she is currently performing. He makes it clear that he is certainly prepared to guarantee her an increased salary, and conditions that are at least equal to those she enjoys at the moment.

You manage to arrange the meeting, and, during lunch, ask Barbara Milson to outline the main aspects of her present job.

'Well, there is a basic requirement to have excellent secretarial skills, and be able to use shorthand or audio machines to produce various types of communication. I'm often simply left with a range of instructions, either in note-form or on tape, and expected to implement them forthwith! Obviously, all incoming mail comes through me, and much of the routine stuff I can deal with without reference to Mary, my boss. Anything which requires her attention is passed to her in order of priority, and when the responses are complete, they go back to her for signing. Copies of all correspondence have to be filed, but I have Jean, a clerk-typist to do this. I set up the filing systems originally, and now simply supervise and monitor Jean's work.

Another area which I consider a separate responsibility is that of specialist communications – you know the sort of thing: press releases; notes for briefings; drafts of articles, leaflets or advertisements; conference programmes; circular letters; invitations, etc. Mary always gives me fairly detailed instructions and guidance on what she wants, but I find it quite a demanding task.

There's plenty of general administration to keep me busy – as if I need to be kept busy! I'm constantly dealing with queries and problems coming through from other departments and sections. It's important to keep channels of communication open and I often have to smooth things over when people get 'uptight'. The day-to-day business of Personnel is quite varied and I have to plan, organise and control all the routine activities. With all this going on I still have a main responsibility to Mary, who can be very demanding and quite short-tempered at times. She insists that I maintain her diary meticulously, ensuring that she is not over-booked or double-booked, and that her commitments are kept to a practical level. It's also important to establish priorities!

As far as the general work is concerned, confidentiality and security of information must be ensured at all times – you know what people are like when things like personnel records are involved! Probably the most boring part of my work is running the petty cash 'Imprest' system – it's about the only bit I don't like. One of the best parts of my job is the special responsibilities I have for the organisation of meetings, conferences, arranging interviews, scheduling appointments and attending meetings as Minutes Secretary. It means I'm involved in all the main decision-making processes, and generally know what's going on throughout the company. Another interesting part of the job is arranging visits abroad for anyone who has to travel on behalf of the company – booking hotels, planning itineraries, and giving my languages a bit of an airing when I ring different countries to make bookings or arrange meetings. Part of my training involved a Secretarial linguist's crash-course, so I welcome any opportunity to practise! Also, my degree was in Modern Languages and it's quite nice to draw on all that academic training and make some use of it.

I should think I've said enough to make you think I run the company, but there are limits to my authority and responsibilities! For example, any decisions which go beyond the actual running of the Personnel Office must be referred to Mary, and the same applies to anything which affects or relates to company policy. If Mary is away, any such decisions must be referred to John Fosdyke, the Company Secretary, or Patricia Winsdale, the M.D. They're the only ones who can give authorisation for any action to be taken.'

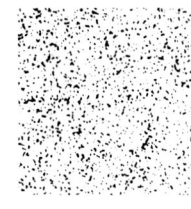

After lunch you go back to the office and after a short briefing session with your senior manager, he asks you to draft a full job specification for his 'new' Personal Secretary's job. He suggests that a 'detailed' job description, incorporating a PIE column, would be useful, and that the personnel specification should include any contra-indications. It's pretty obvious from your conversation with Barbara Milson that the actual job description can be structured according to general areas of responsibility, such as Office Skills, Specialist Communications, Administration, Special Responsibilities and Limit of Authority.

Advertising the job

Once the preliminary documentation has been completed, the next important step is to **advertise the post**. You will have considered the job and the type of person required, and you now have to consider how best to get the right person to apply for the job!

Any advertisement will be fairly specific in content because it will be aimed at a particular audience, i.e. those people who meet the criteria established for the post and who want to apply. The aim of an advertisement is to get as large a response as possible from suitable candidates, and employers have a range of media through which they can contact those who might be interested (see fig. 17.8). If the organisation is big enough, some posts might be advertised internally.

Fig. 17.8

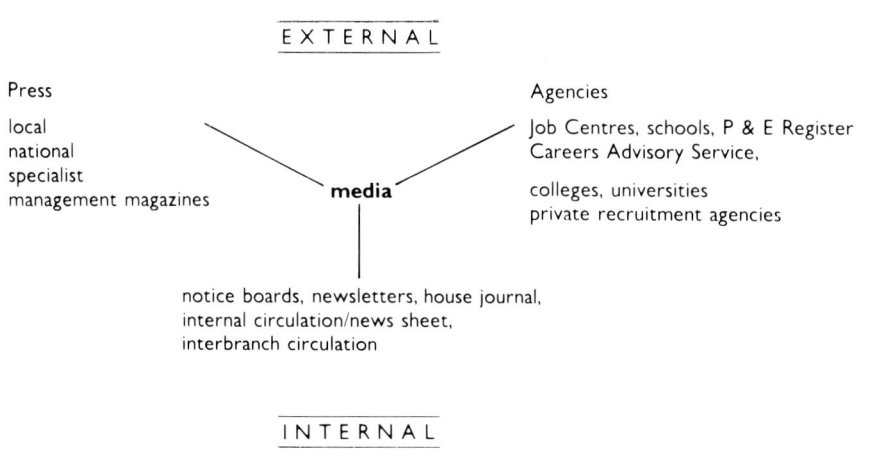

EXTERNAL

Press
local
national
specialist
management magazines

Agencies
Job Centres, schools, P & E Register
Careers Advisory Service,
colleges, universities
private recruitment agencies

media

notice boards, newsletters, house journal,
internal circulation/news sheet,
interbranch circulation

INTERNAL

ACTIVITY

You should have access to a variety of newspapers, magazines and journals which contain advertisements for jobs, through your college library, employer, or at home. Your local newspaper will be quite a good source, as are certain 'nationals' published daily or just at weekends.

Collect examples of six different advertisements, including at least four **display** adverts (the larger ones which are set in their own 'frames'). You can cut them out or photocopy them, and stick them on to a single sheet of A4 paper so that direct comparisons can be made. It would be sensible to ensure that they relate to the types of job you have a knowledge of, so that you can more easily identify the essential requirements.

ACTIVITY

Using a selected range of advertisements as a basis for group discussion, analyse them in terms of the following questions:

1. Which advertisement do you automatically look at first? Why?
2. Are there any techniques used to attract the eye (e.g. frame design, logo, interesting job title, unusual wording, emphasis of particular bits of information, etc.)?
3. To what extent does the type of print affect the readability? How many different types are used? Why?
4. Is display and layout important? Is any one advertisement easier to read than others? Is use made of spacing, paragraphing, indentation, insetting, visual focus points?
5. Is the content as comprehensive as you would want it to be? Is anything particular missing?
6. If you could apply for any one of the jobs, which one would you choose?

Designing a job advertisement

From the previous activities you will have gathered that it is not necessarily an easy task to draft and design advertisements. For anyone finding themselves in this situation, the following guidelines on presentation, display and content should be useful.

- Make sure the job title is prominent and recognisable.
- Give a brief job description and state that applications are required.
- Give an indication of the **type** of person who would be suitable, and what special attributes, talents, skills, qualifications he/she should possess.
- State the salary, or salary range, and outline any conditions you feel are beneficial (e.g. luncheon vouchers, four weeks holiday, company car, etc.)
- Specify what method of application is required and to whom applications should be made.
- Give a reference of some kind for the post.
- State clearly the closing date for applications.
- Include the Company name, address and telephone number, if appropriate.
- Incorporate the Company logo as part of the overall design.
- Use any display techniques with which you are familiar to emphasise particular points.

Note: An important consideration for any organisation is **cost**, and this must be borne in mind at all times. A large display advertisement will cost much more than a two-line insertion in the Situations Vacant column, and you might find that the status of the job will determine how much is spent on advertising the post.

Fig. 17.9

BOLVOR CHEMICALS, LTD

(Member of the CHINSON group)

<u>Job title and grade</u> : Senior Administrative Assistant (new post)

<u>Responsible to</u> : Chief Accountant and Administration Manager

<u>Main purpose of job</u> : To provide a level of administrative support to the Chief Accountant and Administration Manager

<u>Salary scale</u> : £5,000 – £6,500

<u>Duties and responsibilities to include:</u>

1. The drafting of reports, memos, circulars, letters, and minutes of meetings from notes.
2. The provision of financial and other statistical analyses for management information.
3. Dealing with general enquiries from members of public and media.
4. Supervision of the work of the Costing, Wages and General Administration sections.
5. Responsibility for the ordering of all company stationery requirements.

The postholder must also undertake other duties appropriate to the grading of the post, as required by the management. In particular he/she will be expected to assess the extent to which modern technology could be introduced into the company's administrative systems and, where appropriate, introduce such systems and supervise their implementation.

Organisation chart

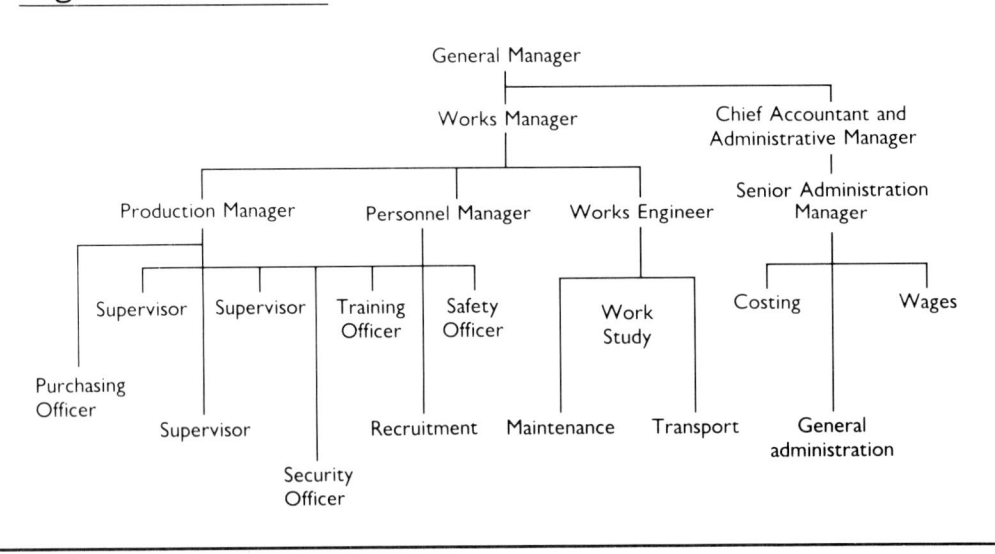

```
                              General Manager
                                    |
                    _____|_____
                    |                               |
              Works Manager              Chief Accountant and
                    |                    Administrative Manager
   _____|_____            |
   |                |              |      Senior Administration
Production     Personnel        Works           Manager
 Manager        Manager        Engineer           |
   |               |              |        _____|_____
   |         _____|_____        |        |      |           |
Supervisor  Training  Safety   Work      Costing             Wages
Supervisor  Officer   Officer  Study
   |
Purchasing
 Officer
                                              General
Supervisor    Recruitment  Maintenance Transport  administration
   |
Security
Officer
```

Filling a vacancy

ACTIVITY

Research a further range of publications which carry job advertisements, and study what techniques are used. Then, using the guidelines given earlier, design a display advertisement for the post outlined in the job description in fig. 17.9. Your final presentation should be on plain paper, using a 12cm × 18cm base-size. Establish the basic size by designing an appropriate frame, and make sure your final presentation is contained within it.

ASSIGNMENT: 'Headhunting' (2)

a   Basing your work on the detailed job specification you drew up for a Personal Secretary in part (1) of this assignment, design a display advertisement which will be used to advertise the post in the local press. Present your advertisement using a 12cm × 18cm format, on plain paper.

b   Produce costings for three insertions of the advertisement on consecutive weekdays beginning with Tuesday. The final size of the advertisement when published will be either 10cm × 1 column width or 10cm × 2 column widths.

You should investigate both possibilities and include appropriate comparative costings in a covering memo to be submitted to Andrew Watson, your Personnel Director, together with the job specification and the draft advertisement.

CHAPTER 18

The job application

In this chapter you will need to look at things from two points of view, because some of you will be looking for guidance on how to get a job, some of you might be looking for a 'refresher' session because you are thinking of changing your job, and some of you undoubtedly anticipate being in a fairly senior position where you will be responsible for recruiting, interviewing and appointing new staff. Each aspect of job finding dealt with here will give you useful information, insights and guidelines to help you understand how the prospective employee prepares for the final interview, and how the recruiter considers and interprets the information received about any applicant.

Personal records

Let's start with the most basic requirement for any person who anticipates applying for a new job

KNOW YOURSELF.

It is amazing how many people are unable, at interview, to give accurate details of their education, qualifications and experience. This points to bad preparation and such candidates should have been 'weeded out' in the short-listing process. As a prospective applicant you should make sure that you are very thorough in recording details of anything which relates to your suitability for jobs. The best approach, whether you are looking for your first job or thinking of a change of job, is to create a **personal record file**, and add to it as your career progresses. This will ensure that you always have essential information at your fingertips, and that there is no chance of any inconsistencies occurring in the information you present to employers. It is not unknown for candidates being interviewed for promotion within their own company to be 'picked up' on information which does not correspond to the records the company already holds. This, of course, can be disastrous.

Fig. 18.1 gives an indication of the sort of information you should hold in a personal record file. Most of it is very obvious.

Obviously, each of the general areas mentioned in fig. 18.1 will require a separate section or sub-section in the file, and it is essential to keep it in order and up-to-date.

The job application

As a recruiter, the guidelines given to job-seekers on keeping a personal record file should indicate to you that there is a wide range of topics about which you can question candidates, and should help you identify any significant omissions in an application.

Fig. 18.1

Personal Details

Full name Tel no.
Address Date of birth

Education

1. Details of secondary education
   Dates, type of school, type of courses followed – GCSE, 'A' level, CPVE, other vocational, etc.
2. Details of further education/training
   Dates, college, courses, professional training, aims, content, vocational elements.
3. Details of higher education
   Polytechnic, university, other?, professional studies, dates, subjects, courses, aims, vocational relevance.

Qualifications achieved

1. At school
   Dates, grades, type of qualification, details of subject areas
2. Vocational
   College course results, grades, subjects, aim of qualification(s), vocational relevance, dates.
3. Higher academic
   Degrees, diplomas, disciplines, dates, results, grades, subjects.

Examinations to be taken

Title, board, level, vocational relevance, subjects, dates, any interim results – e.g. 'mocks'.

Work experience

Part-time or full-time employment. Dates, functions, reasons for leaving, special responsibilities, salary/wages, names of employers, holiday jobs, details of firms you have worked for.

Special activities

Short courses attended, Queen's Scout/Guide, Duke of Edinburgh's Award, voluntary/social work.

Positions of responsibility

1. At school
   Prefect, Year Head, Head Boy/Girl, representing school at sport, captaincies, other responsibilities.
2. Further/higher education
   Student representative, Secretary or President of a society/club, sporting responsibilities, etc.
3. At work
   Supervisory responsibilities, accountability, staff representative, consultative procedures, social secretary, etc.

Spare time/leisure activities

Sport, recreational, list of books read – notes on why you liked/disliked them.

Documentation

1. Certificates and qualifications
2. Testimonials
3. Copies of all previous applications – forms/letters/notes of tel. calls.
4. Results of any assessments/appraisals that have been made of you.
5. Copy of Curriculum Vitae.
6. Checklist of essential documentation.
7. Personal notes on your career objectives, strong points you need to improve on.
8. Advertisements for posts for reference.
9. Job descriptions/specifications.

Current referees

Names, addresses, qualifications, positions (status), tel nos., brief background info. as to why they are suitable referees.

Publications

Any leaflets/pamphlets/articles etc. giving information which could help you.

ACTIVITY

> Start your own personal record file. Create separate sections for each of the main areas indicated earlier in this chapter, and provide a comprehensive summary of your background, experience, education and qualifications up to the present time. Start collecting advertisements and job details in which you are interested, and aim to update your records at regular intervals. At this point you should devote about three hours to establishing the structure and organisation of your file, and inserting basic background information. Remember, this will need to be an on-going activity if it is to be useful to you in the future.

Reading job advertisements

The next thing to think about is the **job advertisement**, and we can concentrate here on how the job-seeker needs to look at the major 'link' between the employer and the prospective employee. In Chapter 17 we considered agencies through which jobs could be advertised, and how advertisements should be structured and designed; but how should you react when you are on the receiving end? As a job-seeker you might have access to all the media dealt with in Chapter 17, and you will undoubtedly be faced with a range of job advertisements to consider. Great care is needed, reinforced by an intelligent approach and a thorough analysis.

ACTIVITY

> Study the two advertisements in fig. 18.2.
>
> Discuss as a group the differences between the two advertisements, and the implications these differences might have for the discerning reader! To start off the discussion, consider the following questions:
>
> - What image do you think each of the employers is projecting?
> - Are there any particular words or phrases which reinforce the image? Examples?
> - Are there any examples of different words being used to express the same thing, but managing to present a different image?
> - Does one of the advertisements present different information from the other? Examples?
> - Is the approach and style less formal in one than the other? Examples?

It will be clear to you from your thoughts and discussion about these two rather obvious examples, that advertisements can provide a wealth of information, not only about the company, but also about the attitudes of the management, and about the kind of person they are really looking for. The type of information put in, what has been left out, and the way in which information is presented, can all give 'pointers' to help you establish an accurate company profile. Nobody can tell you which is the best job for you – only careful consideration and intelligent analysis will enable you to

Fig. 18.2

OFFICE MANAGER/ESS

An old-established local firm of solicitors requires a mature person to organise, delegate and supervise work in a traditional office.

Candidates should be well-qualified in Secretarial Skills and have a formal qualification in Business Administration. Previous experience would be advantageous.

For a suitable candidate the company may be prepared to consider further training in modern office techniques.

Applications should be made in writing to the Senior Partner at the address below, giving full details of qualifications and career to date.

OFFICE MANAGER/ESS

Our successful and expanding law practice is looking for an efficient young Office Manager/ess to take full control of the wide range of current operations in our busy office.

The successful applicant will have been trained in traditional skills, and also have qualifications in administration or office technology.

Previous relevant experience would be useful, and you will be expected to undertake specialist training in modern office techniques with a view to planning and developing technology-based integrated office systems.

You can expect a generous starting salary, excellent working conditions and full support from the Senior Partners.

Telephone John Wyford on 725681 for further details and an application form.

identify a suitable opening for your particular skills and talents. If you are in the position of a recruiter, and have to draft advertisements for the press or other agencies, remember that the type of person you are hoping to employ will probably be shrewd enough to 'read between the lines' and will make a preliminary assessment of your company. Be careful what image you present!

Job applications

The **job application** is a minefield for the inexperienced and experienced alike. Every application will be different, and might require different emphases and a different approach. However, there are certain established guidelines which provide the basis for different methods of application. In this chapter we shall look briefly at the detailed letter of application, the 'cold' letter, the CV (Curriculum Vitae) and covering letter, and the application form.

The 'full' letter

It is unusual nowadays for an organisation to request a full and detailed letter of application for a post, but if the situation does arise it can be useful to have some ideas on what information should be included, and in what sequence it should be presented. The pattern indicated in fig. 18.3 gives a possible structure, but this should be regarded as flexible, and can be adjusted to meet individual needs.

Fig. 18.3

Paragraphs — Example(s)

	Paragraphs	Example(s)
Paragraph 1	reference to source full details of source statement that you wish to apply for the post	Dear Sir, I read with interest your advertisement in the Northern Herald on Wednesday 5th October, and wish to apply for the post of Personnel Officer.
Paragraph 2	state your age summary of secondary education posts of responsibility	names of schools/type explanation of frequent changes courses followed qualifications achieved activities/teams you have been involved in
Paragraph 3	further/higher education specialist training vocational training courses followed subjects studied examinations taken examinations to be taken	College/Polytechnic/University National Diploma/Certificate in Business & Finance Higher National Diploma Diploma in Management Studies Institute of Bankers Part II pass/merit/distinction anticipated results

Paragraph 4	previous employment relevant experience accurate indication of jobs you have had	dates and job titles main duties/responsibilities full-time jobs part-time jobs if they involved relevant skills work experience as part of vocational training
Paragraph 5	any other experience or qualifications relevant to the post interests – recreational/sporting, membership of national schemes or organisations involvement in the community anything that shows independence and initiative	voluntary service Duke of Edinburgh's Award Scheme Queen's Guide/Scout Outward Bound/expedition work instructor's qualifications in any area sporting/recreational activities
Paragraph 6	references testimonials	usually include headteacher or principal of last educational institution full details of names, titles, positions, addresses and telephone numbers copies of testimonials indicate your willingness for references to be taken up
Paragraph 7	conclusion willingness to be available for interview reason for interest in this particular job	as wide a selection of days and times you are available for interview as possible (preferably any time) reputation of company specifically trained for type of work well qualified/experienced

ACTIVITY

1 Make sure you know the difference between a reference and a testimonial.
2 Photocopy and store any testimonials in your personal record file.
3 Decide who you will want to use for referees, and contact them to make sure they agree.
   Note: If one is your past Headteacher or Principal, contact will not normally be necessary.
4 Include **full details** of your referees in your personal record file.

The 'cold' letter

The thing to remember with any letter of application is that it should be friendly and relaxed, but not over-familiar, and should aim to present *you* in the best possible light. This can be even more difficult if you decide to write a 'cold' letter to a number of organisations in the hope that they have a suitable job for you. The problem with the 'cold' letter is that you cannot relate your personal information to a particular job – it is a question of indicating that you are the type of person who not only has skills the employer needs, but are also one who would fit in well with the established workforce and general environment. A possible approach is given in fig. 18.4.

The CV

Assuming that you are responding to an advertisement, the most common approach is to submit a Curriculum Vitae and covering letter. The CV is a summary of your personal details, achievements and experience, and should be presented – preferably on a single sheet of A4 paper – in such a way that a prospective employer can quickly and easily assess your quality and suitability. It should be typed and structured under relevant headings, and, although the example in fig. 18.5 gives you some guidelines, you must be prepared to insert additional sections if you think they are necessary, and omitt any which are not relevant to your own background and experience.

Note: Other possible sections for inclusion in a CV could be: Professional Qualifications, Conferences Attended, Short Courses, Specialist Training Courses, Other Experience (e.g. Youth Leader, Social Work, Expeditions, Outward Bound Activities), Membership of Professional Bodies.

The covering letter

A curriculum vitae will always be submitted with a covering letter, which should not be too long (ideally one side of A4), and should contain fairly limited information to avoid repeating the information you have included in the CV.

The first paragraph must give full source references, as with any letter of application. (See the example in fig. 18.3 earlier in the chapter.)

The main body of the letter can be one or more paragraphs, and should concentrate on relating your training and experience to the requirements of the job i.e. saying why you think you are a suitable candidate. You have to **sell** yourself, and convince the employer that you are worth interviewing, and that you have skills that the company can exploit. It is also useful to indicate that you are aware of the type of work the company is involved in, and of any recent changes, re-organisations, take-overs, etc. in which the organisation might have been involved. If you can,

Fig. 18.4

> 17 Wandle Way,
> Dinsford,
> Sussex.
> SE2 7DN
>
> 15 October 19 —

Mr P. Stanning,
The Personnel Manager,
Johnson Bros. and Associates,
12 Donford Road,
Dinsford,
Sussex.
SE4 8BF

Dear Mr Stanning,

I shall be finishing my vocational training in June of next year, and would like to be considered for a post with your company.

During my time at Winterside Comprehensive School I achieved eight GCSE passes at grade C or above, and am currently working towards the final examinations of the National Diploma in Business and Finance at Wintervale College of Further Education. The course involves a range of study areas including Finance, Economics, Law, Supervision, Industrial Relations, Keyboard Skills, Word Processing and Information Technology (Business Applications). I have also benefited from a period of work-placement with a local firm.

Whilst working for my National Diploma, I have been fully involved in College life, and have represented the College in various sports, including Rugby football, swimming and windsurfing. I have also been a student representative on the Governing Body, and on the Academic Advisory Council.

I am interested in an administrative/clerical position in the Personnel environment, and am aware of the important contribution this department makes to the effective operation of a company like yours. I believe that I would fit well into your organisation, and would welcome the opportunity of discussing the situation further with you, or attending for interview.

Yours sincerely,
J. B. Manville (Ms)

Fig. 18.5

CURRICULUM VITAE

Personal details

Name	:	Peter Michael Trender
Address	:	126, Walkham Rise, Wingbridge, Yorkshire, YE2 8PQ
Telephone no	:	Wingbridge (0738) 927684 (Home)
		Wingbridge (0738) 476766 (Work)
Age	:	19
Date of birth	:	October 15 1970
Personal status	:	Single

Education

Sponsford Comprehensive School Sept. 1982 – July 1987
Yardley College of Further Education Sept. 1987 – July 1989 (Part-time)

Academic qualifications

GCSE: English (B), Maths (C), French (C), History (C), Geography (C), Biology (D), Physics (D), Technology (D) – 1987
National Diploma (BTEC) in Business and Finance – 1989

Examinations to be taken

Chartered Insurance Institute Associateship, three subjects – 1990

Work experience

General Clerk (Claims)	Beacon International Assurance Corporation, York	1987 – 1988
Trainee Underwriter	Menton–Foreshaw Brokers, Wingbridge	1988 – date

Interests/activities

Rugby-football Local Club League
Surfing/sailboarding
Piano (Grade 5)

Referees

Mrs P. Conaghan,
Personnel Manager,
Beacon International Ass. Corpn.,
Beacon House, Wantage Street,
YORK. YE5 7PQ

Mr H. Davies, BSc, FCII,
Senior Partner,
Menton–Foreshaw Brokers,
127 North Hill, Wingbridge,
Yorkshire. YE2 7TD

Ms W. Wingate,
Investment Consultant,
Wanton Investment Services,
173 High Street, YORK. YE7 8PJ

emphasise the good reputation of the company as an employer and in its own field of service or production.

The letter can be finished off by stating that you are enclosing a CV ('details of my education, qualifications and experience') and indicating when you can be available for interview (preferably 'at any time').

Note: A specimen covering letter is **not** included in this text as a deliberate policy. It is not a good idea to be restricted by a suggested style of writing, and you should bear in mind that every letter of application is an **original**, aimed at a particular work situation.

Fig. 18.6

Letters of application checklist

1. **Remember:** the aim of any application is to get an **interview**. No employer will offer a job simply on the strength of a letter (or application form).
2. Don't include too much information. The employer must *want* to find out more about you.
3. Always address your letter to an individual if possible. You might have to ring the company to establish the name and position of the appropriate person.
4. Present a positive image – emphasise things you have done and competences you have demonstrated.
5. **Include** information on team or group activities, situations where you have demonstrated initiative, relevant academic, vocational or professional training.
6. **Exclude** comments on your physical appearance, politics, religion, industrial relations or other possibly contentious subjects.
7. Write in your own handwriting, on white A4 paper. Ideally avoid ballpoint pens or pencils, and do not submit a letter which contains any errors. Make sure your signature can be read easily.
7. Make sure all spelling, punctuation and grammar is correct, and **keep a copy** of the letter.
9. Fold it carefully, a minimum number of times. Don't use a very small envelope.

ACTIVITY

Choose either one of the advertisements in figs. 18.7(a) and (b), *or* find an advertisement for a job in which you would be interested, and submit a full application for the post. Your approach to the application should be based on a CV and covering letter format, and the final submission should be presented to a standard which would be suitable for immediate posting.

Fig. 18.7(a) Advertisement placed in the Northern Gazette, May 20.

FINANCE DEPARTMENT
ACCOUNTANCY ASSISTANT (FAC 2)
up to £10,862

Applications for the above post are invited from qualified members of the Association of Accounting Technicians, or those eligible to enter the final examinations of that body (details of entry requirements can be supplied on request).

The successful candidate will join a small team under the leadership of a qualified IPFA accountant in the Accountancy Section of the Department. The Section is responsible for the preparation of budgets, final accounts, etc.

The duties will provide extensive experience of financial administration in a large local authority with an annual budget of £520 million.

The starting salary will be in accordance with qualifications and experience. If appropriate, day release will be given for examination study.

Apply in writing with CV to the **Director of Finance, PO Box 23, County Hall, Bamsford, Tavyside, TA7 6PT.**
Tel. 0236 872142   Closing date for applications: 12 June

TAVYSIDE COUNTY COUNCIL

Fig. 18.7(b) Advertisement placed in the Southern Evening News, April 27.

SOLVIT CHEMICALS PLC

require

MANAGEMENT ACCOUNTING TRAINEES

for their Industrial and Domestic Chemical Cleaning Products Division (SW England)

This company is established as one of the country's leading suppliers of chemical cleaning products. Recent research has identified numerous potential export markets, and in anticipation of further expansion three posts are being made available for the training of potential senior Management Accountants.

During an initial training period, appointees will gain experience in a variety of departments. They will also be expected to undertake a course of study leading to professional qualifications.

Applicants should be under 20 years of age, and educated to at least 'A' level standard. General Business Studies training/qualifications could be an advantage, but a specific science background or experience of the chemical industry is not necessary.

★ Initial salary: £5,250 per annum (to be reviewed on successful completion of training)

★ Non-contributory pension scheme

★ 3 weeks annual holiday

In the first instance apply in writing to **The Chief Accountant, Trebetherick Road, Wodebridge, Somerset, SE17 8PD.**

Applications must be received not later than 10 May.

The telephone contact

In some circumstances you might wish to respond to an advertisement which asks you to 'telephone for further details', or 'telephone for an application form' or 'telephone for an appointment'. Whatever the wording, you will be under scrutiny and assessment from the moment you 'get through' to the organisation. You can't afford to appear bumbling, disorganised or ill-prepared.

There are certain steps you can take to avoid this situation, and a little careful thought and planning will increase your self-confidence and reduce nervousness.

1 Use a checklist, and tick off things you should have at hand when making a call:

   The advertisement ☑ Pen and paper ☑
   The name of your contact ☑ Your CV ☑
   Details of when you can be available for interview ☑
   A telephone number where you can be contacted ☑

2 During the call, which you should make from a quiet room where disturbance is kept to a minimum, follow these basic guidelines:
   - Speak clearly. Don't gabble.
   - Ask to speak to a specific person, using his/her name.
   - Give your name and state your reason for calling.
   - If it is not convenient for the receiver to talk to you immediately, ask when you can call back, or be prepared to give your contact number.
   - Use your CV as an information source when answering questions. Don't rely on memory!
   - Answer questions concisely. Don't waffle.
   - Make it clear that you would like an interview.
   - Ask for directions and make a note of the time, day, date and place of interview.
   - Conclude the call by thanking the receiver for talking to you.

The application form

All application forms ask for basically the same information, with some variations, particularly in design and layout, from company to company. It is important to be aware of the role of the application form. Like any other method of application, it is a way of trying to secure an interview, and, therefore, presentation, accuracy and an intelligent interpretation of the requirements is essential. Fig. 18.8 gives a fairly comprehensive example.

Fig. 18.8

Application form

(Please answer <u>all</u> sections fully, using block capitals.)

Position applied for: _____

SECTION A — PERSONAL DETAILS

Surname _____	First names _____ Age ___
Permanent address _____	Date of birth _____
_____	Place of birth _____
_____	Nationality _____
_____	Marital status _____
_____	Maiden name _____
_____	No. of children _____
_____	Present position _____
_____	Present salary _____
Telephone no _____	Driver's licence _____
_____	Date available for employment ___

MEDICAL HISTORY

Please give brief details of any serious illnesses, etc., with dates)

_____
_____
_____

Are you registered disabled? _____

NEXT OF KIN

(Name, address and relationship) _____
_____

_____ (Relationship) _____ (Occupation)

SECTION B — EDUCATIONAL DETAILS

SECONDARY EDUCATION

Dates (From — To)	Name and address of school(s)	Type of school (e.g. Comprehensive, Grammar, Technical)
_____	_____	_____
_____	_____	_____
_____	_____	_____
_____	_____	_____

HIGHER/FURTHER EDUCATION AND TRAINING

Dates　　　　Name of college etc.　　　　　　　　　　　　Course taken
(From — To)　　　　　　　　　　　　　　　　　　　　　　(state full- or
　　　　　　　　　　　　　　　　　　　　　　　　　　　　(part-time)

_____　_____　　　_____
_____　_____　　　_____
_____　_____　　　_____
_____　_____　　　_____

TECHNICAL, PROFESSIONAL OR OCCUPATIONAL TRAINING, APPRENTICESHIPS, ETC.

Dates　　　　Type and location of training
(From — To)

_____　_____
_____　_____
_____　_____
_____　_____

QUALIFICATIONS GAINED (Continue on a separate sheet if necessary)

Name of examination　　　　Year taken　　Subjects　　　Level　Result　Grade(s)

_____　　_____　_____　____　____　____
_____　　_____　_____　____　____　____
_____　　_____　_____　____　____　____
_____　　_____　_____　____　____　____
_____　　_____　_____　____　____　____
_____　　_____　_____　____　____　____
_____　　_____　_____　____　____　____

EXAMINATIONS TO BE TAKEN
_____
_____
_____

SECTION C — JOB HISTORY — in chronological order (including H.M. Forces)

Dates　　　　Company, location and nature of business　　Position held and
(From — To)　　　　　　　　　　　　　　　　　　　　　　　　main responsibilities

_____　_____　_____
_____　_____　_____
_____　_____　_____
_____　_____　_____
_____　_____　_____
_____　_____　_____

SECTION D – ADDITIONAL INFORMATION

(Please use this space for further details of knowledge and experience that you consider are relevant.)

_____
_____
_____
_____
_____
_____
_____
_____
_____
_____

SECTION E – LEISURE INTERESTS

(Please give full details, including offices held, past or present and membership of clubs or societies.)

_____
_____
_____
_____
_____
_____

SECTION F – REFERENCES

(Please give the names of two persons who can be consulted regarding your suitability for this post.)

Name   _____
Position _____
Address   _____
          _____

Name   _____
Position _____
Address   _____
          _____
          _____

Signed _____ Date _____

Completing an application form

It is very difficult to give specific advice on how to complete any application form you might come across, but it could be useful to make some general comments which should start you thinking along the right lines. These comments relate to fig. 18.8, but the practical guidance will be relevant to most situations of this type.

1. Take copies of the form as soon as you receive it, and use a copy to draft a 'rough' submission.
2.
   a. It is essential to follow the **instructions**.
   b. If BLOCK CAPITALS are required, then make sure you use them, and maintain a consistent presentation throughout.
   c. Write in ink, with no errors or crossings out.
   d. Answer *all* sections – even if you have to enter 'N/A' (not applicable) in some places.
3. In Section A do not be tempted to leave any part unanswered just because you think it is 'none of their business'. This is a naïve reaction, and you risk not being short-listed.
4. Section B requires full details of all your educational experience, and qualifications gained. If necessary, use a separate sheet to continue the information in any section. If you do this, make a note to this effect on the form and structure your additional sheet in the same way as the original.

   Note: The same principle applies to sections such as Employment Record, Recreational/Leisure Interests and Additional Information. Don't be afraid to continue on another sheet if you feel there is essential information you need to put across. However, *always* insert a note saying 'continued on attached sheet' or 'continued on a separate sheet', and make sure that you use the same layout and format as the original. It is never worth ruining the overall presentation by trying to cram too much information into a small space.
5. The employment history in Section C is very important, and it is essential to present the information in a logical manner. Follow any instructions given, and be **consistent**.
6. The 'Additional Information' section is a favourite of recruiters, as it can provide just the information they require to help them decide who to call for interview. This is the section where you should specifically relate any skills you might have to the requirements of the post, and convince the prospective employer that your past experiences demonstrate your initiative, overall competence and general employability. You *must* convince them that you have something to offer!
7. Leisure Interests are important as they can give an insight into what sort of person you are – introvert or extrovert, good mixer or loner, a thinker or a doer! It is in your interests to indicate that you have a well-balanced personality, but *remember* – you might be questioned closely on this information at interview.

8 The final sections of the form are straightforward, but again, **follow instructions** and give full details.
9 When you have written out the **final** version of the form, take a copy for your personal record file. The original form should then be sent to the company with a very brief covering letter, which should thank them for sending it to you, emphasise that you wish to apply for the post, state that the completed form is enclosed, and indicate when you would be willing/able to attend for interview.

ACTIVITY

1 Collect as many examples of application forms as you can, and keep them in your file. An analysis of a range of forms will give you a clearer insight into what employers are looking for.
2 Using a standard form which your tutor will provide (possibly taking the example in fig. 18.8 as a basic format), make a formal application for a post of your choice based on the advertisements included in this chapter, *or* on an advertisement you have selected from the local, national or specialist press. You should submit a completed application form and covering letter.

CHAPTER 19

Selection and induction

From all the guidance given in the previous chapter on various methods of applying for jobs, you can easily establish for yourself what the employer/recruiter/selector has to look for when considering applicants for a post. Even drawing up a short-list is a demanding and time-consuming task, and the most difficult bit is yet to come.

The interview

We need to consider this from both points of view if you are to be fully aware of the requirements, expectations and implications.

Being interviewed

Most people are aware of the initial considerations in any interview situation (e.g. appropriate dress, punctuality, personal presentation, etc.), but it is often difficult to get guidance on what happens after this, because every interview is different, and every interviewer will take a different approach. All of us can answer questions about our interests, our family background, our work-experience, and demonstrate our general awareness of current affairs, particularly relating to industry and commerce, but many people are never sure what questions they can or are expected to ask, or what general investigative questions they might be asked. To cope with this, plan your approach very carefully, and **do your homework**.

1. Research the company. Be sure you are fully aware of what they do. Are they a subsidiary of a parent company? Are they part of a group? What links are there with other subsidiaries or outside companies? What sort of customers do they have?

2. Clarify details of the job, and be prepared to ask questions about it. Obviously you don't walk into the interview and immediately start questioning the panel, but you should choose your moment carefully and don't be afraid to raise points, particularly if you feel you haven't understood something that has been said. The questions you ask will demonstrate your overall attitude, so don't concentrate on holidays and the length of the working week! However, don't be afraid to query these when all more important topics have been dealt with.

Some questions you might want to ask

Why has the vacancy arisen? Is it because of promotion?
What opportunities are there for advancement?
Will you be given any training?
Is there an induction programme?
Will you be encouraged to improve your qualifications, or go on in-company training courses?
Who will you be working with? How many people?
To whom will you be directly responsible?
Where will you be based?
When does the job commence? When will you be notified?

3   Be prepared to answer open or leading questions/instructions such as:
Why do you want this job?
What qualities do you think you have to offer which will help you in this post?
Tell me about yourself.
What makes you think you will be good at the job?
What is your ultimate ambition? Where do you want to be in five years' time?
What do you do in your spare time?
Have you read any particular books lately? (Be prepared to talk in some detail about this and explain why you enjoyed them, outline the story, and comment on the 'quality' of the author.)
What newspapers do you read? (Be prepared to be questioned on some aspect of current affairs if you claim to read any newspaper regularly.)
What are the most satisfying aspects of your present job?
Is there anything that particularly frustrates you in your present job?
Can you tell us about any incident at work when you have felt particularly effective? Or ineffective?
Tell me something about your present bosses. What kind of people are they? (Be careful not to be tricked into making sweeping criticisms or appearing to gripe about previous colleagues.)

Note   Don't hesitate to ask for clarification if you don't understand a question, or if you are not sure what the interviewer is getting at. **Remember**, the majority of interviewers will not have been trained in the skills of interviewing, and therefore they may not be good enough to conduct the interview in such a way that you are given the opportunity to present yourself in the best light. If this is the case, you must try to guide the conversation towards the important topics you want to bring up, for example, relevant experience, particular expertise, specific qualifications, expression of opinions/attitudes or aspects of the job.

General points

1. When you first enter the interview room, wait until you are asked to sit, and don't make any flippant remarks or attempt to be funny.
2. Be positive in your approach, not hesitant, and (if the situation allows it) be prepared to shake hands with an interviewer. Obviously this wouldn't normally happen if there was a **panel**.
3. Ensure that you know **who** is interviewing you – their names and status (positions in the company).
4. Try to maintain eye-contact with the person to whom you are talking at any one time.
5. At the end of the interview thank the interviewer(s) for giving you the opportunity of discussing the job with them and presenting your 'case'.

Interviewing candidates

As a recruiter and interviewer, you will find that there is a wealth of advice available to you, published by a number of authors or organisations. The activities which you are asked to work on in this part of the chapter will give you the opportunity to investigate some of these, and make up your own mind about the best approach. The basic outline you are given here should get the main principles set in your mind, and you can expand or develop techniques which suit your approach. Remember, many recruiters are bad interviewers – you don't want to be one of them.

The job interview is a two-way exchange of information between the employer (or the employer's representative) and the applicant. In order to get the best out of any 'communicating' situation, thorough planning is essential. As an interviewer, you must prepare yourself with data relating to the situation (e.g. job details, information on the applicant), and should have a written plan containing a checklist of points to be covered, identifiable objectives, and a logical/sequential approach.

First of all . . . get the facts: you will need a **job description** for the post to be filled; a **personnel specification** to identify the qualities and attributes needed to perform the job successfully; the **application**, including all **letters**, **forms**, **CV**, etc.; notes on, or copies of, **references** you have followed up.

Secondly . . . prepare some kind of assessment sheet based on a check-list of points similar to the seven pointplan, or some other grading system (e.g. J. M. Fraser's five-fold grading system, or a weighted points scheme – see activity below).

After that . . . make sure the arrangements are complete. The interview should be held in a suitable place, as private and comfortable as possible, free from stress, interruptions and distractions. You should allow adequate time, and pick a time of day when you and the candidate will not be too tired, or suffering from the after-effects of a large lunch! Obviously, you must ensure that the candidates are notified of the day, date, time and

People in business organisations

place, and on the specified day it creates a good impression if someone is available to receive them and guide them to the waiting area or interview room.

Then . . . assess the candidate's application against the job specification, and, when you are actually interviewing him/her, assess the responses and general personality in the same way. To ensure that you get the best out of the situation, you should, at the beginning of the interview, tell the candidate about the company and the job, and stimulate his/her interest in the post.

Finally . . . develop your interview logically according to a pre-conceived plan. A chronological approach can often be useful – either starting with the current occupation and working backwards, or beginning with childhood (secondary age) and working forwards. Don't introduce contentious points too early, and always try to end each part of the interview on a positive note.

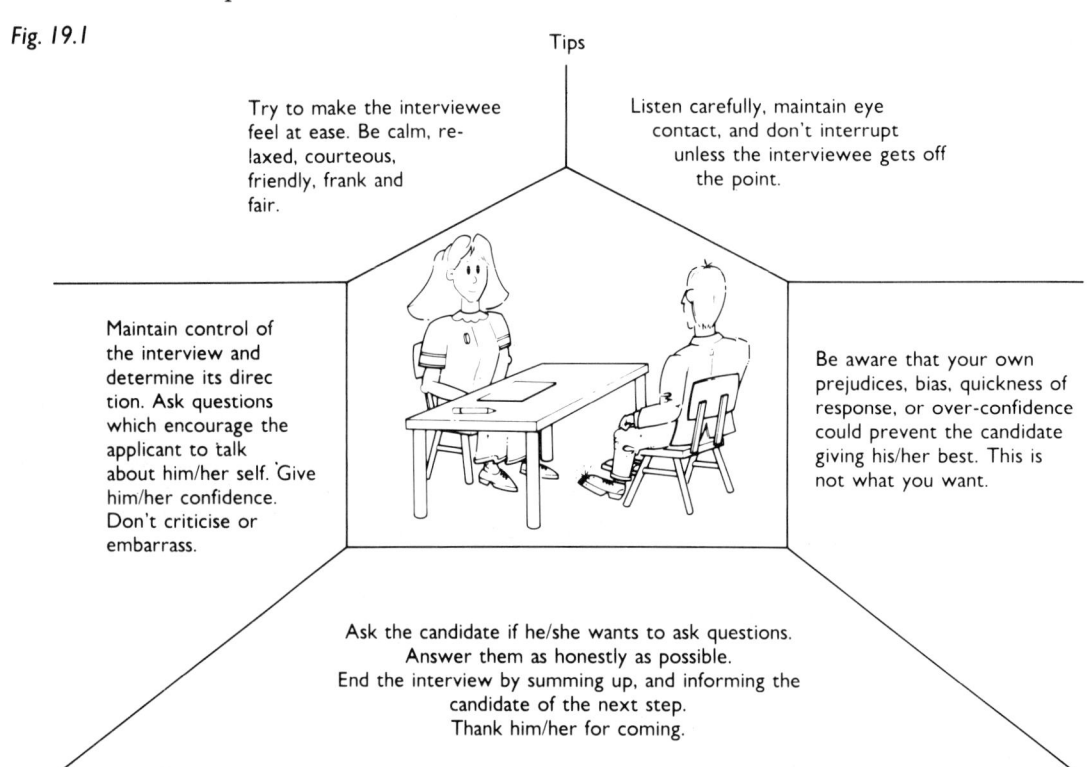

Fig. 19.1

Tips

Try to make the interviewee feel at ease. Be calm, relaxed, courteous, friendly, frank and fair.

Listen carefully, maintain eye contact, and don't interrupt unless the interviewee gets off the point.

Maintain control of the interview and determine its direction. Ask questions which encourage the applicant to talk about him/her self. Give him/her confidence. Don't criticise or embarrass.

Be aware that your own prejudices, bias, quickness of response, or over-confidence could prevent the candidate giving his/her best. This is not what you want.

Ask the candidate if he/she wants to ask questions. Answer them as honestly as possible. End the interview by summing up, and informing the candidate of the next step. Thank him/her for coming.

ACTIVITY 1

Research methods of recording interviewee assessments. Explain how Fraser's five-fold grading system works, and how the weighted-points system is used. Produce copies/examples of appropriate forms which could be used for recording an interviewer's assessment – one form for each of the three main assessment methods.

Selection and induction

ACTIVITY 2

This is a group activity based on films or videos of interview situations. The details of two appropriate audio-visual presentations are given below.

Watch and discuss the videos, building your analysis around a tutor-led discussion. The video can be stopped at crucial stages to emphasise important points.

At the end of the discussion/analysis, you should be prepared to produce a written commentary on your chosen video, clarifying the main points demonstrated.

Useful videos

a *Successful Staff Selection* Guild of Sound & Vision, Ltd.
   6 Royce Road, Peterborough, PE1 5YB

b *Tell Me About Yourself*
   Rank Aldis Training Films & Videos,
   PO Box 70,
   Great West Road,
   Brentford,
   Middlesex TW8 9HR.

Note: Training films and videos of this type do become dated, but the principles are still sound. Your tutor might prefer to select other source material for this activity from the range of films and videos available.

ACTIVITY 3

Set up panels (not more than three people per panel) within your group, and consider a range of applications for particular posts taken from the ones prepared earlier in the chapter. If it is considered more appropriate, a fresh range of advertisements can be used and appropriate applications made.

In consultation with your tutor, two or three will be selected for you to work with, and you should prepare for, and conduct, recruitment interviews for the posts.

The preparation must be done very carefully, making sure that you have as much information as possible available. You will have the advertisement, and from this you can draw up an appropriate outline job description and personnel specification. The application can then be considered in the light of these documents.

Plan your interview carefully – establish roles, approach, techniques, question topics, etc. Decide how your questions will be phrased; you would be advised to do a little research on types of questions and how they should be structured e.g. **open** questions, **closed** questions (to be avoided!), **probe** questions, **counter-productive** questions (can ruin an interview). You should be able to recognise and use various questioning techniques – investigative, reflective, summary, leading, multiple, discriminatory, ambiguous, mirror, interrogative, comparative, hypothetical, etc.

Finally, conduct your interviews. This should not be done in front of the whole group, but simply with an observer (tutor?). If the interview can be recorded on video, this could be very useful for de-briefing and analytical discussion.

People in business organisations

Comments on interviewing and selection

As a last word on this topic, you might find it interesting to read the comments made by a Personnel Officer with wide experience in interviewing and selecting staff:

'Without practice it is impossible for anybody to perform well at interview. I can tell immediately if a candidate is well-prepared and has had previous interview experience. However, for most people who are looking for their first job, or a change of job, the important thing is to perfect their approach to applications. I can't emphasise too much that the purpose of a job application is simply to secure a place on a short-list drawn up from anything up to two hundred applicants. Only about ten will be selected, and these will be those who have made the best applications. I'm sure some of those rejected would make excellent employees, but if they can't produce a comprehensive, relevant and well-presented application, they don't even get given the chance of an interview. The CV and covering letter is the most common method of application, but it is amazing how many people think they can send the same old letter to a whole range of jobs. The letter must always be tailored to the individual application, and a good approach here can mean the difference between being short-listed and being rejected. I'm also very impressed with the applicant who has the sense to follow up an application with a discreet telephone call to 'check' that I have received it, and to carefully inquire how soon decisions will be made. I see this as a sign of enthusiasm, but I don't like people to be 'pushy' – more than one call and I get a bit irritated.

When the candidates come to the interview, there are certain standard things that I like to investigate. It's important to know why they have left previous jobs, for example. I get many answers to this type of question, but what I'm basically looking for is an indication that the move was a **positive** one (such as looking for more scope, more responsibility, or greater challenge) rather than a **negative** one (such as didn't get on with colleagues, found the work boring, or not paid enough). But one of the worst things a candidate can do is spend time criticising previous colleagues, supervisor, boss or management. I also look for intelligent questions which show that the candidate is genuinely interested in the job and the company. Anyone who asks me how much holiday they will get, or whether I will honour their existing holiday arrangements, or how much paid sick leave they can have, or how much Christmas bonus they can expect, or how many tea breaks they're allowed in a day, etc., etc. is **'dead'**!'

Induction

Once an appointment has been made, the successful candidate will be given information on salary, conditions of service, contract of employment and starting date. However, the responsibility of the recruiter does not stop here: the new appointee has a right to expect at least a brief introductory period when he/she can be effectively 'slotted in' to the organisation. This is normally achieved through a formal **induction programme**, designed to integrate the employees into their new environment with as little disruption as possible. Depending on what the company wants to achieve, induction may last one or two days, or be extended over several weeks. Figs. 19.2 and 19.3 give examples of simple induction programmes for employees in (1) a large insurance company, and (2) a retailing organisation.

Selection and induction   219

Fig. 19.2

Induction programme

Post: Administrative Trainee   Dates: 15/16 October

Day 1

0930 Reception by Personnel Officer

0945 Introduction to the company – talk and video covering the activities of the enterprise, organisational structure, functions of various departments, given by the Personnel Manager.

1030 Coffee break

1100 Conducted tour of general facilities and the workplace

1230 Lunch

1330 Introduction to department – welcome by Manager/Supervisor, introduction to staff, detailed look at the work of the department, consideration of job description and identification of role in the department.

1530 Tea followed by Q & A session with Personnel Manager.

Day 2 – in the Department

0900 – ⎫ Systematic introduction to the job – supervisor
1230   ⎭ Preliminary instruction/basic training – colleague

1330 – ⎫ Opportunity to 'try' the job and identify/correct
1730   ⎭ any initial problems. Working *with* colleague.

Fig. 19.3

Induction course

Post: Sales Staff   Dates: 27/28 December

Programme

Day 1

0930 Introduction and welcome – Personnel Assistant

1000 The S & D Stores, Ltd. – talk, Personnel Manager

1115 Coffee

1130 Working for this Company – being an employee, Personnel Assistant

1300 Lunch

1345 The Trade Union – Local Branch Secretary

1400 Reading your pay slip

> 1415 Welcome by Chief Executive
> 1430 Safety at work – Safety Officer
> 1530 Security – Chief Security Officer
> 1630 Open forum – Personnel Manager
> 1645 Close
>
> **Day 2**
>
> 0930 Recap on Day 1 – Personnel Assistant
> 0945 Profitability – talk/film, Personnel Assistant
> 1030 Coffee
> 1045 Customer service – Customer Service Manager
> 1130 Telephone techniques – Personnel Assistant
> 1230 The law and the retailer – Customer Service Manager
> 1250 Course summary – Personnel Manager
> 1300 Lunch
> 1400 The barriers to selling – video, discussion
> 1445 Dealing with complaints – Department Manager
> 1515 Dealing with awkward customers – video, discussion
> 1600 Successful selling – talk, Marketing Manager
> 1630 Open forum
> 1645 Close

As you can see, there is nothing very complicated about an induction programme, but it does need very careful planning and scheduling. Every organisation will have its own ideas about what sort of things should be dealt with, and how long the induction should last, but in general terms the range of topics listed below will provide a core of induction material.

health and safety	reliability	appraisal procedures
company rules	customer relations	training opportunities
safety precautions	colleagues	pay
health hazards/precautions	job description	general standards
fire regulations	sick leave	appearance/dress
fire precautions/procedure	flexitime	speech
accidents at work	hours of work	supervisor
first aid	punctuality	work procedures
reporting accidents	holidays	
overtime	promotion	

In addition, it is usually considered important at the beginning of an induction programme to ensure that the new employee has a basic knowledge of what the company does, how large it is, and what activities

Selection and induction

it is involved in. Anyone joining the organisation will need to be aware of who's who – Who's the Supervisor? Who's the Section Head? Who's the Manager? Who is the Union Representative? Who are the Directors? Who's the Chief Executive? – and it might be useful to know where the cloakroom and lavatories are, whether or not there is a rest-room or recreation room, what the lunch and break arrangements are, and what canteen facilities are available.

Most of these things will be dealt with as part of the general talks given by senior members of staff, and you can probably identify where, in each of the examples given (figs. 19.2 and 19.3), the various topics would be included.

ACTIVITY

1 Earlier in this chapter you were involved with preparing for an interview, and it is likely that you actually conducted an interview for a particular post. Using the range of documents you will have had available for that activity, draw up a comprehensive two-day induction programme for the appointee. The two-day programme should be realistically scheduled, and the timing of the components must be clearly indicated, together with the title/rank/status of the member of staff responsible.

2 Having drawn up your induction programme, produce a detailed breakdown of what information will be dealt with in each of the scheduled 'slots', and what the purpose of including that information is (i.e. why is it important to the employee?). This part of the activity can be structured in whatever way you think appropriate, but probably the easiest way of dealing with it is to use each scheduled item as a sub-heading, and write a brief narrative explanation underneath.

CHAPTER 20

Practical communication skills (3)

You have already worked on two chapters devoted solely to practical communication skills, and guidance on other specific topics has been built into assignments at appropriate points throughout the book. The three topics dealt with in this chapter complete the range of specialist communications of which you should have an awareness and some practical experience.

Committee meetings

Committee meetings are probably one of the most important communicating and decision-making processes employed in business. Whereas the essence of any meeting is discussion, there is a vast amount of paperwork which needs to be completed if the whole proceedings are to run effectively and efficiently.

The main committee documents are the **notice of meeting**, the **agenda paper**, and the **minutes**.

The notice

In order to ensure that the arrangements for, and conduct of, a meeting are not invalidated, certain procedures have to be followed. Initially, **notice** that a meeting is to be held must be sent by the Secretary to all those who are entitled to receive it. There is no set format for a notice, but it must, of course, comply with the established rules and regulations governing the meeting body. A notice should contain the following information:

name of the organisation
name of the meeting body
document identification
time, date and place of meeting
brief details of the purpose of the meeting
signature of the convenor
designation (position) of the convenor
date of issue

In the example in fig. 20.1, you will be able to identify each of these components.

Fig. 20.1

```
Hoarfield Manufacturing PLC
    Sports and Social Club
       Notice of meeting

A meeting of the Executive Committee
will be held at 1930 hours on Thursday
May 17 19— in the Barnford Room at the
Clubhouse, to conduct ordinary and
special business, including arrangements
for the Summer Barbecue.

          A. S. ⟨signature⟩
          ─────────────────
              Secretary

                    April 19 19 —
```

This is a fairly formal style and wording, but is simple to structure. The important thing is to make sure that the meeting is not invalidated before it starts because of a failure to fulfil the basic requirements. Fig. 20.2 gives you some examples of situations in which a meeting would be rendered invalid. Consider these when planning a meeting.

Fig. 20.2

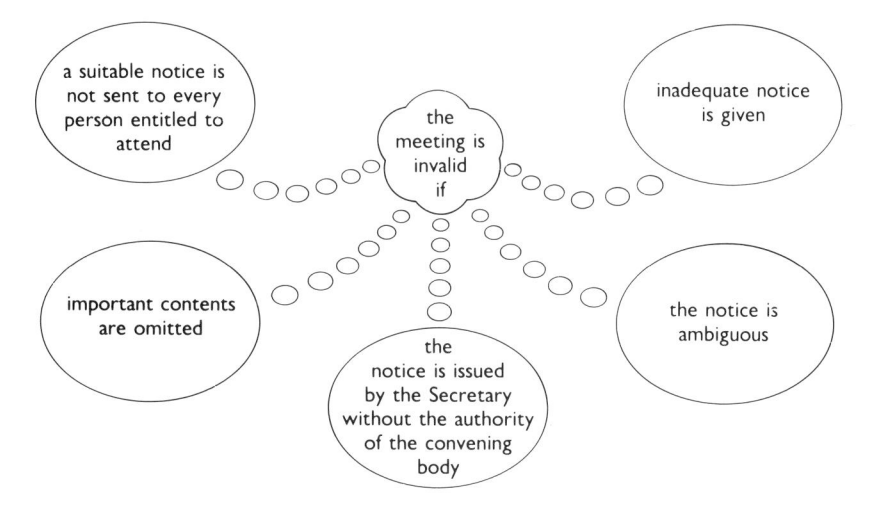

Central node: **the meeting is invalid if**

- a suitable notice is not sent to every person entitled to attend
- inadequate notice is given
- important contents are omitted
- the notice is ambiguous
- the notice is issued by the Secretary without the authority of the convening body

Note: The period of notice required will usually be specified in the regulations governing the meeting, but these guidelines will give you a basis on which to work.

a For a meeting dealing with 'ordinary' business only, 14 clear days is often acceptable.

b For a meeting dealing with 'ordinary' *and* 'special' business, 21 clear days is more appropriate. (The phrase 'clear days' means 'excluding the date of issue and the date of the meeting'.)

ACTIVITY

> As Secretary of the Academic Advisory Council in your college, draft a notice for the next meeting to be held in Committee Room 2 in the Central Administration Block. Provide suitable dates, and indicate that the meeting will be held at 3.15 pm. Business will include a special item on the relocation of the Management Studies Department.

The agenda paper

Usually referred to simply as the **agenda**, this document is prepared by the Secretary, often in conjunction with the Chairperson, and sent out to all those entitled to receive it. The purpose is to give an indication of what will be discussed at the forthcoming meeting. For a normal meeting, which is one in a series of regular meetings, there will be a range of 'ordinary' items of business (i.e. those which occur at every meeting) and a number of 'special' items, dealing with new business and specially requested topics.

Fig. 20.3

```
Hoarfield Manufacturing PLC
   Sports and Social Club

            Agenda

for the meeting to be held at 1930 hrs
on Thursday May 17 19— in the Barnford
Room at the Clubhouse.

       1  Apologies for absence      *
       2  Minutes of last meeting    *
       3  Matters arising            *
       4  Correspondence             =
       5  Summer barbecue            —
       6  Membership fees            —
       7  Any other business         *
       8  Date of next meeting       *
```

Key

*   items of <u>ordinary</u> business
-   items of <u>special</u> business
=   'correspondence' can be regarded as ordinary or special business

Sometimes the notice and the agenda are combined into a single document (see fig. 20.4).

The 'skeleton' agendas shown in figs. 20.3 and 20.4 are adequate for giving a general indication of how the meeting is going to be run, but it is sometimes desirable for committee members to have advance notice of any formal proposals that have been submitted for discussion or decisions.

Practical communication skills

Fig. 20.4

Hoarfield Manufacturing PLC Sports and Social Club

Notice of Meeting

A meeting of the Executive Committee will be held at 1930 hrs on Thursday May 17 19— in the Barnford Room at the Clubhouse, to conduct ordinary and special business as itemised below.

L.M. Barbe
Secretary

April 19 19—

Agenda

1. Apologies for absence
2. Minutes of last meeting
3. Matters arising
4. Correspondence
5. Summer barbecue
6. Membership fees
7. Any other business
8. Date of next meeting

Fig. 20.5

Hoarfield Manufacturing PLC Sports and Social Club

Committee Members' Agenda

for the meeting to be held at 1930 hrs on Thursday May 17 19— in the Barnford Room at the Clubhouse.

1. Apologies for absence
2. Minutes of last meeting
3. Matters arising
4. Correspondence
5. Summer barbecue

   Proposal for venue:

   That the barbecue will be held at Cliffside Beach rather than on the Company playing field.
   Proposer: Mr J. North
   Seconder: Mrs M. Hocking

6. Membership fees

   Proposal to raise membership fees:

   That the membership fees should be raised by £5.00 per year per employee member in order that the cover charge of 10p per person per visit can be cancelled for members' families.
   Proposer: Mr E. Booth
   Seconder: Mr F. Carper

7. Any other business
8. Date of next meeting

Chairman: A. J. Prendle   Vice Chairman: R. S. Vaughan
Secretary: B. J. Jonson   Treasurer: C. E. Austen
Committee Members: J. North E. Booth F. Carper N. Hocking
Secretary's Address: 3, Bixton Close, Wilford, Surrey, SE1 5PJ. Tel. Wilford 756392

The **detailed** or **committee members' agenda** in fig. 20.5 fulfils this role. Note the inclusion of the committee details at the end.

As the drafting of these documents usually falls to the Secretary, you can see what a crucial role he or she plays in the running of a committee.

People in business organisations

ACTIVITY

Your Departmental Manager, Teresa Willoughby, has been sent on an Information Technology up-dating course, and will be away for a week. When you arrived at the office this morning, you found the note shown in fig. 20.6, on your desk.

From the file, you establish that Mr F. Forsyth is Vice-Chairman of the Committee, that the other members are Mrs V. Spanner, Miss W. Shelling, and Mr S. Shriver (Safety Officer), and that Freddie Forsyth wants monthly practices for evacuation procedures, under the control and direction of the Safety Officer.

Fig. 20.6

You're in charge this week!

Sorry to load you with extra work, but as Secretary of the Safety Committee, I've been asked by Bill Scott, the chairman, to call a meeting for the first possible Thursday — Can you set things in motion? I'll want you there as minutes secretary. The file is with this note and contains minutes, circulation list etc. You'll need to issue the notice in my name, and draft the agenda. I suggest you send out a combined notice and skeleton agenda, and then put together a committee members Agenda separately. It can be sent out a little later. I'm pretty well booked up for the next three weeks, but the Thursday after that will do.

The meetings are usually held in the Financial Director's Office at about 4.30 pm. The reason for this particular meeting is that the Local Authority Inspector is coming here in August, and we need to clear up one or two things before he starts snooping around. Bill wants to discuss the fitting of safety alarms to our trucks for use when reversing into the loading bays. The supervisor down there was nearly crushed a couple of weeks ago! He's asked me to make a formal proposal for the fitting of these — over to you!! He will second me.

Other things to be discussed will be the fire doors and evacuation procedures in case of fire. In the file you will see that Freddie Forsythe has submitted a proposal for regular fire 'practices' — see if you can draft this in an appropriate form.

Apart from Freddie, Bill and myself, there are three others on the committee — details in the file.

Thanks for your help,
Teresa

The chairperson's agenda

Another preliminary task can be the preparation of a **chairperson's agenda**. This single-copy document is designed to help the chairperson run the meeting, and has two distinctive characteristics.

1 A column is ruled and left blank down the right-hand side of the agenda, headed 'Chairperson's Notes'. This is to enable the Chairperson to jot down his or her own comments as the meeting progresses, to help him in recalling accurately what decisions are made, and to record any significant observations.

2 Under each item of business, the Secretary will include any relevant information, guidelines, suggestions or warnings which might help the Chairperson run the meeting effectively.

The general layout of a chairperson's agenda is given in fig. 20.7.

Fig. 20.7

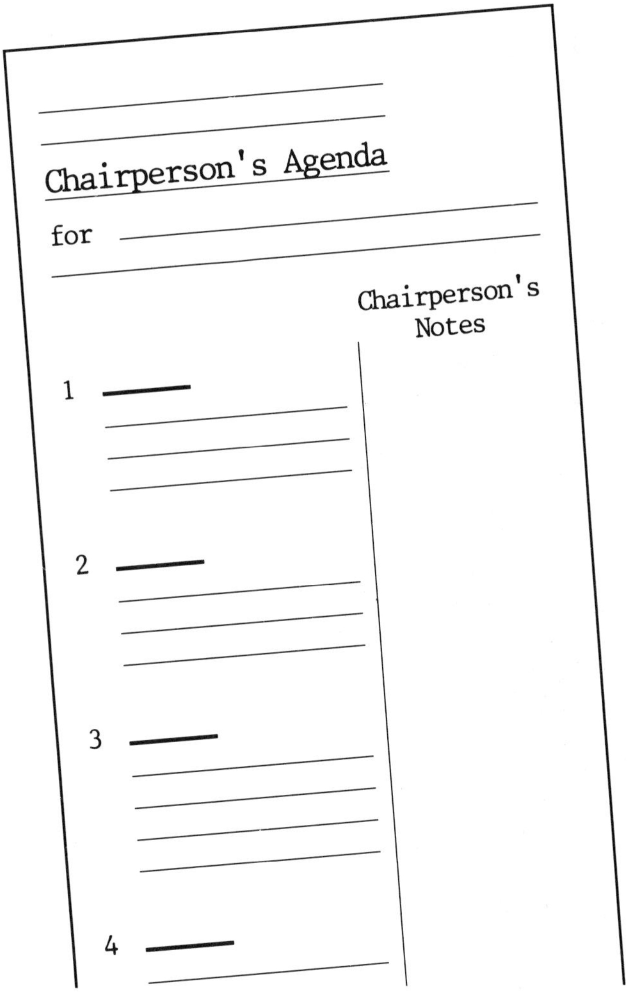

Fig. 20.8

Management Committee Agenda Notes

Sorry about these 'random jottings' — had to note in haste:
 Mrs Benson just resigned from Restaurant Manageress post — agreed to work notice 2 weeks.
Recv'd follwg today:
 That consideration be given by the Management Committee to requesting the Board of Directors to examine the possibility of establishing a training Department to coordinate current and future training needs.
 It's been proposed by Mrs. Chesterton with Miss Watson as seconder.
Letter (attached) arrived yestd. — H.O.D. Marford Coll Techn., Mgt and Bus. St. Dept. wants to know if we can help with work experience, placements. Rang Peter Kent, Personnel Mgr. — in favour if enough time given. N.B. MD on Coll Gov. Body as I recall.
N.B. No. of complaints re Staff Restaurant — cold, small portions etc., also, Gordon Price to give rept. on running costs — expect fireworks here from C'tee grapevine grumbles.
Have rec'd 10 copies of Marford Coll. Techn. Mgt. and Bus. Studies Prospectus — ought to explore day release possibilities.
Mrs Bately to retire next month — 22 yrs as Co. Sec. MD keen on approp. ceremony and present — C'tee to decide.
Have note from Gordon Price — re item 6 last mtg mins: figure for microwave ovens shd read £1540 and not £1940 in estimates.
N.B. Jack Barton rang to-day. He's away for next fortnight on course — 'Robotics, Friend or Foe?' (sounds very foe to me!)
Mrs Trenton stopped me in corridor — still on about cost of vending machine drinks (again!) — likely to raise but fully debated two months ago — Co. already selling at cost.
Almost forgot — Jack Barton offered his wife's help with Restaurant — apparently Inst. Catering quals. — cd be delicate situation.
Hope you can make sense of this — if not ring me tonight, as out all day tomorrow.
 Many thanks,
  J.L.

ACTIVITY

Part of your duties as deputy to Mrs Joy Lawson, Office Administration Manager of Sherwood Furniture Ltd., is to assist her generally in her capacity as Secretary to the firm's Management Committee.

The Committee meets monthly and acts in an advisory capacity to Mr Stephen Watkins, Managing Director, and his board of directors. It is mainly concerned with internal company matters.

The Committee is made up as follows:

Mr John Howard (Chairman)	Deputy Managing Director
Mrs Joy Lawson (Secretary)	Office Administration Manager
Mr Jack Barton	Production Manager
Mrs Lucy Chesterton	Sales Manager
Mr Richard French	Chief Purchasing Officer
Mr Gordon Price	Assistant Accounts Manager
Mrs Pamela Trenton	Senior Secretarial Supervisor
Miss Naomi Watson	Assistant Personnel Manager

Earlier today, Mrs Lawson raised the work of the Committee in this context:

> Look, I'm sorry to have to burden you with this, but if I'm to get out to see Mr Perkins this afternoon, I simply won't have time to draw up the agenda and chairman's agenda for the Management Committee's meeting next Wednesday week at 4.30 in the Conference Room.
> If I leave you the essential information later this morning, I'm sure you could manage them for me to submit to Mr Howard.

As promised, Mrs Lawson left you the hurried notes in fig. 20.8.

Using Mrs Lawson's notes as a guide, compose a **chairman's agenda** for Mr Howard's use at the next Management Committee meeting.

Minutes of meetings

The conduct of any meeting is closely controlled by the Chairperson, but, as with preparatory work (e.g. notice, agenda, etc.) the responsibility for recording what goes on usually falls on the Secretary. Some meeting bodies have a separate Minutes Secretary in order to lighten the workload.

There are two main types of minutes which you are likely to come across: resolution minutes and narrative minutes.

Resolution minutes are usually very brief and just record the decisions reached, giving only the information necessary for implementation. Not all organisations would adopt this approach, but it can be useful when the executive body needs to maintain a united front, and demonstrate collective responsibility. The advantage is that strong disagreements between those involved in the decision-making process can be concealed from junior staff.

Narrative minutes are by far the most common form, and are designed to give a summary of the main points of discussion leading up to a decision. The essence of writing narrative minutes is to record all important aspects without including every little comment made by every speaker.

Fig. 20.9

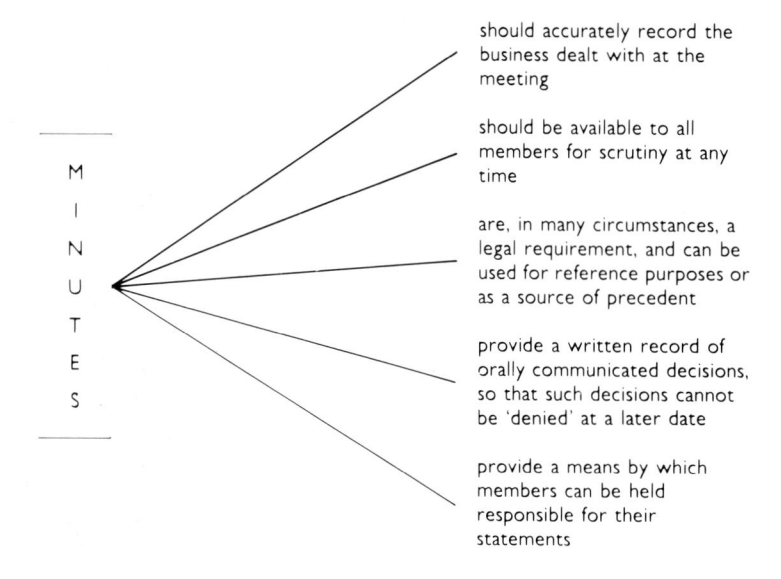

MINUTES
- should accurately record the business dealt with at the meeting
- should be available to all members for scrutiny at any time
- are, in many circumstances, a legal requirement, and can be used for reference purposes or as a source of precedent
- provide a written record of orally communicated decisions, so that such decisions cannot be 'denied' at a later date
- provide a means by which members can be held responsible for their statements

Examples

(The number 5 refers to the item number on the agenda.)

Resolution minutes

(5) It was resolved that the Marketplan Advertising Agency be appointed to create and implement an advertising and marketing strategy for the launch of the new PC2000 desk-top publishing system.

Narrative minutes

The same item might be recorded as follows:

(5) The Chairwoman referred the meeting to Mrs Dyson's proposal recorded on the Agenda Paper for the meeting relating to the appointment of the Marketplan Advertising Agency. She asked Mr Dyson to speak on the motion, and then invited discussion. John Swift commented that he was not confident that a relatively small local firm should be entrusted with such an important project, and suggested that it would be safer to appoint a company with a national reputation. Mrs Copple pointed out that Marketplan had been very successful in orchestrating the launch of the W. B. Conder PLC's new product range, but agreed that they did not have any particular expertise or experience in the computer field. In view of the conflicting views expressed by the various members, the Chairwoman asked that a vote be taken and on a vote of 5 to 3 it was:

RESOLVED that the Marketplan Advertising Agency be appointed to create and implement an advertising and marketing strategy for the launch of the new PC2000 desk-top publishing system.

Practical communication skills 231

Basic style and technique

Minutes must be written in **reported speech**. In effect, the Secretary is **reporting** what went on at the meeting, and must present the minutes in the appropriate style when formally writing them up afterwards.

Often the most difficult task is actually taking notes during the meeting. The Secretary must try to record things exactly as they are spoken, or might make abbreviated notes.

Example

At a meeting the Treasurer might say:

> ❛ I'm a bit worried about increasing the amount we spend on advertising. We've already agreed to increase the fees we pay to speakers, and are committed to keeping members informed by sending regular mail-shots. ❜

The Secretary might make brief notes like this:

> Treasurer worried about spending more on adv. – already increased speakers' fees and members info.

The **minutes** would read like this:

> The Treasurer expressed his concern at any prospective increase in advertising expenditure in view of the agreed increases for speakers' fees and the mail-shots to members.

Fig. 20.10

> MEMBERSHIP: overall increase – some decline in support for certain events. Not enough people prepared to organise. Functions Secretary often ran events single-handed. Need for more to serve on Committee. 2 resignations during year – pressure of work – criticism from members.
>
> EVENTS: Summer Barbecue successful – thanks to John Server and his staff for catering, etc.
> Athletics team did well – 3rd overall in area meeting.
> Cricket & football teams v. successful – football won Grinstead League Cup – cricket runners-up in John Sayer competition.
>
> FINANCIAL: Treasurer to report – generally good year showing healthy balance of £1272.46. Hope to renew old equipment.
>
> Future: number of events planned inc. shopping trip to France. With support could be just as successful as those events which everyone enjoyed last year.

People in business organisations

ACTIVITY

The Annual General Meeting of the Hoarfield Manufacturing Sports and Social Club has recently been held, and as Minutes Secretary you made some rough notes during the meeting on each item of business. One of the main items was the Chairman's Report, and the notes you have are shown in fig. 20.10.

Using these as a guide, draft the narrative minutes for this agenda item. Remember the reported speech style, and make sure that you include all the information you have available. If you have any doubts about what any of the notes mean, interpret them in an appropriate way to fit in with the sense of the Chairman's comments.

Format and presentation

There are a number of different ways in which minutes can be set out on paper, but certain basic principles should be applied.

1. A complete and explanatory title must be provided.
2. The attendance list must be recorded. This is often done by giving details of the 'Officers' present, and then indicating how many 'other members' attended, e.g.
   A. J. Rendle, Chairperson; R. S. Vaughan, Vice-Chairman; B. J. Jonson, Secretary; C. E. Anstey, Treasurer; J. North. E. Booth, F. Carper, M. Hocking and those 23 ordinary members whose names are recorded on the attendance sheet.
3. Apologies for absence must be recorded.
4. Agenda items such as 'Minutes of Last Meeting', 'Matters Arising', and 'Any Other Business' must be recognised and recorded appropriately.
5. The sequence of items on the agenda must be followed.
6. Intelligent use of spacing and layout should be used to help the reader identify headings and individual agenda items.
7. Reported statements should be clearly attributed to identified speakers, whose names and designations should be given.
8. Decisions should be recorded appropriately and accurately.
9. The correct sequence and format for 'special' or *'ad hoc'* meetings should be used:
   for example no 'minutes of last meeting' or 'matters arising' – these items often being replaced by 'Chairperson's Introduction' or 'Briefing'.
10. Accurate use of the following terms is essential:
    a. **Proposal**: the name given to an item for discussion submitted in written form before the meeting takes place.
    b. **Motion**: the name given to a proposal when it is being discussed at a meeting.
    c. **Resolution**: the name given to a motion which has been passed or carried – used after a decision has been reached.

Practical communication skills

11 When recording minutes, always indicate that they are to be validated by the Chairperson. It can be done by using these devices at the end:

Signed .... (Chairperson)

Date ....

ACTIVITY

Most Business Studies textbooks which deal with Communication and Administration will include a section on meetings' documents. Using whatever resources you have available to you, acquire examples or copies of two different styles of presenting minutes. You should aim to get *complete* examples, rather than extracts, and these should be analysed in the light of the requirements indicated in the previous section on format and presentation. Don't write a separate analysis or commentary, but simply work through each set of minutes, annotating them at particular points where you think comment is useful. The aim is not necessarily to identify faults or omissions, but to recognise where established principles have been applied. An appreciation of different styles should help you when you have to produce a full set of minutes yourself.

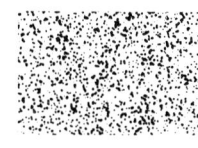

ASSIGNMENT

Prepare minutes for the meeting of the Wickborough County Players Association, amplifying the information given in fig. 20.11.

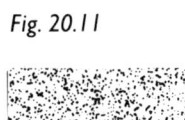

Fig. 20.11

THE WICKBOROUGH COUNTY PLAYERS ASSOCIATION

Notice of Annual General Meeting

The fourteenth Annual General Meeting of the Wickborough County Players Association will be held in Room 224, The Guildhall, Castle Street, Wickborough, on Tuesday 16 June, 199– at 7 pm.

AGENDA

1 Apologies for absence.
2 Minutes of previous meeting.
3 Matters arising from the minutes.
4 Secretary's Report.
5 Treasurer's Report.
6 Elections: Officers of the Association.
              Members of the Committee.
              Honorary Auditor.
7 Any other business.

J.J. Horner
Secretary

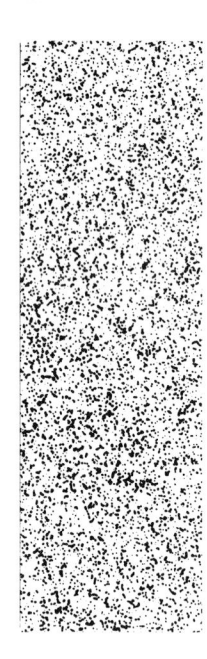

Synopsis

Five named officer holders and committee members attend, along with twenty-five ordinary members. Guy Harding (committee) is in hospital. The Secretary pays tribute to the late James Hennessey, OBE, formerly patron of the Association. The year's main stage productions are reviewed: Alan Bennett's *Habeas Corpus*, Bolt's *A Man for All Seasons* and Alan Ayckbourn's *Absent Friends*; two principal players are praised for their performances. The organised visits to Stratford and one other (named) venue are mentioned. Current membership is reviewed and Jean Johnson's special efforts in forming a Youth section of the Association are noted. The Secretary concludes on a note of optimism.

The Treasurer points to certain items on the Income and Expenditure Account and Balance Sheet before the members, notably the disturbing rise in the costs of props and costumes. Fund-raising efforts are called for. Some stage lighting needs replacing. While *Habeas Corpus* and *Absent Friends* show a profit of £17.26, *A Man for All Seasons* has made a loss of £64.33.

The final financial position is announced. Elections and re-elections take place. Any Other Business includes an enquiry whether money can be had from the local authority: the Secretary will explore possibilities. The Committee and all who have helped them with productions are thanked.

(RSA Diploma for Personal Assistants examination, 1981.)

Visual presentation of data

You have now experienced the written formality of various meetings' documents, and will appreciate how much care and attention to detail is needed to ensure that things run smoothly. Visual communication is often regarded as much more informal, and as having more immediacy of impact. However in many circumstances visual presentations have as much formality and convention associated with them as any written format.

One of the easiest ways of demonstrating this is through **visual presentation of data** (i.e. charts and diagrams). Very often, the aim of these visual presentations is to convey information in a such a way that it is easily and quickly comprehensible without in-depth analysis. The problem is that, in order to produce these visual delights, a great deal of skill is required in analysing the background information, assessing the audience, identifying the function of the presentation, and choosing the most effective method. Accuracy is essential, and reader-comprehension must be a major consideration. There are various ways of presenting statistical information, and the four most common ones are given below.

Tabular

Numerical information is presented in columns under appropriate headings. Simple cross-referencing is normally required.
Example: fig. 20.12.

Graphical

Graphs are often used to show quantities in relation to the movement of time. Other variations are possible.
Example: fig. 20.13.

Practical communication skills

Fig. 20.12
The numbers and value of off-road vehicles delivered from the manufacturers to retailers, and the numbers and value exported during the last four years.

Year	Petrol	Diesel	Value	Petrol	Diesel	Value
	(Total Number)		(£000)	(Total Number)		(£000)
1	15 621	13 204	288 200	7 752	3862	116 100
2	17 109	14 877	319 800	8 878	4357	132 300
3	18 399	15 868	357 000	9 607	5484	160 000
4	19 017	16 697	357 100	10 741	6752	174 900

Fig. 20.13
Graph to show the monthly profit on sales of video recorders by 'Playback' Ltd during their first two years of trading.

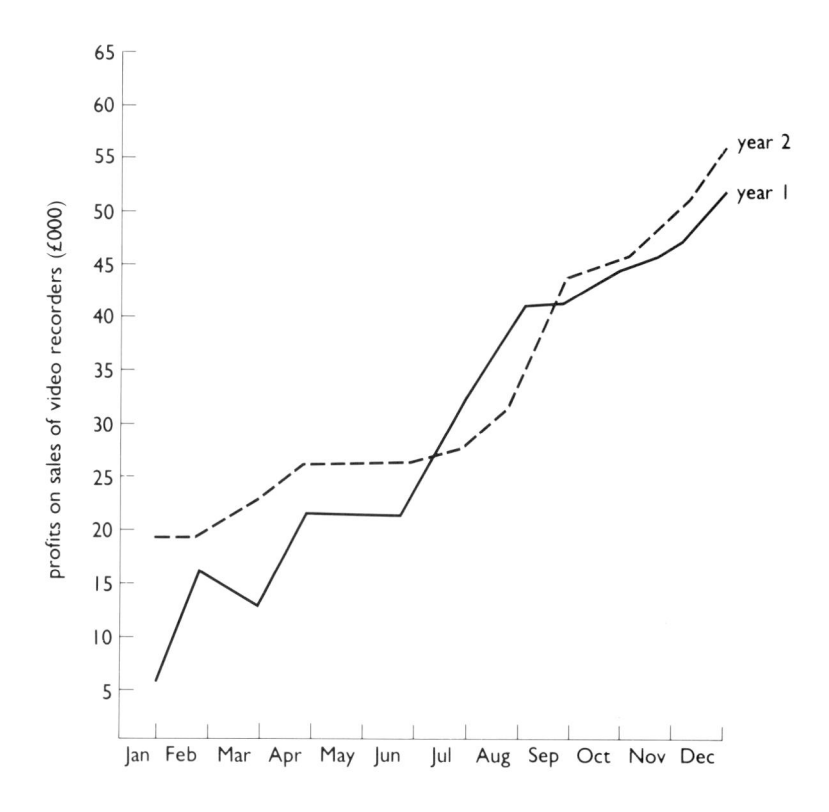

Proportional

Proportions or percentages are shown by different-sized blocks (bar chart) or by a segmented circle (pie chart).
Example: charts (a) and (b) in fig. 20.14.

Pictogram

Pictures are used to represent a certain number of items.
Example: fig. 20.15.

*Fig. 20.14(a)
Big chart*

food	travel	entertainment	books/stationery	other items
£10.00	£5.00	£5.00	£3.00	£2.00

*Fig. 20.14(b)
Pie chart*

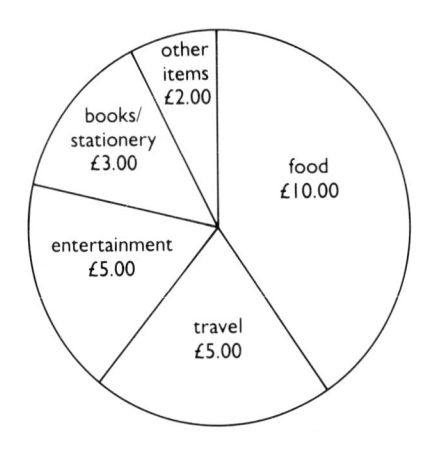

- other items £2.00
- books/stationery £3.00
- entertainment £5.00
- travel £5.00
- food £10.00

*Fig. 20.15
Pictogram showing placements/occupations of full-time BTEC students leaving college last July.*

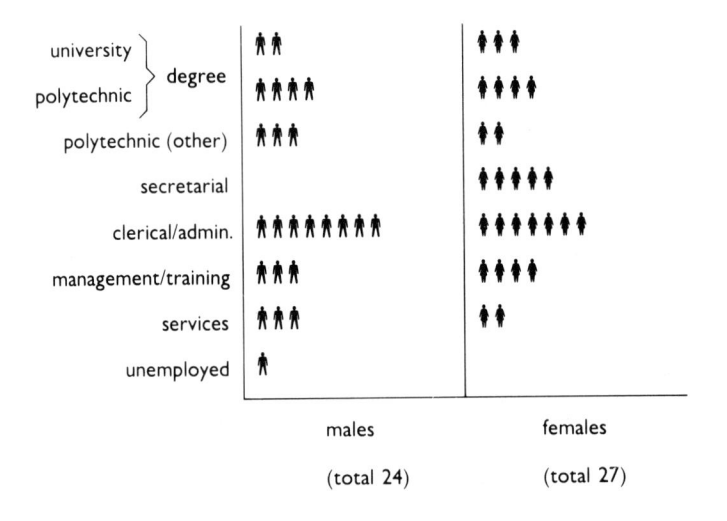

	males (total 24)	females (total 27)
university ⎫ degree	2	3
polytechnic ⎭	4	4
polytechnic (other)	3	2
secretarial		5
clerical/admin.	8	7
management/training	3	4
services	3	1
unemployed	1	

ACTIVITY

> Using any source available to you, acquire an example (photocopy) of each of the types of visual presentation demonstrated above. Your examples should be real ones, taken from such publications as the *Annual Abstract of Statistics*, *The Economist*, one of the major bank reviews, *Economic Progress Reports*, *Financial Times* etc. Your tutors should be able to guide you to an appropriate source.
>
> Write a commentary on each of your examples, saying how effective you think it is, how easy it is to understand, assessing its visual impact, describing the context in which it was produced, and identifying the particular function/audience for which it was intended.

Preparing a visual presentation

The task of representing numerical data in a more 'visual' format is not an easy one, and a detailed mathematical or statistical explanation of how the various charts are constructed is inappropriate here. With a little basic guidance and common sense you should be able to use any of the standard types dealt with in this chapter.

The first step is to determine exactly what you want your chart to **show**. The best way of doing this is to write a full and explanatory **title** which will establish your terms of reference, and set the parameters within which you are working. Examples of appropriate titles are given in figs. 20.12 – 20.15, and you should have others associated with the charts dealt with in the previous activity.

Another preliminary decision is which method of presentation is most **appropriate** for the information you are dealing with. Which will make it easier to understand? Important considerations here will be:

What is its function?
Who is it aimed at?

If the format you choose is based on horizontal and vertical axes you must decide what information is to be recorded on each one. Remember, there will often be different ways of doing it, but **one** will be much more visually effective than the others. You must find this **one**.

The **scales** you decide to use are also important, as they must be structured in such a way that your chart or diagram is 'useable' (i.e. not too big; not too small; not too complex; not too simplistic). It is quite acceptable to round up or round down certain figures, but it is essential to be consistent, and a statement to this effect should be incorporated into the overall presentation.

ACTIVITY

> As Personnel Assistant at Johnby, Johnby & Grout, Ltd, a local electronic component manufacturer, you have been asked to produce an analysis showing the age composition of the workforce over the last five years. You consult the personnel files, and draw up the table shown in fig. 20.16.

> When you pass this information on to Belinda Charles, the Personnel Manager, she says:
> 'I think we could use this data in the Annual Report this year – not the official Company Report, but the general one we publish for all employees, giving them a run-down on what's happening in the Company, and how we're doing. However, I can't see anybody wanting to plough through all these figures, so see if you can present them in an easily-readable visual format. I've also got some figures here relating to the state of our pension fund, and what we have paid out over the last five years. Employees are always keen to see what they can get out of the Company, so juggle these about and create a nice visual presentation for them as well. You'd better note this down as I read it out to you:
> "Over the five year period the contributions paid by the Company – given in millions of pounds – were 4.3, 6.0, 7.4, 8.3 and 8.5 consecutively. In the same period, corresponding employee contributions were 0.6, 1.3, 1.3, 1.3 and 1.5 million. The really interesting information is shown in the benefits paid out by the company over these five years. In year one it was 4.1 million; year two, 6.1 million; year three, 8.5; years four and five, 9.5 million each!"
> Remember that these must be easy to understand at a glance, and should show the company in the best possible light. See what you can do with them, and let me have the "visuals" by next week.'

Fig. 20.16

Age	Year 1	2	3	4	5
16–18	256	261	249	232	209
19–25	1905	1826	1832	1786	1928
26–35	3037	2896	2806	2780	2886
36–45	2235	2292	2091	2136	2282
46–55	1472	1466	1435	1538	1542
56–65	309	321	329	317	268

Using the media

Statistical data is one small part of the information published by organisations for general consumption, and most companies have regular contact with the various branches of the media in one form or another – it might be advertising material, a feature article, a new product launch or an interview with a senior manager. There is a whole range of circumstances in which **contacts with the media** are useful, particularly on the Public Relations side.

Public Relations is generally a very sensitive area for most organisations, and is often handled by a specialist PR department. Contact can be made on a formal or an informal basis, but in normal circumstances a company would discourage formal contacts between employees and the media because confusion, conflict or 'misunderstanding' might arise between the company viewpoint and the individual's point of view.

Formal contacts can be closely monitored and controlled, and adequate preparations made to ensure that an appropriate company image is presented to the public.

Fig. 20.17 Methods of contact with the media.

Other than routine communications, there are recognised ways of establishing media contact in specific circumstances, as illustrated in fig. 20.17.

The press briefing

These are normally arranged to give specialist writers and commentators the background to some specific event, incident, or development, and to 'guide' their interpretation of the situaton. This device is often used in the political arena when a senior government official wants to brief a small number of knowledgeable journalists on a current development.

The press reception

Usually regarded as a 'social' event, this type of gathering is normally more appropriate when the news story is 'soft'. It might herald the launching of a new product or a range of fashion-wear, and often involves substantial refreshments.

The press release

This is a very different method of contact relying on a written presentation, which must conform to accepted conventions of style, content and layout.

The news conference

This type of meeting is generally called because there is specific news to give of major importance; for example, the discovery of a new oil-field, or the signing of a long-sought trade agreement.

The Press Release

This is a formal statement issued by an organisation in the hope that it will be newsworthy enough to justify an editor devoting 'copy' to it. Recognition of the role of the editor is crucial to an understanding of how a Press Release should be written. It must be 'targeted' specifically at the editor and will need to demonstrate news value, coherence, sound organisation and structure. It must be factual and as concise as possible so that the theme can be quickly identified and assessed. An important thing to remember at all times is that a Release will not automatically be printed. It is being submitted for consideration, and you cannot assume that the editor or staff will have any inherent interest in, or knowledge of, the topic.

Consider the example of a Press Release in fig. 20.18.

Fig. 20.18

PRESS RELEASE

Date: June 15 1988

Further information:

   contact Charles Kent
   extension 812
   After office hours;
   Bridlingford (723) 84621

Brink Autofuels, Ltd.
Brink Mansions
Watts Street
London NW2 4SW
Tel: 01-426 7788

BRINK ENTERS SPORTSWEAR BUSINESS

The Brinkmanship Collection, a range of sportswear recently launched by this major company will be distributed through a nationwide network of service stations from July 1 1990.

The main customer is seen as the sports enthusiast with a requirement for high-quality, hard-wearing sports clothes, and the 15 piece collection is distinctively styled using the striking company livery as its theme. The range includes all basic clothing from tracksuits to T-shirts and slacks to ski-jackets. Most of the garments are designed to look equally stylish on men or women, and the 'Mini' range will cope with the younger members of the family.

Brink has aimed to provide high quality at a price below that of the high street multiples, and the choice of cotton and nylon/polyester fabrics ensures hard-wearing garments which are machine washable and need no special care.

This is the latest move by Brink Autofuels, Ltd. to expand its range of own-brand products beyond the standard fuel and lubricant market, and will establish the company firmly in the field of leisure accessories as well as reinforce the brand image in traditional areas such as motorists supplies, batteries and tyres.

As you will have noticed, there is a careful avoidance of unnecessary 'padding', and the aim is to emphasise a positive Company image and convince the editor that the readers will be interested to hear about these products. The style is formal and abstract (i.e. written in the 'third person') and it is important to adopt this style consistently throughout the Release.

The conventions of presentation demand that a Press Release would normally be submitted on a single sheet of A4, typed in double line spacing, and would contain the following components:

Practical communication skills

- document title
- name of company
- address and telephone number of company
- date of issue
- contact for further information
- main heading
- main body of the Release

Note A Company logo is often incorporated if there is one.

Additional guidelines for drafting Press Releases are:

1. The heading must *not* be a **'headline'** – it should be a label or caption, clearly stating the topic.
2. The first paragraph must give essential information – Where? When? Why? How? Who? – and should clearly summarise the essential facts.
3. Any supporting technical or background information should *not* be incorporated into the Release – it should be attached as appendices.
4. Any embargo or restriction on use should be prominently placed, underlined, and clearly worded.

Example

<u>NOT FOR PUBLICATION BEFORE MORNING PAPERS ON
FRIDAY, JUNE 18th, 19—</u>

ACTIVITY

Progress in Renaissance Kitchens is now evident, and with substantial capital investment further premises have been acquired, machinery purchased and installed, and general preparations made for increasing production within the next two weeks. The original business has been maintained throughout this busy period, and signs are good for the future. Also, at a recent Trade Fair, discussions with a major distributor and furnishing house led to an agreement to set up exhibition/demonstration tableaux in all their main stores, and this is likely to lead to many more direct orders from customers. Extra staff have been engaged and it is anticipated that over the next twelve months a number of trainee places will be available to school leavers.

In 300 – 350 words, write a Press Release for local circulation in which you emphasise the success of the firm as reflected in its current expansion, talk about the benefits the extra employment brings to the local community, mention that the new premises will be officially opened by the Mayor, and include appropriate comments/quotations from the Chairperson of the local Chamber of Commerce.